C-640   CAREER EXAMINATION SERIES

*This is your
PASSBOOK for...*

Police Administrative Aide

**Test Preparation Study Guide
Questions & Answers**

NATIONAL LEARNING CORPORATION®

COPYRIGHT NOTICE

This book is SOLELY intended for, is sold ONLY to, and its use is RESTRICTED to individual, bona fide applicants or candidates who qualify by virtue of having seriously filed applications for appropriate license, certificate, professional and/or promotional advancement, higher school matriculation, scholarship, or other legitimate requirements of education and/or governmental authorities.

This book is NOT intended for use, class instruction, tutoring, training, duplication, copying, reprinting, excerption, or adaptation, etc., by:

1) Other publishers
2) Proprietors and/or Instructors of "Coaching" and/or Preparatory Courses
3) Personnel and/or Training Divisions of commercial, industrial, and governmental organizations
4) Schools, colleges, or universities and/or their departments and staffs, including teachers and other personnel
5) Testing Agencies or Bureaus
6) Study groups which seek by the purchase of a single volume to copy and/or duplicate and/or adapt this material for use by the group as a whole without having purchased individual volumes for each of the members of the group
7) Et al.

Such persons would be in violation of appropriate Federal and State statutes.

PROVISION OF LICENSING AGREEMENTS – Recognized educational, commercial, industrial, and governmental institutions and organizations, and others legitimately engaged in educational pursuits, including training, testing, and measurement activities, may address request for a licensing agreement to the copyright owners, who will determine whether, and under what conditions, including fees and charges, the materials in this book may be used them. In other words, a licensing facility exists for the legitimate use of the material in this book on other than an individual basis. However, it is asseverated and affirmed here that the material in this book CANNOT be used without the receipt of the express permission of such a licensing agreement from the Publishers. Inquiries re licensing should be addressed to the company, attention rights and permissions department.

All rights reserved, including the right of reproduction in whole or in part, in any form or by any means, electronic or mechanical, including photocopying, recording, or by any information storage and retrieval system, without permission in writing from the Publisher.

Copyright © 2024 by
National Learning Corporation

212 Michael Drive, Syosset, NY 11791
(516) 921-8888 • www.passbooks.com
E-mail: info@passbooks.com

PASSBOOK® SERIES

THE *PASSBOOK® SERIES* has been created to prepare applicants and candidates for the ultimate academic battlefield – the examination room.

At some time in our lives, each and every one of us may be required to take an examination – for validation, matriculation, admission, qualification, registration, certification, or licensure.

Based on the assumption that every applicant or candidate has met the basic formal educational standards, has taken the required number of courses, and read the necessary texts, the *PASSBOOK® SERIES* furnishes the one special preparation which may assure passing with confidence, instead of failing with insecurity. Examination questions – together with answers – are furnished as the basic vehicle for study so that the mysteries of the examination and its compounding difficulties may be eliminated or diminished by a sure method.

This book is meant to help you pass your examination provided that you qualify and are serious in your objective.

The entire field is reviewed through the huge store of content information which is succinctly presented through a provocative and challenging approach – the question-and-answer method.

A climate of success is established by furnishing the correct answers at the end of each test.

You soon learn to recognize types of questions, forms of questions, and patterns of questioning. You may even begin to anticipate expected outcomes.

You perceive that many questions are repeated or adapted so that you can gain acute insights, which may enable you to score many sure points.

You learn how to confront new questions, or types of questions, and to attack them confidently and work out the correct answers.

You note objectives and emphases, and recognize pitfalls and dangers, so that you may make positive educational adjustments.

Moreover, you are kept fully informed in relation to new concepts, methods, practices, and directions in the field.

You discover that you are actually taking the examination all the time: you are preparing for the examination by "taking" an examination, not by reading extraneous and/or supererogatory textbooks.

In short, this PASSBOOK®, used directedly, should be an important factor in helping you to pass your test.

POLICE ADMINISTRATIVE AIDE

DUTIES
Police Administrative Aides, under supervision, with some latitude for independent action, initiative or decision, perform responsible and difficult clerical, typing, word processing and data entry tasks in a police station or other department unit, command or office. They perform administrative work of moderate difficulty involving the handling of confidential and other information and material; refer members of the public who ask for assistance to the appropriate City agency; utilize manual and automated office systems; type records, reports, forms and schedules; review and verify written information; receive, send, separate and distribute mail; obtain from and transmit information to the public or members of the police department: occasionally perform cashier or messenger duties; and perform related work.

EXAMPLES OF TYPICAL TASKS
Performs responsible clerical and typing work in a police station or other department unit, command or office of the Police Department. Receives emergency phone calls and puts information into a computer. Refers members of the public who ask for assistance to appropriate city agencies. Receives, sends, separates and distributes mail. Keeps records; files, shelves, stores and retrieves correspondence, records, reports, manuals or other material. Types records, reports, communications, forms and schedules. Reviews and verifies written information. Completes department forms. Obtains from and transmits information to the public or members of the Police Department. Writes reports and communications.

SCOPE OF THE EXAMINATION
The written test will be of the multiple-choice type and may consist of questions related to extracting pertinent information from written materials, organizing information in a logical order, writing grammatically correct English, spelling, record keeping and filing operations, performing basic mathematical computations and other related areas, including written comprehension; written expression; memorization; problem sensitivity; deductive reasoning; inductive reasoning; information ordering; spatial orientation; number facility; and time sharing.

HOW TO TAKE A TEST

I. YOU MUST PASS AN EXAMINATION

A. *WHAT EVERY CANDIDATE SHOULD KNOW*

Examination applicants often ask us for help in preparing for the written test. What can I study in advance? What kinds of questions will be asked? How will the test be given? How will the papers be graded?

As an applicant for a civil service examination, you may be wondering about some of these things. Our purpose here is to suggest effective methods of advance study and to describe civil service examinations.

Your chances for success on this examination can be increased if you know how to prepare. Those "pre-examination jitters" can be reduced if you know what to expect. You can even experience an adventure in good citizenship if you know why civil service exams are given.

B. *WHY ARE CIVIL SERVICE EXAMINATIONS GIVEN?*

Civil service examinations are important to you in two ways. As a citizen, you want public jobs filled by employees who know how to do their work. As a job seeker, you want a fair chance to compete for that job on an equal footing with other candidates. The best-known means of accomplishing this two-fold goal is the competitive examination.

Exams are widely publicized throughout the nation. They may be administered for jobs in federal, state, city, municipal, town or village governments or agencies.

Any citizen may apply, with some limitations, such as the age or residence of applicants. Your experience and education may be reviewed to see whether you meet the requirements for the particular examination. When these requirements exist, they are reasonable and applied consistently to all applicants. Thus, a competitive examination may cause you some uneasiness now, but it is your privilege and safeguard.

C. *HOW ARE CIVIL SERVICE EXAMS DEVELOPED?*

Examinations are carefully written by trained technicians who are specialists in the field known as "psychological measurement," in consultation with recognized authorities in the field of work that the test will cover. These experts recommend the subject matter areas or skills to be tested; only those knowledges or skills important to your success on the job are included. The most reliable books and source materials available are used as references. Together, the experts and technicians judge the difficulty level of the questions.

Test technicians know how to phrase questions so that the problem is clearly stated. Their ethics do not permit "trick" or "catch" questions. Questions may have been tried out on sample groups, or subjected to statistical analysis, to determine their usefulness.

Written tests are often used in combination with performance tests, ratings of training and experience, and oral interviews. All of these measures combine to form the best-known means of finding the right person for the right job.

II. HOW TO PASS THE WRITTEN TEST

A. NATURE OF THE EXAMINATION

To prepare intelligently for civil service examinations, you should know how they differ from school examinations you have taken. In school you were assigned certain definite pages to read or subjects to cover. The examination questions were quite detailed and usually emphasized memory. Civil service exams, on the other hand, try to discover your present ability to perform the duties of a position, plus your potentiality to learn these duties. In other words, a civil service exam attempts to predict how successful you will be. Questions cover such a broad area that they cannot be as minute and detailed as school exam questions.

In the public service similar kinds of work, or positions, are grouped together in one "class." This process is known as *position-classification*. All the positions in a class are paid according to the salary range for that class. One class title covers all of these positions, and they are all tested by the same examination.

B. FOUR BASIC STEPS

1) Study the announcement

How, then, can you know what subjects to study? Our best answer is: "Learn as much as possible about the class of positions for which you've applied." The exam will test the knowledge, skills and abilities needed to do the work.

Your most valuable source of information about the position you want is the official exam announcement. This announcement lists the training and experience qualifications. Check these standards and apply only if you come reasonably close to meeting them.

The brief description of the position in the examination announcement offers some clues to the subjects which will be tested. Think about the job itself. Review the duties in your mind. Can you perform them, or are there some in which you are rusty? Fill in the blank spots in your preparation.

Many jurisdictions preview the written test in the exam announcement by including a section called "Knowledge and Abilities Required," "Scope of the Examination," or some similar heading. Here you will find out specifically what fields will be tested.

2) Review your own background

Once you learn in general what the position is all about, and what you need to know to do the work, ask yourself which subjects you already know fairly well and which need improvement. You may wonder whether to concentrate on improving your strong areas or on building some background in your fields of weakness. When the announcement has specified "some knowledge" or "considerable knowledge," or has used adjectives like "beginning principles of…" or "advanced … methods," you can get a clue as to the number and difficulty of questions to be asked in any given field. More questions, and hence broader coverage, would be included for those subjects which are more important in the work. Now weigh your strengths and weaknesses against the job requirements and prepare accordingly.

3) Determine the level of the position

Another way to tell how intensively you should prepare is to understand the level of the job for which you are applying. Is it the entering level? In other words, is this the position in which beginners in a field of work are hired? Or is it an intermediate or advanced level? Sometimes this is indicated by such words as "Junior" or "Senior" in the class title. Other jurisdictions use Roman numerals to designate the level – Clerk I, Clerk II, for example. The word "Supervisor" sometimes appears in the title. If the level is not indicated by the title, check the description of duties. Will you be working under very close supervision, or will you have responsibility for independent decisions in this work?

4) Choose appropriate study materials

Now that you know the subjects to be examined and the relative amount of each subject to be covered, you can choose suitable study materials. For beginning level jobs, or even advanced ones, if you have a pronounced weakness in some aspect of your training, read a modern, standard textbook in that field. Be sure it is up to date and has general coverage. Such books are normally available at your library, and the librarian will be glad to help you locate one. For entry-level positions, questions of appropriate difficulty are chosen -- neither highly advanced questions, nor those too simple. Such questions require careful thought but not advanced training.

If the position for which you are applying is technical or advanced, you will read more advanced, specialized material. If you are already familiar with the basic principles of your field, elementary textbooks would waste your time. Concentrate on advanced textbooks and technical periodicals. Think through the concepts and review difficult problems in your field.

These are all general sources. You can get more ideas on your own initiative, following these leads. For example, training manuals and publications of the government agency which employs workers in your field can be useful, particularly for technical and professional positions. A letter or visit to the government department involved may result in more specific study suggestions, and certainly will provide you with a more definite idea of the exact nature of the position you are seeking.

III. KINDS OF TESTS

Tests are used for purposes other than measuring knowledge and ability to perform specified duties. For some positions, it is equally important to test ability to make adjustments to new situations or to profit from training. In others, basic mental abilities not dependent on information are essential. Questions which test these things may not appear as pertinent to the duties of the position as those which test for knowledge and information. Yet they are often highly important parts of a fair examination. For very general questions, it is almost impossible to help you direct your study efforts. What we can do is to point out some of the more common of these general abilities needed in public service positions and describe some typical questions.

1) General information

Broad, general information has been found useful for predicting job success in some kinds of work. This is tested in a variety of ways, from vocabulary lists to questions about current events. Basic background in some field of work, such as sociology or economics, may be sampled in a group of questions. Often these are principles which have become familiar to most persons through exposure rather than through formal training. It is difficult to advise you how to study for these questions; being alert to the world around you is our best suggestion.

2) Verbal ability

An example of an ability needed in many positions is verbal or language ability. Verbal ability is, in brief, the ability to use and understand words. Vocabulary and grammar tests are typical measures of this ability. Reading comprehension or paragraph interpretation questions are common in many kinds of civil service tests. You are given a paragraph of written material and asked to find its central meaning.

3) Numerical ability

Number skills can be tested by the familiar arithmetic problem, by checking paired lists of numbers to see which are alike and which are different, or by interpreting charts and graphs. In the latter test, a graph may be printed in the test booklet which you are asked to use as the basis for answering questions.

4) Observation

A popular test for law-enforcement positions is the observation test. A picture is shown to you for several minutes, then taken away. Questions about the picture test your ability to observe both details and larger elements.

5) Following directions

In many positions in the public service, the employee must be able to carry out written instructions dependably and accurately. You may be given a chart with several columns, each column listing a variety of information. The questions require you to carry out directions involving the information given in the chart.

6) Skills and aptitudes

Performance tests effectively measure some manual skills and aptitudes. When the skill is one in which you are trained, such as typing or shorthand, you can practice. These tests are often very much like those given in business school or high school courses. For many of the other skills and aptitudes, however, no short-time preparation can be made. Skills and abilities natural to you or that you have developed throughout your lifetime are being tested.

Many of the general questions just described provide all the data needed to answer the questions and ask you to use your reasoning ability to find the answers. Your best preparation for these tests, as well as for tests of facts and ideas, is to be at your physical and mental best. You, no doubt, have your own methods of getting into an exam-taking mood and keeping "in shape." The next section lists some ideas on this subject.

IV. KINDS OF QUESTIONS

Only rarely is the "essay" question, which you answer in narrative form, used in civil service tests. Civil service tests are usually of the short-answer type. Full instructions for answering these questions will be given to you at the examination. But in case this is your first experience with short-answer questions and separate answer sheets, here is what you need to know:

1) Multiple-choice Questions

Most popular of the short-answer questions is the "multiple choice" or "best answer" question. It can be used, for example, to test for factual knowledge, ability to solve problems or judgment in meeting situations found at work.

A multiple-choice question is normally one of three types—
- It can begin with an incomplete statement followed by several possible endings. You are to find the one ending which *best* completes the statement, although some of the others may not be entirely wrong.
- It can also be a complete statement in the form of a question which is answered by choosing one of the statements listed.

- It can be in the form of a problem – again you select the best answer.

Here is an example of a multiple-choice question with a discussion which should give you some clues as to the method for choosing the right answer:

When an employee has a complaint about his assignment, the action which will *best* help him overcome his difficulty is to
- A. discuss his difficulty with his coworkers
- B. take the problem to the head of the organization
- C. take the problem to the person who gave him the assignment
- D. say nothing to anyone about his complaint

In answering this question, you should study each of the choices to find which is best. Consider choice "A" – Certainly an employee may discuss his complaint with fellow employees, but no change or improvement can result, and the complaint remains unresolved. Choice "B" is a poor choice since the head of the organization probably does not know what assignment you have been given, and taking your problem to him is known as "going over the head" of the supervisor. The supervisor, or person who made the assignment, is the person who can clarify it or correct any injustice. Choice "C" is, therefore, correct. To say nothing, as in choice "D," is unwise. Supervisors have and interest in knowing the problems employees are facing, and the employee is seeking a solution to his problem.

2) True/False Questions

The "true/false" or "right/wrong" form of question is sometimes used. Here a complete statement is given. Your job is to decide whether the statement is right or wrong.

SAMPLE: A roaming cell-phone call to a nearby city costs less than a non-roaming call to a distant city.

This statement is wrong, or false, since roaming calls are more expensive.

This is not a complete list of all possible question forms, although most of the others are variations of these common types. You will always get complete directions for answering questions. Be sure you understand *how* to mark your answers – ask questions until you do.

V. RECORDING YOUR ANSWERS

Computer terminals are used more and more today for many different kinds of exams.

For an examination with very few applicants, you may be told to record your answers in the test booklet itself. Separate answer sheets are much more common. If this separate answer sheet is to be scored by machine – and this is often the case – it is highly important that you mark your answers correctly in order to get credit.

An electronic scoring machine is often used in civil service offices because of the speed with which papers can be scored. Machine-scored answer sheets must be marked with a pencil, which will be given to you. This pencil has a high graphite content which responds to the electronic scoring machine. As a matter of fact, stray dots may register as answers, so do not let your pencil rest on the answer sheet while you are pondering the correct answer. Also, if your pencil lead breaks or is otherwise defective, ask for another.

Since the answer sheet will be dropped in a slot in the scoring machine, be careful not to bend the corners or get the paper crumpled.

The answer sheet normally has five vertical columns of numbers, with 30 numbers to a column. These numbers correspond to the question numbers in your test booklet. After each number, going across the page are four or five pairs of dotted lines. These short dotted lines have small letters or numbers above them. The first two pairs may also have a "T" or "F" above the letters. This indicates that the first two pairs only are to be used if the questions are of the true-false type. If the questions are multiple choice, disregard the "T" and "F" and pay attention only to the small letters or numbers.

Answer your questions in the manner of the sample that follows:

32. The largest city in the United States is
    A. Washington, D.C.
    B. New York City
    C. Chicago
    D. Detroit
    E. San Francisco

1) Choose the answer you think is best. (New York City is the largest, so "B" is correct.)
2) Find the row of dotted lines numbered the same as the question you are answering. (Find row number 32)
3) Find the pair of dotted lines corresponding to the answer. (Find the pair of lines under the mark "B.")
4) Make a solid black mark between the dotted lines.

VI. BEFORE THE TEST

Common sense will help you find procedures to follow to get ready for an examination. Too many of us, however, overlook these sensible measures. Indeed, nervousness and fatigue have been found to be the most serious reasons why applicants fail to do their best on civil service tests. Here is a list of reminders:

- Begin your preparation early – Don't wait until the last minute to go scurrying around for books and materials or to find out what the position is all about.
- Prepare continuously – An hour a night for a week is better than an all-night cram session. This has been definitely established. What is more, a night a week for a month will return better dividends than crowding your study into a shorter period of time.
- Locate the place of the exam – You have been sent a notice telling you when and where to report for the examination. If the location is in a different town or otherwise unfamiliar to you, it would be well to inquire the best route and learn something about the building.
- Relax the night before the test – Allow your mind to rest. Do not study at all that night. Plan some mild recreation or diversion; then go to bed early and get a good night's sleep.
- Get up early enough to make a leisurely trip to the place for the test – This way unforeseen events, traffic snarls, unfamiliar buildings, etc. will not upset you.
- Dress comfortably – A written test is not a fashion show. You will be known by number and not by name, so wear something comfortable.

- Leave excess paraphernalia at home – Shopping bags and odd bundles will get in your way. You need bring only the items mentioned in the official notice you received; usually everything you need is provided. Do not bring reference books to the exam. They will only confuse those last minutes and be taken away from you when in the test room.
- Arrive somewhat ahead of time – If because of transportation schedules you must get there very early, bring a newspaper or magazine to take your mind off yourself while waiting.
- Locate the examination room – When you have found the proper room, you will be directed to the seat or part of the room where you will sit. Sometimes you are given a sheet of instructions to read while you are waiting. Do not fill out any forms until you are told to do so; just read them and be prepared.
- Relax and prepare to listen to the instructions
- If you have any physical problem that may keep you from doing your best, be sure to tell the test administrator. If you are sick or in poor health, you really cannot do your best on the exam. You can come back and take the test some other time.

VII. AT THE TEST

The day of the test is here and you have the test booklet in your hand. The temptation to get going is very strong. Caution! There is more to success than knowing the right answers. You must know how to identify your papers and understand variations in the type of short-answer question used in this particular examination. Follow these suggestions for maximum results from your efforts:

1) Cooperate with the monitor

The test administrator has a duty to create a situation in which you can be as much at ease as possible. He will give instructions, tell you when to begin, check to see that you are marking your answer sheet correctly, and so on. He is not there to guard you, although he will see that your competitors do not take unfair advantage. He wants to help you do your best.

2) Listen to all instructions

Don't jump the gun! Wait until you understand all directions. In most civil service tests you get more time than you need to answer the questions. So don't be in a hurry. Read each word of instructions until you clearly understand the meaning. Study the examples, listen to all announcements and follow directions. Ask questions if you do not understand what to do.

3) Identify your papers

Civil service exams are usually identified by number only. You will be assigned a number; you must not put your name on your test papers. Be sure to copy your number correctly. Since more than one exam may be given, copy your exact examination title.

4) Plan your time

Unless you are told that a test is a "speed" or "rate of work" test, speed itself is usually not important. Time enough to answer all the questions will be provided, but this does not mean that you have all day. An overall time limit has been set. Divide the total time (in minutes) by the number of questions to determine the approximate time you have for each question.

5) Do not linger over difficult questions
If you come across a difficult question, mark it with a paper clip (useful to have along) and come back to it when you have been through the booklet. One caution if you do this – be sure to skip a number on your answer sheet as well. Check often to be sure that you have not lost your place and that you are marking in the row numbered the same as the question you are answering.

6) Read the questions
Be sure you know what the question asks! Many capable people are unsuccessful because they failed to *read* the questions correctly.

7) Answer all questions
Unless you have been instructed that a penalty will be deducted for incorrect answers, it is better to guess than to omit a question.

8) Speed tests
It is often better NOT to guess on speed tests. It has been found that on timed tests people are tempted to spend the last few seconds before time is called in marking answers at random – without even reading them – in the hope of picking up a few extra points. To discourage this practice, the instructions may warn you that your score will be "corrected" for guessing. That is, a penalty will be applied. The incorrect answers will be deducted from the correct ones, or some other penalty formula will be used.

9) Review your answers
If you finish before time is called, go back to the questions you guessed or omitted to give them further thought. Review other answers if you have time.

10) Return your test materials
If you are ready to leave before others have finished or time is called, take ALL your materials to the monitor and leave quietly. Never take any test material with you. The monitor can discover whose papers are not complete, and taking a test booklet may be grounds for disqualification.

VIII. EXAMINATION TECHNIQUES

1) Read the general instructions carefully. These are usually printed on the first page of the exam booklet. As a rule, these instructions refer to the timing of the examination; the fact that you should not start work until the signal and must stop work at a signal, etc. If there are any *special* instructions, such as a choice of questions to be answered, make sure that you note this instruction carefully.

2) When you are ready to start work on the examination, that is as soon as the signal has been given, read the instructions to each question booklet, underline any key words or phrases, such as *least, best, outline, describe* and the like. In this way you will tend to answer as requested rather than discover on reviewing your paper that you *listed without describing*, that you selected the *worst* choice rather than the *best* choice, etc.

3) If the examination is of the objective or multiple-choice type – that is, each question will also give a series of possible answers: A, B, C or D, and you are called upon to select the best answer and write the letter next to that answer on your answer paper – it is advisable to start answering each question in turn. There may be anywhere from 50 to 100 such questions in the three or four hours allotted and you can see how much time would be taken if you read through all the questions before beginning to answer any. Furthermore, if you come across a question or group of questions which you know would be difficult to answer, it would undoubtedly affect your handling of all the other questions.

4) If the examination is of the essay type and contains but a few questions, it is a moot point as to whether you should read all the questions before starting to answer any one. Of course, if you are given a choice – say five out of seven and the like – then it is essential to read all the questions so you can eliminate the two that are most difficult. If, however, you are asked to answer all the questions, there may be danger in trying to answer the easiest one first because you may find that you will spend too much time on it. The best technique is to answer the first question, then proceed to the second, etc.

5) Time your answers. Before the exam begins, write down the time it started, then add the time allowed for the examination and write down the time it must be completed, then divide the time available somewhat as follows:
    - If 3-1/2 hours are allowed, that would be 210 minutes. If you have 80 objective-type questions, that would be an average of 2-1/2 minutes per question. Allow yourself no more than 2 minutes per question, or a total of 160 minutes, which will permit about 50 minutes to review.
    - If for the time allotment of 210 minutes there are 7 essay questions to answer, that would average about 30 minutes a question. Give yourself only 25 minutes per question so that you have about 35 minutes to review.

6) The most important instruction is to *read each question* and make sure you know what is wanted. The second most important instruction is to *time yourself properly* so that you answer every question. The third most important instruction is to *answer every question*. Guess if you have to but include something for each question. Remember that you will receive no credit for a blank and will probably receive some credit if you write something in answer to an essay question. If you guess a letter – say "B" for a multiple-choice question – you may have guessed right. If you leave a blank as an answer to a multiple-choice question, the examiners may respect your feelings but it will not add a point to your score. Some exams may penalize you for wrong answers, so in such cases *only*, you may not want to guess unless you have some basis for your answer.

7) Suggestions
    a. Objective-type questions
        1. Examine the question booklet for proper sequence of pages and questions
        2. Read all instructions carefully
        3. Skip any question which seems too difficult; return to it after all other questions have been answered
        4. Apportion your time properly; do not spend too much time on any single question or group of questions

5. Note and underline key words – *all, most, fewest, least, best, worst, same, opposite*, etc.
6. Pay particular attention to negatives
7. Note unusual option, e.g., unduly long, short, complex, different or similar in content to the body of the question
8. Observe the use of "hedging" words – *probably, may, most likely,* etc.
9. Make sure that your answer is put next to the same number as the question
10. Do not second-guess unless you have good reason to believe the second answer is definitely more correct
11. Cross out original answer if you decide another answer is more accurate; do not erase until you are ready to hand your paper in
12. Answer all questions; guess unless instructed otherwise
13. Leave time for review

b. Essay questions
 1. Read each question carefully
 2. Determine exactly what is wanted. Underline key words or phrases.
 3. Decide on outline or paragraph answer
 4. Include many different points and elements unless asked to develop any one or two points or elements
 5. Show impartiality by giving pros and cons unless directed to select one side only
 6. Make and write down any assumptions you find necessary to answer the questions
 7. Watch your English, grammar, punctuation and choice of words
 8. Time your answers; don't crowd material

8) Answering the essay question

Most essay questions can be answered by framing the specific response around several key words or ideas. Here are a few such key words or ideas:

M's: manpower, materials, methods, money, management
P's: purpose, program, policy, plan, procedure, practice, problems, pitfalls, personnel, public relations

 a. Six basic steps in handling problems:
  1. Preliminary plan and background development
  2. Collect information, data and facts
  3. Analyze and interpret information, data and facts
  4. Analyze and develop solutions as well as make recommendations
  5. Prepare report and sell recommendations
  6. Install recommendations and follow up effectiveness

 b. Pitfalls to avoid
  1. *Taking things for granted* – A statement of the situation does not necessarily imply that each of the elements is necessarily true; for example, a complaint may be invalid and biased so that all that can be taken for granted is that a complaint has been registered

2. *Considering only one side of a situation* – Wherever possible, indicate several alternatives and then point out the reasons you selected the best one
3. *Failing to indicate follow up* – Whenever your answer indicates action on your part, make certain that you will take proper follow-up action to see how successful your recommendations, procedures or actions turn out to be
4. *Taking too long in answering any single question* – Remember to time your answers properly

IX. AFTER THE TEST

Scoring procedures differ in detail among civil service jurisdictions although the general principles are the same. Whether the papers are hand-scored or graded by machine we have described, they are nearly always graded by number. That is, the person who marks the paper knows only the number – never the name – of the applicant. Not until all the papers have been graded will they be matched with names. If other tests, such as training and experience or oral interview ratings have been given, scores will be combined. Different parts of the examination usually have different weights. For example, the written test might count 60 percent of the final grade, and a rating of training and experience 40 percent. In many jurisdictions, veterans will have a certain number of points added to their grades.

After the final grade has been determined, the names are placed in grade order and an eligible list is established. There are various methods for resolving ties between those who get the same final grade – probably the most common is to place first the name of the person whose application was received first. Job offers are made from the eligible list in the order the names appear on it. You will be notified of your grade and your rank as soon as all these computations have been made. This will be done as rapidly as possible.

People who are found to meet the requirements in the announcement are called "eligibles." Their names are put on a list of eligible candidates. An eligible's chances of getting a job depend on how high he stands on this list and how fast agencies are filling jobs from the list.

When a job is to be filled from a list of eligibles, the agency asks for the names of people on the list of eligibles for that job. When the civil service commission receives this request, it sends to the agency the names of the three people highest on this list. Or, if the job to be filled has specialized requirements, the office sends the agency the names of the top three persons who meet these requirements from the general list.

The appointing officer makes a choice from among the three people whose names were sent to him. If the selected person accepts the appointment, the names of the others are put back on the list to be considered for future openings.

That is the rule in hiring from all kinds of eligible lists, whether they are for typist, carpenter, chemist, or something else. For every vacancy, the appointing officer has his choice of any one of the top three eligibles on the list. This explains why the person whose name is on top of the list sometimes does not get an appointment when some of the persons lower on the list do. If the appointing officer chooses the second or third eligible, the No. 1 eligible does not get a job at once, but stays on the list until he is appointed or the list is terminated.

X. HOW TO PASS THE INTERVIEW TEST

The examination for which you applied requires an oral interview test. You have already taken the written test and you are now being called for the interview test – the final part of the formal examination.

You may think that it is not possible to prepare for an interview test and that there are no procedures to follow during an interview. Our purpose is to point out some things you can do in advance that will help you and some good rules to follow and pitfalls to avoid while you are being interviewed.

What is an interview supposed to test?

The written examination is designed to test the technical knowledge and competence of the candidate; the oral is designed to evaluate intangible qualities, not readily measured otherwise, and to establish a list showing the relative fitness of each candidate – as measured against his competitors – for the position sought. Scoring is not on the basis of "right" and "wrong," but on a sliding scale of values ranging from "not passable" to "outstanding." As a matter of fact, it is possible to achieve a relatively low score without a single "incorrect" answer because of evident weakness in the qualities being measured.

Occasionally, an examination may consist entirely of an oral test – either an individual or a group oral. In such cases, information is sought concerning the technical knowledges and abilities of the candidate, since there has been no written examination for this purpose. More commonly, however, an oral test is used to supplement a written examination.

Who conducts interviews?

The composition of oral boards varies among different jurisdictions. In nearly all, a representative of the personnel department serves as chairman. One of the members of the board may be a representative of the department in which the candidate would work. In some cases, "outside experts" are used, and, frequently, a businessman or some other representative of the general public is asked to serve. Labor and management or other special groups may be represented. The aim is to secure the services of experts in the appropriate field.

However the board is composed, it is a good idea (and not at all improper or unethical) to ascertain in advance of the interview who the members are and what groups they represent. When you are introduced to them, you will have some idea of their backgrounds and interests, and at least you will not stutter and stammer over their names.

What should be done before the interview?

While knowledge about the board members is useful and takes some of the surprise element out of the interview, there is other preparation which is more substantive. It *is* possible to prepare for an oral interview – in several ways:

1) Keep a copy of your application and review it carefully before the interview

This may be the only document before the oral board, and the starting point of the interview. Know what education and experience you have listed there, and the sequence and dates of all of it. Sometimes the board will ask you to review the highlights of your experience for them; you should not have to hem and haw doing it.

2) Study the class specification and the examination announcement

Usually, the oral board has one or both of these to guide them. The qualities, characteristics or knowledges required by the position sought are stated in these documents. They offer valuable clues as to the nature of the oral interview. For example, if the job involves supervisory responsibilities, the announcement will usually indicate that knowledge of modern supervisory methods and the qualifications of the candidate as a supervisor will be tested. If so, you can expect such questions, frequently in the form of a hypothetical situation which you are expected to solve. NEVER go into an oral without knowledge of the duties and responsibilities of the job you seek.

3) Think through each qualification required

Try to visualize the kind of questions you would ask if you were a board member. How well could you answer them? Try especially to appraise your own knowledge and background in each area, *measured against the job sought*, and identify any areas in which you are weak. Be critical and realistic – do not flatter yourself.

4) Do some general reading in areas in which you feel you may be weak

For example, if the job involves supervision and your past experience has NOT, some general reading in supervisory methods and practices, particularly in the field of human relations, might be useful. Do NOT study agency procedures or detailed manuals. The oral board will be testing your understanding and capacity, not your memory.

5) Get a good night's sleep and watch your general health and mental attitude

You will want a clear head at the interview. Take care of a cold or any other minor ailment, and of course, no hangovers.

What should be done on the day of the interview?

Now comes the day of the interview itself. Give yourself plenty of time to get there. Plan to arrive somewhat ahead of the scheduled time, particularly if your appointment is in the fore part of the day. If a previous candidate fails to appear, the board might be ready for you a bit early. By early afternoon an oral board is almost invariably behind schedule if there are many candidates, and you may have to wait. Take along a book or magazine to read, or your application to review, but leave any extraneous material in the waiting room when you go in for your interview. In any event, relax and compose yourself.

The matter of dress is important. The board is forming impressions about you – from your experience, your manners, your attitude, and your appearance. Give your personal appearance careful attention. Dress your best, but not your flashiest. Choose conservative, appropriate clothing, and be sure it is immaculate. This is a business interview, and your appearance should indicate that you regard it as such. Besides, being well groomed and properly dressed will help boost your confidence.

Sooner or later, someone will call your name and escort you into the interview room. *This is it.* From here on you are on your own. It is too late for any more preparation. But remember, you asked for this opportunity to prove your fitness, and you are here because your request was granted.

What happens when you go in?

The usual sequence of events will be as follows: The clerk (who is often the board stenographer) will introduce you to the chairman of the oral board, who will introduce you to the other members of the board. Acknowledge the introductions before you sit down. Do not be surprised if you find a microphone facing you or a stenotypist sitting by. Oral interviews are usually recorded in the event of an appeal or other review.

Usually the chairman of the board will open the interview by reviewing the highlights of your education and work experience from your application – primarily for the benefit of the other members of the board, as well as to get the material into the record. Do not interrupt or comment unless there is an error or significant misinterpretation; if that is the case, do not hesitate. But do not quibble about insignificant matters. Also, he will usually ask you some question about your education, experience or your present job – partly to get you to start talking and to establish the interviewing "rapport." He may start the actual questioning, or turn it over to one of the other members. Frequently, each member undertakes the questioning on a particular area, one in which he is perhaps most competent, so you can expect each member to participate in the examination. Because time is limited, you may also expect some rather abrupt switches in the direction the questioning takes, so do not be upset by it. Normally, a board member will not pursue a single line of questioning unless he discovers a particular strength or weakness.

After each member has participated, the chairman will usually ask whether any member has any further questions, then will ask you if you have anything you wish to add. Unless you are expecting this question, it may floor you. Worse, it may start you off on an extended, extemporaneous speech. The board is not usually seeking more information. The question is principally to offer you a last opportunity to present further qualifications or to indicate that you have nothing to add. So, if you feel that a significant qualification or characteristic has been overlooked, it is proper to point it out in a sentence or so. Do not compliment the board on the thoroughness of their examination – they have been sketchy, and you know it. If you wish, merely say, "No thank you, I have nothing further to add." This is a point where you can "talk yourself out" of a good impression or fail to present an important bit of information. Remember, *you close the interview yourself*.

The chairman will then say, "That is all, Mr. _____, thank you." Do not be startled; the interview is over, and quicker than you think. Thank him, gather your belongings and take your leave. Save your sigh of relief for the other side of the door.

How to put your best foot forward

Throughout this entire process, you may feel that the board individually and collectively is trying to pierce your defenses, seek out your hidden weaknesses and embarrass and confuse you. Actually, this is not true. They are obliged to make an appraisal of your qualifications for the job you are seeking, and they want to see you in your best light. Remember, they must interview all candidates and a non-cooperative candidate may become a failure in spite of their best efforts to bring out his qualifications. Here are 15 suggestions that will help you:

1) Be natural – Keep your attitude confident, not cocky

If you are not confident that you can do the job, do not expect the board to be. Do not apologize for your weaknesses, try to bring out your strong points. The board is interested in a positive, not negative, presentation. Cockiness will antagonize any board member and make him wonder if you are covering up a weakness by a false show of strength.

2) Get comfortable, but don't lounge or sprawl

Sit erectly but not stiffly. A careless posture may lead the board to conclude that you are careless in other things, or at least that you are not impressed by the importance of the occasion. Either conclusion is natural, even if incorrect. Do not fuss with your clothing, a pencil or an ashtray. Your hands may occasionally be useful to emphasize a point; do not let them become a point of distraction.

3) Do not wisecrack or make small talk

This is a serious situation, and your attitude should show that you consider it as such. Further, the time of the board is limited – they do not want to waste it, and neither should you.

4) Do not exaggerate your experience or abilities

In the first place, from information in the application or other interviews and sources, the board may know more about you than you think. Secondly, you probably will not get away with it. An experienced board is rather adept at spotting such a situation, so do not take the chance.

5) If you know a board member, do not make a point of it, yet do not hide it

Certainly you are not fooling him, and probably not the other members of the board. Do not try to take advantage of your acquaintanceship – it will probably do you little good.

6) Do not dominate the interview

Let the board do that. They will give you the clues – do not assume that you have to do all the talking. Realize that the board has a number of questions to ask you, and do not try to take up all the interview time by showing off your extensive knowledge of the answer to the first one.

7) Be attentive

You only have 20 minutes or so, and you should keep your attention at its sharpest throughout. When a member is addressing a problem or question to you, give him your undivided attention. Address your reply principally to him, but do not exclude the other board members.

8) Do not interrupt

A board member may be stating a problem for you to analyze. He will ask you a question when the time comes. Let him state the problem, and wait for the question.

9) Make sure you understand the question

Do not try to answer until you are sure what the question is. If it is not clear, restate it in your own words or ask the board member to clarify it for you. However, do not haggle about minor elements.

10) Reply promptly but not hastily

A common entry on oral board rating sheets is "candidate responded readily," or "candidate hesitated in replies." Respond as promptly and quickly as you can, but do not jump to a hasty, ill-considered answer.

11) Do not be peremptory in your answers

A brief answer is proper – but do not fire your answer back. That is a losing game from your point of view. The board member can probably ask questions much faster than you can answer them.

12) Do not try to create the answer you think the board member wants

He is interested in what kind of mind you have and how it works – not in playing games. Furthermore, he can usually spot this practice and will actually grade you down on it.

13) Do not switch sides in your reply merely to agree with a board member

Frequently, a member will take a contrary position merely to draw you out and to see if you are willing and able to defend your point of view. Do not start a debate, yet do not surrender a good position. If a position is worth taking, it is worth defending.

14) Do not be afraid to admit an error in judgment if you are shown to be wrong

The board knows that you are forced to reply without any opportunity for careful consideration. Your answer may be demonstrably wrong. If so, admit it and get on with the interview.

15) Do not dwell at length on your present job

The opening question may relate to your present assignment. Answer the question but do not go into an extended discussion. You are being examined for a *new* job, not your present one. As a matter of fact, try to phrase ALL your answers in terms of the job for which you are being examined.

Basis of Rating

Probably you will forget most of these "do's" and "don'ts" when you walk into the oral interview room. Even remembering them all will not ensure you a passing grade. Perhaps you did not have the qualifications in the first place. But remembering them will help you to put your best foot forward, without treading on the toes of the board members.

Rumor and popular opinion to the contrary notwithstanding, an oral board wants you to make the best appearance possible. They know you are under pressure – but they also want to see how you respond to it as a guide to what your reaction would be under the pressures of the job you seek. They will be influenced by the degree of poise you display, the personal traits you show and the manner in which you respond.

ABOUT THIS BOOK

This book contains tests divided into Examination Sections. Go through each test, answering every question in the margin. We have also attached a sample answer sheet at the back of the book that can be removed and used. At the end of each test look at the answer key and check your answers. On the ones you got wrong, look at the right answer choice and learn. Do not fill in the answers first. Do not memorize the questions and answers, but understand the answer and principles involved. On your test, the questions will likely be different from the samples. Questions are changed and new ones added. If you understand these past questions you should have success with any changes that arise. Tests may consist of several types of questions. We have additional books on each subject should more study be advisable or necessary for you. Finally, the more you study, the better prepared you will be. This book is intended to be the last thing you study before you walk into the examination room. Prior study of relevant texts is also recommended. NLC publishes some of these in our Fundamental Series. Knowledge and good sense are important factors in passing your exam. Good luck also helps. So now study this Passbook, absorb the material contained within and take that knowledge into the examination. Then do your best to pass that exam.

EXAMINATION SECTION

EXAMINATION SECTION

TEST 1

DIRECTIONS: Each question or incomplete statement is followed by several suggested answers or completions. Select the one that BEST answers the question or completes the statement. *PRINT THE LETTER OF THE CORRECT ANSWER IN THE SPACE AT THE RIGHT.*

Questions 1-6.

DIRECTIONS: Questions 1 through 6 are to be answered SOLELY on the basis of the numbered boxes on the Arrest Report and paragraph below.

ARREST REPORT

1. Arrest Number	2. Precinct of Arrest	3. Date/Time of Arrest	4. Defendant's Name	5. Defendant's Address
6. Defendant's Date of Birth	7. Sex	8. Race	9. Height	10. Weight	11. Location of Arrest	12. Date and Time of Occurrence
13. Location of Occurrence	14. Complaint Number	15. Victim's Name	16. Victim's Address	17. Victim's Date of Birth
18. Precinct of Complaint	19. Arresting Officer's Name	20. Shield Number	21. Assigned Unit Precinct	2. Date of Complaint

On Friday, December 13 at 11:45 P.M., while leaving a store at 235 Spring Street, Grace O'Connell, a white female, 5'2" 130 lbs., was approached by a white male, 5'11", 200 lbs., who demanded her money and jewelry. As the man ran and turned down River Street, Police Officer William James, Shield Number 31724, assigned to the 14th Precinct, gave chase and apprehended him in front of 523 River Street. The prisoner, Gerald Grande, who resides at 17 Water Street, was arrested at 12:05 A.M., was charged with robbery, and taken to the 13th Precinct, where he was assigned Arrest Number 53048. Miss O'Connell, who resides at 275 Spring St., was given Complaint Number 822460.

1. On the basis of the Arrest Report and the above paragraph, the CORRECT entry for Box Number 3 should be
   A. 11:45 P.M., 12/13 B. 11:45 P.M., 12/14
   C. 12:05 A.M., 12/13 D. 12:05 A.M., 12/14

   1._____

2. On the basis of the Arrest Report and the above paragraph, the CORRECT entry for Box Number 21 should be
   A. 12th Precinct B. 14th Precinct
   C. Mounted Unit D. 32nd Precinct

   2._____

3. On the basis of the Arrest Report and the above paragraph, the CORRECT entry for Box Number 11 should be
   A. 235 Spring St.
   B. 523 River St.
   C. 275 Spring St.
   D. 17 Water St.

4. On the basis of the Arrest Report and the above paragraph, the CORRECT entry for Box Number 2 should be
   A. 13th Precinct
   B. 14th Precinct
   C. Mounted Unit
   D. 32nd Precinct

5. On the basis of the Arrest Report and the above paragraph, the CORRECT entry for Box Number 13 should be
   A. 523 River St.
   B. 17 Water St.
   C. 275 Spring St.
   D. 235 Spring St.

6. On the basis of the Arrest Report and the above paragraph, the CORRECT entry for Box Number 14 should be
   A. 53048   B. 31724   C. 12/13   D. 82460

Questions 7-10.

DIRECTIONS: Questions 7 through 10 are to be answered SOLELY on the basis of the following information.

You are required to file various documents in file drawers which are labeled according to the following pattern:

DOCUMENTS

MEMOS		LETTERS		REPORTS		INQUIRIES	
File	Subject	File	Subject	File	Subject	File	Subject
84PM1	(A-L)	84PC1	(A-L)	84PR1	(A-L)	84PQ1	(A-L)
84PM2	(M-Z)	84PC2	(M-Z)	84PR2	(M-Z)	84PQ2	(M-Z)

7. A letter dealing with a burglary should be filed in the drawer labeled
   A. 84PM1   B. 84PC1   C. 84PR1   D. 84PQ2

8. A report on *Statistics* should be found in the drawer labeled
   A. 84PM1   B. 84PC2   C. 84PR2   D. 84PQ2

9. An inquiry is received about parade permit procedures. It should be filed in the drawer labeled
   A. 84PM2   B. 84PC1   C. 84PR1   D. 84PQ2

10. A police officer has a question about a robbery report you filed. You should pull this file from the drawer labeled
    A. 84PM1   B. 84PM2   C. 84PR1   D. 84PR2

Questions 11-18.

DIRECTIONS: Questions 11 through 18 are to be answered SOLELY on the basis of the following information.

Below are listed the code number, name, and area of investigation of six detective units. Each question describes a crime.
For each question, choose the option (A, B, C, or D) which contains the code number for the detective unit responsible for handling that crime.

DETECTIVE UNITS

Unit Code No.	Unit Name	Unit's Area of Investigation
01	Senior Citizens Unit	All robberies of senior citizens 65 years or older
02	Major Case Unit	Any bank robbery; a commercial robbery where value of goods or money stolen is over $25,000
03	Robbery Unit	Any commercial, non-bank robbery where the value of the stolen goods or money is $25,000 or less; robberies of individuals under 65 years of age
04	Fraud and Larceny Unit	Confidence games and pickpockets
05	Special Investigations Unit	Burglaries of premises where the value of goods removed or monies taken is $15,000 or less
06	Burglary Unit	Burglaries of premises where the value of goods removed or monies taken is over $15,000

11. Mrs. Green calls the precinct and reports that her apartment was burglarized while she was on vacation and that precious jewelry and silverware, valued at $27,000, were taken.
    To which unit code number should her complaint be referred?
    A. 05   B. 02   C. 03   D. 06

12. Sylvia Bailey, Manager of the Building and Loan Savings Bank, reports that a man handed one of her tellers a note stating, *This is a robbery*. He had a gun and demanded money. The teller gave the man $500 in small bills, and the man then left.
    To which unit code should the complaint be referred?
    A. 02   B. 06   C. 03   D. 05

13. Mrs. Miniver, a 67-year-old widow, states that she was beaten and robbed by two men in the elevator of her apartment building.
    To which unit code number should the complaint be referred?
    A. 06   B. 01   C. 03   D. 02

14. Mr. Whipple, Manager of T.V.A. Supermarket, reports that during the night someone entered the store and removed merchandise valued at $12,500.
    To which unit code number should the complaint be referred?
    A. 05   B. 03   C. 06   D. 02

15. Mr. Gold, owner of Gold's Jewelry Exchange, reports that two men, armed with shotguns, robbed his store and removed money and jewelry valued at $28,000.
    To which unit code number should the complaint be referred?
    A. 05   B. 03   C. 06   D. 02

16. Mr. Watson, a 62-year-old man, was walking in Central Park when he was approached by a man with a knife and was robbed of $72.
    To which unit code number should the complaint be referred?
    A. 01   B. 06   C. 03   D. 02

17. The Ace Jewelry Manufacturing Company was broken into over the weekend when the building was closed. The owner stated that $35,000 in gold, silver, diamonds, and jewelry were taken.
    To which unit code number should the complaint be referred?
    A. 02   B. 03   C. 06   D. 05

18. Mrs. Vargas, 62, reports that she gave Mr. Greene of the Starlite Realty Corporation $1,000 to locate a new apartment for her family. A week went by, and she never heard from Mr. Greene. She called the Starlite Realty Corporation, and they informed her that Mr. Greene never worked for Starlite Realty Corporation and that they have no record of the $1,000 deposit of Mrs. Vargas.
    To which unit code number should the complaint be referred?
    A. 04   B. 03   C. 01   D. 05

Questions 19-24.

DIRECTIONS: Questions 19 through 24 consist of sentences which contain examples of correct or incorrect English usage. Examine each sentence with reference to grammar, spelling, punctuation, and capitalization. Choose one of the following options that would be BEST for correct English usage:
A. The sentence is correct.
B. There is one mistake.
C. There are two mistakes.
D. There are three mistakes.

19. Mrs. Fitzgerald came to the 59th Precinct to retreive her property which were stolen earlier in the week.

20. The two officer's responded to the call, only to find that the perpatrator and the   20.____
    victim have left the scene.

21. Mr. Coleman called the 61st Precinct to report that, upon arriving at his store,   21.____
    he discovered that there was a large hole in the wall and that three boxes of
    radios were missing

22. The Administrative Leiutenant of the 62nd Precinct held a meeting which was   22.____
    attended by all the civilians, assigned to the Precinct.

23. Three days after the robbery occured the detective apprahended two   23.____
    suspects and recovered the stolen items.

24. The Community Affairs Officer of the 64th Precinct is the liaison between   24.____
    the Precinct and the community; he works closely with various community
    organizations, and elected officials.

Questions 25-32.

DIRECTIONS: Questions 25 through 32 are to be answered on the basis of the following
              paragraph, which contains some deliberate errors in spelling and/or grammar
              and/or punctuation. Each line of the paragraph is preceded by a number.
              There are 9 lines and 9 numbers.

Line No.	Paragraph Line
1	The protection of life and property are, one of
2	the oldest and most important functions of a city.
3	New York city has its own full-time police Agency.
4	The police Department has the power an it shall
5	be there duty to preserve the Public piece,
6	prevent crime detect and arrest offenders, suppress
7	riots, protect the rites of persons and property, etc.
8	The maintainance of sound relations with the community they
9	serve is an important function of law enforcement officers.

25. How many errors are contained in line one?   25.____
    A. One   B. Two   C. Three   D. None

26. How many errors are contained in line two?   26.____
    A. One   B. Two   C. Three   D. None

27. How many errors are contained in line three?   27.____
    A. One   B. Two   C. Three   D. None

28. How many errors are contained in line four?   28.____
    A. One   B. Two   C. Three   D. None

29. How many errors are contained in line five?
    A. One   B. Two   C. Three   D. None

30. How many errors are contained in line six?
    A. One   B. Two   C. Three   D. None

31. How many errors are contained in line seven?
    A. One   B. Two   C. Three   D. None

32. How many errors are contained in line eight?
    A. One   B. Two   C. Three   D. None

Questions 33-40.

DIRECTIONS: Questions 33 through 40 are to be answered on the basis of the material contained in the INDEX OF CRIME IN CENTRAL CITY, U.S.A. 2011-2020 appearing below. Certain information is various columns is deliberately left blank.
The correct answer (A, B, C, or D) to these questions requires you to make computations that will enable you to fill in the blanks correctly.

INDEX OF CRIME IN CENTRAL CITY, U.S.A., 2011-2020									
	Crime Index Total	Violent Crime[1]	Property Crime[2]	Murder	Forcible Rape	Robbery	Aggravated Assault	Burglary	Larceny Theft	Motor Vehicle Theft
2011	8,717	875		19	51	385	420	2,565	4,347	930
2012	10,252	974	9278	20	55	443	456		5,262	977
2013	11,256	1,026	10,230	20		465	485	3,253	5,977	1,000
2014	11,304	986		18	58	420	490	3,089	6,270	959
2015	10,935	1,009	9,926	19	63	405	522	3,053	5,605	968
2016	11,140	1,061	10,079	19	67	417	558	3,104	5,983	992
2017	12,152	1,178	10,974	23	75	466	614	3,299	6,578	1,097
2018	13,294	1,308	11,986	23	83		654	3,759	7,113	1,114
2019	13,289	1,321	11,968	22	82	574	643	3,740	7,154	1,074
2020	12,856	1,285	11,571	22	77	536	650	3,415	7,108	1,048

33. What was the TOTAL number of Property Crimes in 2011?
    A. 9,740   B. 10,252   C. 16,559   D. 7,842

34. What was the TOTAL number of Burglaries for 2012?
    A. 2,062   B. 3,039   C. 3,259   D. 4,001

35. In 2020, the total number of Aggravated Assaults was MOST NEARLY what percent of the total number of Violent Crimes for that year?
    A. 49.1   B. 46.3   C. 50.6   D. 41.7

36. In 2015, Property Crime was MOST NEARLY what percent of the Crime Index Total?
    A. 90.8   B. 9.3   C. 10.1   D. 89.9

37. What was the TOTAL number of Property Crimes for 2014? 37.____
    A. 10,318   B. 11,304   C. 98   D. 10,808

38. What was the TOTAL number of Robberies for 2018? 38.____
    A. 654   B. 571   C. 548   D. 1,202

39. Robbery made up what percent of the TOTAL number of Violent Crimes for 2020? 39.____
    A. 68.8%   B. 4.1%   C. 21.9%   D. 41.7%

40. What was the TOTAL number of Forcible Rapes for 2013? 40.____
    A. 47   B. 56   C. 55   D. 101

KEY (CORRECT ANSWERS)

1.	D	11.	D	21.	A	31.	A
2.	B	12.	A	22.	C	32.	A
3.	B	13.	B	23.	C	33.	D
4.	A	14.	A	24.	B	34.	B
5.	D	15.	D	25.	C	35.	C
6.	D	16.	C	26.	D	36.	A
7.	B	17.	C	27.	C	37.	A
8.	C	18.	A	28.	B	38.	C
9.	D	19.	C	29.	C	39.	D
10.	D	20.	D	30.	B	40.	B

TEST 2

DIRECTIONS: Each question or incomplete statement is followed by several suggested answers or completions. Select the one that BEST answers the question or completes the statement. *PRINT THE LETTER OF THE CORRECT ANSWER IN THE SPACE AT THE RIGHT.*

Questions 1-8.

DIRECTIONS: Each of Questions 1 through 8 consists of three lines of code letters and numbers. The numbers on each line should correspond to the code letters on the same line in accordance with the table below.

Code Letter	X	B	L	T	V	M	P	F	J	S
Corresponding Number	0	1	2	3	4	5	6	7	8	9

On some of the lines, an error exists in the coding. Compare the letters and numbers in each question carefully. If you find an error or errors on:
Only <u>one</u> of the lines in the question, mark your answer A;
Any <u>two</u> of the lines in the question, mark your answer B;
All <u>three</u> lines in the question, mark your answer C;
<u>None</u> of the lines in the question, mark your answer D.

SAMPLE QUESTION: MSXVLPT—5904263
SBFJLTP—9178246
XVMBTPF—8451367

In the above sample, the first line is correct since each code letter listed has the correct corresponding number. On the second line, an error exists because code letter T should have number 3 instead of number 4. On the third line, an error exists because the code letter X should have the number 0 instead of the number 8. Since there are errors on two of the three lines, the correct answer is B.

1. VFSTPLM—4793625
   SBXFLTP—9017236
   BT[JFSV—1358794

2. TSLFVPJ—3927468
   JLFTVXS—8273409
   MVSXBFL—5490172

3. XFTJSVT—0739843
   VFMTFLB—4753721
   LTFJSFM—2378985

4. SJMSJVL—9859742
   VFBXMPF—3710568
   PFPXLBS—7670219

1.____

2.____

3.____

4.____

2 (#2)

5. MFPXVFP—5764076
    PTFJBLX—6378120
    VXSVSTB—4094931
                                                                                    5.____

6. BXFPVJT—1076483
    STFMVLT—9375423
    TXPBTTM—3061335
                                                                                    6.____

7. VLSBLVP—4290246
    FPSFBMV—7679154
    XTMXMLL—0730522
                                                                                    7.____

8. JFVPMTJ—8746538
    TFPMXBL—3765012
    TJSFMFX—4987570
                                                                                    8.____

Questions 9-18.

DIRECTIONS: Questions 9 through 18 each consists of two columns, each containing four lines of names, numbers and/or addresses. For each question, compare the lines in Column I with the lines in Column II to see if they match exactly, and mark your answer (A, B, C, or D) according to the following instructions:
A. all four lines match exactly
B. only three lines match exactly
C. only two lines match exactly
D. only one line matches exactly

9. (1) Earl Hodgson   Earl Hodgson
    (2) 1409870   1408970
    (3) Shore Ave.   Schore Ave.
    (4) Macon Rd.   Macon Rd.

10. (1) 9671485   9671485
    (2) 470 Astor Court   470 Astor Court
    (3) Halprin, Phillip Halperin, Phillip
    (4) Frank D. Poliseo Frank D. Poliseo

11. (1) Tandem Associates   Tandom Associates
    (2) 144-17 Northern Blvd. 144-17 Northern Blvd.
    (3) Alberta Forchi   Albert Forchi
    (4) Kings Park, NY 10751 Kings Point, NY 10751

12. (1) Bertha C. McCormack Bertha C. McCormack
    (2) Clayton, MO   Clayton, MO
    (3) 976-4242   976-4242
    (4) New City, NY 10951   New City, NY 10951

13. (1) George C. Morill   George C. Morrill   13._____
    (2) Columbia, SC 29201   Columbia, SD 29201
    (3) Louis Ingham   Louis Ingham
    (4) 3406 Forest Ave.   3406 Forest Ave.

14. (1) 506 S. Elliott Pl.   506 S. Elliott Pl.   14._____
    (2) Herbert Hall   Hurbert Hall
    (3) 4712 Rockaway Pkway   4712 Rockaway Pkway
    (4) 169 E. 7 St.   169 E. 7 St.

15. (1) 345 Park Ave.   345 Park Pl.   15._____
    (2) Colman Oven Corp.   Coleman Oven Corp.
    (3) Robert Conte   Robert Conti
    (4) 6179846   6179846

16. (1) Grigori Schierber   Grigori Schierber   16._____
    (2) Des Moines, Iowa   Des Moines, Iowa
    (3) Gouverneur Hospital   Gouverneur Hospital
    (4) 91-35 Cresskill Pl.   91-35 Cresskill Pl.

17. (1) Jeffery Janssen   Jeffrey Janssen   17._____
    (2) 8041071   8041071
    (3) 40 Rockefeller Plaza   40 Rockafeller Plaza
    (4) 407 6 St.   406 7 St.

18. (1) 5971996   5871996   18._____
    (2) 3113 Knickerbocker Ave. 3113 Knickerbocker Ave.
    (3) 8434 Boston Post Rd.   8424 Boston Post Rd.
    (4) Penn Station   Penn Station

Questions 19-22.

DIRECTIONS: Questions 19 through 22 are to be answered by looking at the 4 groups of names and addresses listed below (I, II, III, and IV) and then finding out the number of groups that have their corresponding numbered lines exactly the same.

Group I
Line 1 Ingersoll Public Library
Line 2 Reference and Research Dept.
Line 3 95-12 238 St.
Line 4 East Elmhurst, N.Y. 11357

Group II
Ingersoil Public Library
Reference and Research Dept.
95-12 238 St.
East Elmhurst, N.Y. 11357

Group III
Line 1 Ingersoll Public Library
Line 2 Reference and Research Dept.
Line 3 92-15 283 St.
Line 4 East Elmhurst, N.Y. 11357

Group IV
Ingersoll Poblic Library
Referance and Research Dept.
95-12 283 St.
East Elmhurst, N.Y. 1357

4 (#2)

19. In how many groups is line one exactly the same?   19._____
    A. Two B. Three C. Four D. None

20. In how many groups is line two exactly the same?   20._____
    A. Two B. Three C. Four D. None

21. In how many groups is line three exactly the same?   20._____
    A. Two B. Three C. Four D. None

22. In how many groups is line four exactly the same?   22._____
    A. Two B. Three C. Four E. None

Questions 23-26.

DIRECTIONS: Questions 23 through 26 are to be answered by looking at the 4 groups of names and addresses listed below (I, II, III, and IV) and then finding out the number of groups that have their corresponding numbered lines exactly the same.

Group I
Line 1 Richmond General Hospital
Line 2 Geriatric Clinic
Line 3 3975 Paerdegat St.
Line 4 Loudonville, New York 11538

Group II
Richman General Hospital
Geriatric Clinic
3975 Peardegat St.
Londonville, New York 11538

Group III
Line 1 Richmond General Hospital
Line 2 Geriatric Clinic
Line 3 3795 Paerdegat St.
Line 4 Loudonville, New York 11358

Group IV
Richmend General Hospital
Geriatric Clinic
3975 Paerdegat St.
Loudonville, New York 11538

23. In how many groups is line one exactly the same?   23._____
    A. Two B. Three C. Four D. None

24. In how many groups is line two exactly the same?   24._____
    A. Two B. Three C. Four D. None

25. In how many groups is line three exactly the same?   25._____
    A. Two B. Three C. Four D. None

26. In how many groups is line four exactly the same?   26._____
    A. Two B. Three C. Four D. None

Questions 27-34.

DIRECTIONS: Each of Questions 27 through 34 consists of four or six numbered names. For each question, choose the option (A, B, C, or D) which indicates the order in which the names should be filed in accordance with the following file instructions:

11

5 (#2)

- File alphabetically according to last name, then first name, then middle initial.
- File according to each successive letter within a name.
- When comparing two names where the letters in the longer name are identical with the corresponding letters in the shorter name, the shorter name is filed first.
- When the last names are the same, initials are always filed before names beginning with the same letter.

27. I. Ralph Robinson
    II. Alfred Ross
    III. Luis Robles
    IV. James Roberts
    The CORRECT filing sequence for the above names should be
    A. IV, II, I, III   B. I, IV, III, II   C. III, IV, I, II   D. IV, I, III, II

28. I. Irwin Goodwin
    II. Inez Gonzalez
    III. Irene Goodman
    IV. Ira S. Goodwin
    V. Ruth I. Goldstein
    VI. M.B. Goodman
    The CORRECT filing sequence for the above names should be
    A. V, II, I, IV, III, VI   B. V, II, VI, III, IV, I
    C. V, II, III, VI, IV, I   D. V, II, III, VI, I, IV

29. I. George Allan
    II. Gregory Allen
    III. Gary Allen
    IV. George Allen
    The CORRECT filing sequence for the above names should be
    A. IV, III, I, II   B. I, IV, II, III   C. III, IV, I, II   D. I, III, IV, II

30. I. Simon Kauffman
    II. Leo Kauffman
    III. Robert Kaufmann
    IV. Paul Kauffman
    The CORRECT filing sequence for the above names should be
    A. I, IV, II, III   B. II, IV, I, III   C. III, II, IV, I   D. I, II, III, IV

31. I. Roberta Williams
    II. Robin Wilson
    III. Roberta Wilson
    IV. Robin Williams
    The CORRECT filing sequence for the above names should be
    A. III, II, IV, I   B. I, IV, III, II   C. I, II, III, IV   D. III, I, II, IV

32. I. Lawrence Shultz
    II. Albert Schultz
    III. Theodore Schwartz
    IV. Thomas Schwarz
    V. Alvin Schultz
    VI. Leonard Shultz
    The CORRECT filing sequence for the above names should be
    A. II, V, III, IV, I, VI
    B. IV, III, V, I, II, VI
    C. II, V, I, VI, III, IV
    D. I, VI, II, V, III, IV

33. I. McArdle
    II. Mayer
    III. Maletz
    IV. McNiff
    V. Meyer
    VI. MacMahon
    The CORRECT filing sequence for the above names should be
    A. I, IV, VI, III, II, V
    B. II, I, IV, VI, III, V
    C. VI, III, II, I, IV, V
    D. VI, III, II, V, I, IV

34. I. Jack E. Johnson
    II. R.H. Jackson
    III. Bertha Jackson
    IV. J.T. Johnson
    V. Ann Johns
    VI. John Jacobs
    The CORRECT filing sequence for the above names should be
    A. II, III, VI, V, IV, I
    B. III, II, VI, V, IV, I
    C. VI, II, III, I, V, IV
    D. III, II, VI, IV, V, I

Questions 35-40.

DIRECTIONS: Questions 35 through 40 are to be answered SOLELY on the basis of the following passage.

An aide assigned to the Complaint Room must be familiar with the various forms used by that office. Some of these forms and their uses are:

Complaint Report:	Used to record information on or information about crimes reported to the Police Department.
Complaint Report Follow-Up:	Used to record additional information after the initial complaint report has been filed
Aided Card:	Used to record information pertaining to sick and injured persons aided by the police.
Accident Report:	Used to record information on or information about injuries and/or property damage involving motorized vehicles.
Property Vouch:	Used to record information on or information about property which comes into possession of the Police Department. (Motorized vehicles are not included.)

Auto Voucher: Used to record information on or information about a motorized vehicle which comes into possession of the Police Department.

35. Mr. Brown walks into the police precinct and informs the Administrative Aide that, while he was at work, someone broke into his apartment and removed property belonging to him. He does not know everything that was taken, but he wants to make a report now and will make a list of what was taken and bring it in later.
According to the above passage, the CORRECT form to use in this situation should be the
   A. Property Voucher
   B. Complaint Report
   C. Complaint Report Follow-Up
   D. Aided Card

36. Mrs. Wilson telephones the precinct and informs the Administrative Aide she wishes to report additional property which was taken from her apartment. The Administrative Aide finds a Complaint Report had been previously filed for Mrs. Wilson.
According to the above passage, the CORRECT form to use in this situation should be the
   A. Property Voucher
   B. Complaint Report
   C. Complaint Report Follow-Up
   D. Aided Card

37. Police Officer Jones walks into the Complaint Room and informs the Administrative Aide that, while he was on patrol, he observed a woman fall to the sidewalk and remain there, apparently hurt. He comforted the injured woman and called for an ambulance, which came and brought the woman to the hospital.
According to the above passage, the CORRECT form on which to record this information should be the
   A. Accident Report
   B. Complaint Report
   C. Complaint Report Follow-Up
   D. Aided Card

38. Police Officer Smith informed the Administrative Aide assigned to the Complaint Room that Mr. Green, while crossing the street, was struck by a motorcycle and had to be taken to the hospital.
According to the above passage, the facts regarding this incident should be recorded on which one of the following forms?
   A. Accident Report
   B. Complaint Report
   C. Complaint Report Follow-Up
   D. Aided Card

39. Police Officer Williams reports to the Administrative Aide assigned to the Complaint Room that he and his partner, Police Officer Murphy, found an auto which was reported stolen and had the auto towed into the police garage.
Of the following forms listed in the above passage, which is the CORRECT one to use to record this information?
   A. Property Voucher
   B. Auto Voucher
   C. Complaint Report Follow-Up
   D. Complaint Report

40. Administrative Aide Lopez has been assigned to the Complaint Room. During her tour of duty, a person who does not identify herself hands Ms. Lopez a purse. The person states that she found the purse on the street. She then leaves the station house.
   According to the information in the above passage, which is the CORRECT form to fill out to record the incident?
   A. Property Voucher
   B. Auto Voucher
   C. Complaint Report Follow-Up
   D. Complaint Report

KEY (CORRECT ANSWERS)

1.	B	11.	D	21.	A	31.	B
2.	D	12.	A	22.	C	32.	A
3.	B	13.	C	23.	A	33.	C
4.	C	14.	B	24.	C	34.	B
5.	A	15.	D	25.	A	35.	B
6.	D	16.	A	26.	A	36.	C
7.	C	17.	D	27.	D	37.	D
8.	A	18.	C	28.	C	38.	A
9.	C	19.	A	29.	D	39.	B
10.	B	20.	B	30.	B	40.	A

EXAMINATION SECTION
TEST 1

DIRECTIONS: Each question or incomplete statement is followed by several suggested answers or completions. Select the one that BEST answers the question or completes the statement. *PRINT THE LETTER OF THE CORRECT ANSWER IN THE SPACE AT THE RIGHT.*

1. As an administrative aide, it is your job to type reports prepared by several police officers. These reports are then returned to them for review and signature. Officer X consistently submits reports to you which contain misspellings and incorrect punctuation.
    Of the following, the BEST action for you to take is to
    A. tell your supervisor that something must be done about Officer X's poor English
    B. ask Officer X for permission to correct any mistakes
    C. assemble all of the officers and tell them that you refuse to correct their mistakes
    D. tell Officer X to be more careful

1.____

2. On a chart used in your precinct, there appear small figures of men, women, and children to denote population trends. Your supervisor assigns you to suggest possible symbols for a char which will be used to indicate daily vehicular traffic flow in the area covered by this precinct.
    In this situation, your BEST course of action would be to
    A. tell your supervisor an artist should be hired to draw these symbols
    B. make up a list of possible symbols, such as cars and trucks
    C. say that any decision as to the symbols to be used should be made at a higher level
    D. find out how many vehicles use the area

2.____

3. As an administrative aide, you are assigned to the telephone switchboard. An extremely irate citizen calls complaining in bigoted terms about a group of Black teenagers who congregate in front of his house. The caller insists on speaking to whoever is in charge. At the moment, Sergeant X, a black man, is in charge.
    The BEST course of action for you to take is to
    A. inform the caller that the teenagers may meet wherever they wish
    B. tell the caller that Sergeant X, a black man, is in charge, and ask him to call back later when a white man will be there
    C. tell the caller that you resent his bigotry and insist that he call back when he has calmed down
    D. acquaint Sergeant X with the circumstances and connect the caller with him

3.____

4. Assume that you have access to restricted materials such as conviction records. A friend asks you, unofficially, if a man he has recently met has a record of conviction.
   The BEST thing for you to do is to
   A. give your friend the information he wants and inform your supervisor of your actions
   B. tell your friend that you are not allowed to give out such information
   C. tell your friend you will try to get the information for him but do not take any action
   D. give him the information because it is a matter of public record

5. Assume that you are an administrative aide assigned to a busy telephone information center.
   Of the following, which is the MOST important technique to use when answering the telephone?
   A. Using many technical police terms
   B. Speaking slowly, in a monotone, for clarity
   C. Using formal English grammar
   D. Speaking clearly and distinctly

6. As an administrative aide, you are asked by an officer working in an adjacent office to type a very important letter without mistakes or corrections exactly as he has prepared it. As you are typing, you notice a word which, according to the dictionary, is misspelled.
   Under the circumstances, you should
   A. ignore the error and type it exactly as prepared
   B. change the spelling without telling the officer
   C. ask the officer if you should change the spelling
   D. change the spelling and tell the officer

7. As am administrative aide, you are in charge of a large complex of files. In an effort to be helpful, some officers who frequently use the file have begun to refile material they had been using. Unfortunately, they often make errors.
   Of the following, your BEST course of action is to
   A. ask them to leave the files for you to put away
   B. ask your supervisor to reprimand them
   C. frequently check the whole filing system for errors
   D. tell them they are making mistakes and insist they leave the files alone

8. One afternoon several of the police officers ask you to do different tasks. Each task will take about a day to complete, but each officer insists that his work must be completed immediately.
   Your BEST course of action is to
   A. do a little of each assignment given to you
   B. ask your fellow workers to help you with the assignment
   C. speak to your supervisor in order to determine the priority of the assignments
   D. do the work in the order of the rank of the officers giving the assignments

Questions 9-12.

DIRECTIONS: Questions 9 through 12 are to be answered on the basis of the following passage.

It should be emphasized that one goal of law enforcement is the reduction of stress between one population group and another. When no stress exists between populations, law enforcement can deal with other tensions or simply perform traditional police functions. However, when stress between populations does exist, law enforcement, in its efforts to prevent disruptive behavior, becomes committed to reducing that stress (if for no other reason than its responsibility to maintain an orderly environment). The type of stress to be reduced, unlike the tension stemming from social change, is stress generated through intergroup and interracial friction. Of course, all sources of tension are inextricably interrelated, but friction between different populations in the community is of immediate concern to law enforcement.

9. The above passage emphasizes that, during times of stress between groups in the community, it is necessary for the police to attempt to
   A. continue their traditional duties
   B. eliminate tension resulting from social change
   C. reduce intergroup stress
   D. punish disruptive behavior

10. Based on the above passage, police concern with tension among groups in a community is MOST likely to stem primarily from their desire to
   A. establish racial justice   B. prevent violence
   C. protect property   D. unite the diverse groups

11. According to the above passage, enforcers of the law are responsible for
   A. analyzing consequences of population-group hostility
   B. assisting social work activities
   C. creating order in the environment
   D. explaining group behavior

12. The factor which produces the tension accompanying social change is
   A. a disorderly environment
   B. disruptive behavior
   C. inter-community hostility
   D. not discussed in the above passage

Questions 13-19.

DIRECTIONS: Questions 13 through 19 are to be answered on the basis of the information given in the following passage.

From a nationwide point of view, the need for new housing units during the years immediately ahead will be determined by four major factors. The most important factor is the net change in household formations—that is, the difference between the number of new households that are formed and the number of existing households that are dissolved, whether by death or other circumstances. During the 1990's, as the children born during the decades of the 60's and 70's come of age and marry, the total number of households is expected to increase at a rate of more than 1,000,000 annually. The second factor affecting the need for new housing units is *removals*—that is, existing units that are demolished, damaged beyond repair, or otherwise removed from the housing supply. A third factor is the number of existing vacancies. To some extent, vacancies can satisfy the housing demand caused by increases in total number of households or by removals, although population shifts that are already under way mean that some areas will have a surfeit of vacancies and other areas will be faced with serious shortages of housing. A final factor, and one that has only recently assumed major importance, is the increasing demand for second homes. These may take any form from a shack in the woods for the city dweller to a *pied-a-terre* in the city for a suburbanite. Whatever the form, however, it is certain that increasing leisure time, rising amounts of discretionary income, and improvements in transportation are leading more and more Americans to look on a second home not as a rich man's luxury but as the common man's right.

13. The above passage uses the term *housing units* to refer to
    A. residences of all kinds
    B. apartment buildings only
    C. one-family houses only
    D. the total number of families in the United States

14. The passage uses the word *removals* to mean
    A. the shift of population from one area to another
    B. vacancies that occur when families move
    C. financial losses suffered when a building is damaged or destroyed
    D. former dwellings that are demolished or can no longer be used for housing

15. The expression *pied-a-terre* appears in the next-to-last sentence in the passage. A person who is not familiar with the expression should be able to tell from the way it is used here that it probably means
    A. a suburban home owned by a commuter
    B. a shack in the woods
    C. a second home that is used from time to time
    D. overnight lodging for a traveler in a strange city

16. Of the factors described in the passage as having an important influence on the demand for housing, which factor—taken alone—is LEAST likely to encourage the construction of new housing?
    The
    A. net change in household formations
    B. destruction of existing housing
    C. existence of vacancies
    D. use of second homes

17. Based on the above passage, the TOTAL increase in the number of households during the 1990's is expected to be MOST NEARLY
    A. 1,000,000
    B. 10,000,000
    C. 100,000,000
    D. 1,000,000,000

18. Which one of the following conclusions could MOST logically be drawn from the information given in the passage?
    A. The population of the United States is increasing at the rate of about 1,000,000 people annually.
    B. There is already a severe housing shortage in all parts of the country.
    C. The need for additional housing units is greater in some parts of the country than in others.
    D. It is still true that only wealthy people can afford to keep up more than one home.

19. Which one of the following conclusions could NOT logically be drawn from the information given in the passage?
    A. The need for new housing will be even greater in the 2000's than in the 1990's.
    B. Demolition of existing housing must be taken into account in calculating the need for new housing construction.
    C. Having a second home is more common today than it was in the 1960's.
    D. Part of the housing needs of the 1990's can be met by vacancies.

20. You are making a report on the number of incoming calls handled by two different switchboards. Over a five-day period, the total count of incoming calls per day for both switchboards together was 2,773. The average number of incoming calls per day for Switchboard A was 301. You cannot find one day's tally for Switchboard B, but the total for the other four days for Switchboard B come to 1,032.
    Determine from this how many incoming calls must have been reported on the *missing* tally for Switchboard B.
    A. 236   B. 259   C. 408   D. 1,440

21. Assume that one-page notices for distribution may be reproduced by photocopy or by a designer. The cost for photocopying is 5½ cents per copy. It can also be reproduced by a designer for an initial preparation cost of $1.38 plus a per-copy cost of one cent.
    Strictly according to cost, which of the following is the LOWEST number of copies at which it would be more economical to choose the designer instead of photocopying?
    A. 15   B. 30   C. 45   D. 138

22. An employee completed 75% of a clerical assignment in four days.
    How much of it did he complete in the last two days if he finished 3/8 of it in the first two days?
    A. 1/4   B. 3/8   C. 5/8   D. 3/4

23. Seven hundred people are to be scheduled for interviews.
    If 58% of these 700 people have already been scheduled, how many more must be scheduled?
    A. 138   B. 294   C. 406   D. 410

24. In recent years, an average of 35% of the violations reported in any given month have been corrected by the time of a follow-up inspection one month later. Last month, 240 violations were reported, and this month's follow-up inspections show that 93 of them have been corrected.
How many more violations have been corrected than would have been expected based on the average rate?
   A. 5   B. 9   C. 33   D. 58

25. Suppose that, on a scaled drawing of an office floor plan, ½ inch equals 2 feet. An office that is actually 12 feet wide and 17 feet long has which of the following dimensions on this scaled drawing?
   _____ wide and _____.
   A. 3"; 4.25"   B. 6"' 8.5"   C. 12"; 17"   D. 24"; 34"

KEY (CORRECT ANSWERS)

1.	B		11.	C
2.	B		12.	D
3.	D		13.	A
4.	B		14.	D
5.	D		15.	C
6.	C		16.	C
7.	A		17.	B
8.	C		18.	C
9.	C		19.	A
10.	B		20.	A

21.	C
22.	B
23.	B
24.	B
25.	A

TEST 2

DIRECTIONS: Each question or incomplete statement is followed by several suggested answers or completions. Select the one that BEST answers the question or completes the statement. *PRINT THE LETTER OF THE CORRECT ANSWER IN THE SPACE AT THE RIGHT.*

1. Suppose that employees in a certain division put in a total of 1,250 hours of overtime in 2019. In 2020, total overtime hours for the same division were 2% less than in 2019, but in 2021 overtime hours increased by 8% over the 2020 total.
   How many overtime hours were worked by the staff of this division in 2021?
   A. 1,323   B. 1,331   C. 1,350   D. 1,375

   1.____

2. A particular operation currently involves 75 employees, 80% of whom work in the field and the rest of whom are office staff. A management study has shown that in order to be truly efficient, the operation should have a ratio of at least 1 office employee to every 3 field employees, and the study recommends that the number of field employees remain the same as at present.
   What is the MINIMUM number of employees needed to carry out the operation efficiently, according to this recommendation?
   A. 65   B. 75   C. 80   D. 100

   2.____

Questions 3-6.

DIRECTIONS: Questions 3 through 6 are to be answered on the basis of the information given in the following passage.

Data processing is by no means a new invention. In one form or another, it has been carried on throughout the entire history of civilization. In its most general sense, data processing means organizing data so that it can be used for a specific purpose, a procedure commonly known simply as *record-keeping* or paperwork. With the development of modern office equipment, and particularly with the recent introduction of computers, the techniques of data processing have become highly elaborate and sophisticated, but the basic purpose remains the same: turning raw data into useful information.

The key concept here is usefulness. The data, or input, that is to be processed can be compared to the raw material that is to go into a manufacturing process. The information, or output, that results from data processing—like the finished product of a manufacturer—should be clearly usable. A collection of data has little value unless it is converted into information that serves a specific function.

3. The expression *paperwork*, as it is used in this passage,
   A. shows that the author regards such operations as a waste of time
   B. has the same general meaning as *data processing*
   C. refers to methods of record-keeping that are no longer in use
   D. indicates that the public does not understand the purpose of data processing

   3.____

4. The passage indicates that the use of computers has 4.____
   A. greatly simplified the clerical work in an office
   B. led to more complicated systems for the handling of data
   C. had no effect whatsoever on data processing
   D. made other modern office machines obsolete

5. Which of the following BEST expresses the basic principle of data processing 5.____
   as it is described in the passage?
   A. Input – processing – output
   B. Historical record-keeping – modern techniques – specific functions
   C. Office equipment – computer – accurate data
   D. Raw material – manufacturer - retailer

6. According to the above passage, data processing may be described as 6.____
   A. a new management technique   B. computer technology
   C. information output   D. record-keeping

Questions 7-10.

DIRECTIONS: Questions 7 through 10 are to be answered on the basis of the following passage.

Analysis of current data reveals that motor vehicle transportation actually requires less space than was used for other types of transportation in the pre-automobile era, even including the substantial area taken by freeways. The reason is that when the fast-moving through traffic is put on built-for-the-purpose arterial roads, then the amount of ordinary space needed for strictly local movement and for access to property drops sharply. Even the amount of land taken for urban expressways turns out to be surprisingly small in terms either of total urban acreage or of the volume of traffic they carry. No existing or contemplated urban expressway system requires as much as 3 percent of the land in the areas it serves, and this would be exceptionally high. The Los Angeles freeway system, when complete, will occupy only 2 percent of the available land; the same is true of the District of Columbia, where only 0.75 percent will be pavement, with the remaining 1.25 percent as open space. California studies estimate that, in a typical California urban community, 1.6 to 2 percent of the area should be devoted to freeways, which will handle 50 to 60 percent of all traffic needs, and about ten times as much land to the ordinary roads and streets that carry the rest of the traffic. By comparison, when John A. Sutter laid out Sacramento in 1850, he provided 38 percent of the area for streets and sidewalks. The French architect, Pierre L'Enfant, proposed 59 percent of the area of the District of Columbia for roads and streets; urban renewal in Southwest Washington, incorporating a modern street network, reduced the acreage of space for pedestrian and vehicular traffic in the renewal area from 48.2 to 41.5 percent of the total. If we are to have a reasonable consideration of the impact of highway transportation on contemporary urban development, it would be well to understand these relationships.

7. The author of this passage says that 7.____
   A. modern transportation uses less space than was used for transportation before the auto age
   B. expressways require more space than streets in terms of urban acreage

C. typical urban communities were poorly designed in terms of relationship between space used for traffic and that used for other purposes
D. the need for local and access roads would increase if the number of expressways were increased

8. According to the above passage, it was originally planned that the percent of the area to be used for roads and streets in the District of Columbia should be MOST NEARLY
   A. 40%   B. 45%   C. 505   D. 60%

9. The above passage states that the amount of space needed for local traffic
   A. *increases* when arterial highways are constructed
   B. *decreases* when arterial highways are constructed
   C. *decreases* when there is more land available
   D. *increases* when there is more land available

10. According to the above passage, studies estimate that, in a typical California urban community, the amount of land devoted to ordinary roads and streets as compared with that devoted to freeways should be MOST NEARLY _____ as much.
    A. one-half   B. one-tenth   C. twice   D. ten times

Questions 11-13.

DIRECTIONS: Questions 11 through 13 are to be answered on the basis of the following passage.

A glaring exception to the usual practice of the judicial trial as a means of conflict resolution is the utilization of administrative hearings. The growing tendency to create administrative bodies with rule-making and quasi-judicial powers has shattered many standard concepts. A comprehensive examination of the legal process cannot neglect these newer patterns.

In the administrative process, the legislative, executive, and judicial functions are mixed together, and many functions, such as investigating, advocating, negotiating, testifying, rule-making an adjudicating, are carried out by the same agency. The reason for the breakdown of the separation-of-powers formula is not hard to find. It was felt by Congress, and state and municipal legislatures, that certain regulatory tasks could not be performed efficiently, rapidly, expertly, and with due concern for the public interest by the traditional branches of government. Accordingly, regulatory agencies were delegated powers to consider disputes from the earliest stage of investigation to the final stages of adjudication entirely within each agency itself, subject only to limited review in the regular courts.

11. The above passage states that the usual means for conflict resolution is through the use of
    A. judicial trial   B. administrative hearing
    C. legislation   D. regulatory agencies

12. The above passage *implies* that the use of administrative hearing in resolving conflict is a(n) _____ approach.
    A. traditional
    B. new
    C. dangerous
    D. experimental

13. The above passage states that the reason for the breakdown of the separation-of-powers formula in the administrative process is that
    A. Congress believed that certain regulatory tasks could be better performed by separate agencies
    B. legislative and executive functions are incompatible in the same agency
    C. investigative and regulatory functions are not normally reviewed by the courts
    D. state and municipal legislatures are more concerned with efficiency than with legality

14. An employee examining the summonses of individuals appearing for hearings noticed that the address on one summons was the same as that of an individual who had appeared earlier that day. He asked the second respondent if he knew the first respondent.
    The MOST appropriate evaluation of the employee's behavior is that he should
    A. not have mentioned any other respondent to the second respondent
    B. not waste time inspecting summonses in such detail
    C. be commended for inspecting summonses so carefully
    D. be commended for his investigation of the respondents

15. An employee is assigned to maintain all types of frequently used reference materials such as booklets and technical papers. He keeps these in a pile on a shelf in order of arrival. When new material arrives, he put it on top of the pile.
    Which of the following BEST evaluates the employee's handling of this reference material?
    His system is MOST likely to result in _____ filing and _____ retrieval.
    A. fast; slow   B. slow; slow   C. fast; fast   D. slow; fast

16. An employee computes statistics relating to proceeding. The method he devised consists of organizing his source and summary documents in such a manner that at any time another employee can assume the work. This method takes a little more time than other possible methods.
    Which of the following statements BEST evaluates the judgment of the employee in devising such a method?
    The employee has used
    A. *good* judgment because it is important to provide for continuity
    B. *poor* judgment because he is not using the fastest method
    C. *good* judgment because, if a job is done as fast as possible, it becomes tiring
    D. *poor* judgment because it is not an employee's responsibility to prepare for a replacement

5 (#2)

17. Assume that it is your job to receive incoming telephone calls. Those calls which you cannot handle yourself have to be transferred to the appropriate office.
    If you receive an outside call for an extension line which is busy, the one of the following which you should do FIRST is to
    A. interrupt the person speaking on the extension and tell him a call is waiting
    B. tell the caller the line is busy and let him know every thirty seconds whether or not it is free
    C. leave the caller on *hold* until the extension is free
    D. tell the caller the line is busy and ask him if he wishes to wait

17.____

18. On one occasion in a certain office, an elderly employee collapsed, apparently the victim of a heart attack. Chaos broke out in the office as several people tried to help him and several others tried to get assistance.
    Of the following, the MOST certain way of avoiding such chaos in the future is to
    A. keep a copy of heart attack procedures on file so that it can be referenced to by any member of the staff when an emergency occurs
    B. provide each member of the staff with a first aid book which is to be kept in an accessible location
    C. train all members of the staff in the proper procedure for handling such emergencies, assigning specific responsibilities
    D. post, in several places around the office, a list of specific procedures to follow in each of several different emergencies

18.____

19. Your superior has subscribed to several publications directly related to your divisions work, and he has asked you to see to it that the publications are circulated among the supervisory personnel in the division. There are eight supervisors involved.
    The BEST method of insuring that all eight see these publications is to
    A. place the publication in the division's general reference library as soon as it arrives
    B. inform each supervisor whenever a publication arrives and remind all of them that they are responsible for reading it
    C. prepare a standard slip that can be stapled to each publication, listing the eight supervisors and saying, *Please read, initial your name, and pass along*
    D. send a memo to the eight supervisors saying that they may wish to purchase individual subscriptions in their own names if they are interested in seeing each issue

19.____

20. Assume that you have been asked to prepare a narrative summary of the monthly reports submitted by employees in your division.
    In preparing your summary of this month's reports, the FIRST step to take is to
    A. read through the reports, noting their general content and any unusual features
    B. decide how many typewritten pages your summary should contain

20.____

C. make a written summary of each separate report, so that you will not have to go back to the original reports again
D. ask each employee which points he would prefer to see emphasized in your summary

21. Your superior has telephoned a number of key officials in your agency to ask whether they can meet at a certain time next month. He has found that they can all make it, and he has asked you to confirm the meeting.
Which of the following is the BEST way to confirm such a meeting?
    A. Note the meeting on your superior's calendar
    B. Post a notice of the meeting on the agency bulletin board
    C. Call the officials on the day of the meeting to remind them of the meeting
    D. Write a memo to each official involved repeating the time and place of the meeting

22. Of the following, the worker who is MOST likely to create a problem in maintaining safety is one who
    A. disregards hazards
    B. feels tired
    C. resents authority
    D. gets bored

23. Assume that a new regulation requires that certain kinds of private organizations file information forms with your department. You have been asked to write the short explanatory message that will be printed on the front cover of the pamphlet containing the forms and instructions.
Which of the following would be the MOST appropriate way of beginning this message?
    A. Get the readers' attention by emphasizing immediately that there are legal penalties for organizations that fail to file before a certain date
    B. Briefly state the nature of the enclosed forms and the types of organizations that must file
    C. Say that your department is very sorry to have to put organizations to such an inconvenience
    D. Quote the entire regulation adopted by the city, even if it is quite long and is expressed in complicated legal language

24. Suppose that you have been told to make up the vacation schedule for the 15 employees in a particular unit. In order for the unit to operate effectively, only a few employees can be on vacation at the same time.
Which of the following is the MOST advisable approach in making up the schedule?
    A. Draw up a schedule assigning vacations in alphabetical order
    B. Find out when the supervisors want to take their vacations, and randomly assign whatever periods are left to the non-supervisory personnel
    C. Assign the most desirable times to employees of longest standing, and the least desirable times to the newest employees
    D. Have all employees state their own preferences, and then work out any conflicts in consultation with the people involved

25. Assume that you have been asked to prepare job descriptions for various positions in your department.
Which of the following are the BASIC points that should be covered in a job description?
   A. General duties and responsibilities of the position, with examples of day-to-day tasks
   B. Comments on the performances of present employees
   C. Estimates of the number of openings that may be available in each category during the coming year
   D. Instructions for carrying out the specific tasks assigned to your department

25.____

KEY (CORRECT ANSWERS)

1.	A	11.	A
2.	C	12.	B
3.	B	13.	A
4.	B	14.	A
5.	A	15.	A
6.	D	16.	A
7.	A	17.	D
8.	D	18.	C
9.	B	19.	C
10.	D	20.	A

21.	D
22.	A
23.	B
24.	D
25.	A

TEST 3

DIRECTIONS: Each question or incomplete statement is followed by several suggested answers or completions. Select the one that BEST answers the question or completes the statement. *PRINT THE LETTER OF THE CORRECT ANSWER IN THE SPACE AT THE RIGHT.*

Questions 1-6.

DIRECTIONS: Questions 1 through 6 consist of sets of names and addresses. In each question, the name and address in Column II should be an exact copy of the name and address in Column I. If there is:
a mistake only in the name, mark your answer A;
a mistake only in the address, mark your answer B;
a mistake in both name and address, mark your answer C;
NO mistake in either name or address, mark your answer D.

SAMPLE QUESTION

COLUMN I	COLUMN II
Christina Magnusson	Christina Magnusson
288 Greene Street	288 Greene Street
New York, NY 10003	New York, NY 10013

Since there is a mistake only in the address (the zone number should be 10003 instead of 10013), the answer to the sample question is B.

	COLUMN I	COLUMN II	
1.	Ms. Joan Kelly 313 Franklin Ave. Brooklyn, NY 11202	Ms. Joan Kielly 318 Franklin Ave. Brooklyn, NY 11202	1.____
2.	Mrs. Eileen Engel 47-24 86 Road Queens, NY 11122	Mrs. Ellen Engel 47-24 86 Road Queens, NY 11122	2.____
3.	Marcia Michaels 213 E. 81 St. New York, NY 10012	Marcia Michaels 213 E. 81 St. New York, NY 10012	3.____
4.	Rev. Edward J. Smyth 1401 Brandeis Street San Francisco, CA 96201	Rev. Edward J. Smyth 1401 Brandies Street San Francisco, CA 96201	4.____
5.	Alicia Rodriguez 24-68 81 St. Elmhurst, NY 11122	Alicia Rodriguez 2468 81 St. Elmhurst, NY 11122	5.____

COLUMN I	COLUMN II	
6. Ernest Eisemann
21 Columbia St.
New York, NY 10007	Ernest Eisermann
21 Columbia St.
New York, NY 10007	6._____

Questions 7-11.

DIRECTIONS: Questions 7 through 11 each consist of five serial numbers which must be arranged according to the directions given below.

The serial numbers of dollar bills in Column I begin and end with a capital letter and have an eight-digit number in between. They are to be arranged as follows:

First: In alphabetical order according to the first letter.
Second: When two or more serial numbers have the same first letter, in alphabetical order according to the last letter.
Third: When two or more serial numbers have the same first and last letters, in numerical order, beginning with the lowest number.

The serial numbers in Column I are numbered (1) through (5) in the order in which they are listed. In Column II, the numbers (1) through (5) are arranged in four different ways to show different arrangements of the corresponding serial numbers. Choose the answer in Column II in which the serial numbers are arranged according to the above rules.
SAMPLE QUESTION:

	COLUMN I		COLUMN II
(1)	E75044127B	(A)	4, 1, 3, 2, 5
(2)	B96399104A	(B)	4, 1 2, 3, 5
(3)	B93939086A	(C)	4, 3, 2 5, 1
(4)	B47064465H	(D)	3, 2, 5, 4, 1
(5)	B99040922A		

In the sample question, the four serial numbers starting with B should be put before the serial numbers starting with E. The serial numbers starting with B and ending with A should be put before the serial number starting with B and ending with H. The three serial numbers starting with B and ending with A should be listed in numerical order, beginning with the lowest number. The correct way to arrange the serial numbers, therefore, is

(3) B93939086A
(2) B96399104A
(5) B99040922A
(4) B47064465H
(1) B75044127B

Since the order of arrangement is 3, 2, 5, 4, 1, the answer to the sample question is (D).

	COLUMN I		COLUMN II		
7.	(1)	S55126179E	A.	1, 5, 2, 3, 4	7._____
	(2)	R55136177Q	B.	3, 4, 1, 5, 2	
	(3)	P55126177R	C.	3, 5, 2, 1, 4	
	(4)	S55126178R	D.	4, 3, 1, 5, 2	
	(5)	R55126180P			
8.	(1)	T64217813Q	A.	4, 1, 3, 2, 5	8._____
	(2)	I642178170	B.	2, 4, 3, 1, 5	
	(3)	T642188O	C.	4, 1, 5, 2, 3	
	(4)	I64217811Q	D.	2, 3, 4, 1, 5	
	(5)	T64217816Q			
9.	(1)	C83261824G	A.	2, 4, 1, 5, 3	9._____
	(2)	C78361833C	B.	4, 2, 1, 3, 5	
	(3)	G83261732G	C.	3, 1, 5, 2, 4	
	(4)	C88261823C	D.	2, 3, 5, 1, 4	
	(5)	G83261743C			
10.	(1)	A11710107H	A.	2, 1, 4, 3, 5	10._____
	(2)	H17110017A	B.	3, 1, 5, 2, 4	
	(3)	A11170707A	C.	3, 4, 1, 5, 2	
	(4)	II17170171H	D.	3, 5, 1, 2, 4	
	(5)	A11710177A			
11.	(1)	R26794821S	A.	3, 2, 4, 1, 5	11._____
	(2)	O26794821T	B.	3, 4, 2, 1, 5	
	(3)	M26794827Z	C.	4, 2, 1, 3, 5	
	(4)	Q26794821R	D.	5, 4, 1, 2, 3	
	(5)	S26794821P			

Questions 12-16.

DIRECTIONS: Questions 12 through 16 each consist of three lines of code letters and numbers. The numbers on each line should correspond with the code letters on the same line in accordance with the table below.

Code Letters	Q	S	L	Y	M	O	U	N	W	Z
Corresponding Numbers	1	2	3	4	5	6	7	8	9	0

On some of the lines, an error exists in the coding. Compare the letters and numbers in each question carefully. If you find an error on:
  only ONE of the lines in the question, mark your answer A;
  any TWO lines in the question, mark your answer B;
  all THREE lines in the question, mark your answer C;
  NONE of the lines in the question, mark your answer D.

SAMPLE: MOQNWZQS – 56189012
QWNMOLYU – 19865347
LONLMYWN – 36835489

In the above sample, the first line is correct since each code letter, as listed, has the correct corresponding number. On the second line, an error exists because code letter M should have the letter number 5 instead of the number 6. On the third line, an error exists because the code letter W should have the number 9 instead of the number 8. Since there are errors on two of the three lines, the correct answer is B.

12.	SMUWOLQN ULSQNMZL NMYQZUSL	25796318 73218503 85410723	12.____
13.	YUWWMYQZ SOSOSQSO ZUNLWMYW	47995410 26262126 07839549	13.____
14.	QULSWZYN ZYLQWOYW QLUYWZSO	17329045 04319639 13749026	14.____
15.	NLQZOYUM SQMUWZOM MMYWMZSQ	83106475 21579065 55498021	15.____
16.	NQLOWZZU SMYLUNZO UWMSNZOL	81319007 25347806 79528013	16.____

Questions 17-24.

DIRECTIONS: Each of Questions 17 through 24 represents five cards to be filed, numbered 1 through 5 in Column I. Each card is made up of the employee's name, the date of a work assignment, and the work assignment code number shown in parentheses. The cards are to be filed according to the following rules.

    First: File in alphabetical order.
    Second: When two or more cards have the same employee's name, file according to the assignment date beginning with the earliest date.
    Third: When to or more cards have the same employee's name and the same date, file according to the work assignment number beginning with the lowest number.

Column II shows the cards arranged in four different orders. Pick the answer (A, B, C, or D) in Column which shows the cards arranged correctly according to the above filing rules.

5 (#3)

SAMPLE QUESTION

COLUMN I
(1) Cluney   4/8/19   (486503)
(2) Roster   5/10/18   (246611)
(3) Altool   10/15/18 (711433)
(4) Cluney   2/18/19   (527610)
(5) Cluney   4/8/19   (486500)

COLUMN II
A. 2, 3, 4, 1, 5
B. 2, 5, 1, 3, 4
C. 3, 2, 1, 4, 5
D. 3, 5, 1, 4, 2

The correct way to file the cards is:
(3) Altool   10/15/18 (711433)
(5) Cluney   4/8/19   (486500)
(1) Cluney   4/8/19   (486503)
(4) Cluney   12/18/19 (527610)
(2) Roster   5/10/18   (246611)

The correct filing order is shown by the numbers in front of each name (3, 5, 1, 4, 2). The answer to the sample question is the letter in Column II in front of the numbers 3, 5, 1, 4, 2. This answer is D.

Now answer Questions 17 through 24 according to these rules.

COLUMN I   COLUMN II

17. (1) Kohls   4/2/19   (125677)   A. 1, 2, 3, 4, 5   17.____
    (2) Keller   3/21/19   (129698)   B. 3, 2, 1, 4, 5
    (3) Jackson   4/10/19   (213541)   C. 3, 1, 2, 4, 5
    (4) Richards   1/9/20   (347236)   D. 5, 2, 1, 3, 4
    (5) Richmond   12/11/18 (379321)

18. (1) Burroughs 5/27/19   (237896)   A. 1, 4, 3, 2, 5   18.____
    (2) Charlson   1/16/19   (114537)   B. 4, 1, 5, 2, 2
    (3) Carlsen   12/2/19   (114377)   C. 1, 4, 3, 5, 2
    (4) Burton   5/1/19   (227096)   D. 4, 1, 3, 5, 2
    (5) Charlson   12/2/19   (114357)

19. (1) Ungerer   11/11/19 (537924)   A. 1, 5, 3, 2, 4   19.____
    (2) Winters   11/10/19 (657834)   B. 5, 1, 3, 4, 2
    (3) Ventura   12/1/19   (698694)   C. 3, 5, 1, 2, 4
    (4) Winters   10/11/18 (675654)   D. 1, 5, 3, 4, 2
    (5) Ungaro   11/10/19 (684325)

20. (1) Norton   3/12/20   (071605)   A. 1, 4, 2, 3, 5   20.____
    (2) Morris   2/26/20   (068931)   B. 3, 5, 2, 4, 1
    (3) Morse   5/12/20   (142358)   C. 2, 4, 3, 5, 1
    (4) Morris   2/26/20   (068391)   D. 4, 2, 5, 3, 1
    (5) Morse   2/26/20   (068391)

21.	(1) Eger	4/19/19	(874129)	A. 3, 4, 1, 2, 5		21._____
	(2) Eihler	5/19/20	(875329)	B. 1, 4, 5, 2, 3		
	(3) Ehrlich	11/19/19	(874839)	C. 4, 1, 3, 2, 5		
	(4) Eger	4/19/19	(876129)	D. 1, 4, 3, 5, 2		
	(5) Eihler	5/19/19	(874239)			
22.	(1) Johnson	12/21/19	(786814)	A. 2, 4, 3, 5, 1		22._____
	(2) Johns	12/21/20	(801024)	B. 4, 2, 5, 3, 1		
	(3) Johnson	12/12/20	(762814)	C. 4, 5, 3, 1, 2		
	(4) Jackson	12/12/20	(862934)	D. 5, 3, 1, 2, 4		
	(5) Johnson	12/12/20	(762184)			
23.	(1) Fuller	7/12/19	(598310)	A. 2, 1, 5, 4, 3		23._____
	(2) Fuller	7/2/19	(598301)	B. 1, 2, 4, 5, 3		
	(3) Fuller	7/22/19	(598410)	C. 1, 4, 5, 2, 3		
	(4) Fuller	7/17/20	(598710)	D. 2, 1, 3, 5, 3		
	(5) Fuller	7/17/20	(598701)			
24.	(1) Perrine	10/27/16	(637096)	A. 3, 4, 5, 1, 2		24._____
	(2) Perrone	11/14/19	(767609)	B. 3, 2, 5, 4, 1		
	(3) Perrault	10/15/15	(629706)	C. 5, 3, 1, 4, 2		
	(4) Perrine	10/17/19	(373656)	D. 4, 5, 1, 2, 3		
	(5) Perine	10/17/18	(376356)			

Questions 25-30.

DIRECTIONS: Questions 25 through 30 are to be answered on the basis of the information given in the following passage.

It is often said that no system will work if the people who carry it out do not want it to work. In too many cases, a departmental reorganization that seemed technically sound and economically practical has proved to be a failure because the planners neglected to take the human factor into account. The truth is that employees are likely to feel threatened when they learn that a major change is in the wind. It does not matter whether or not the change actually poses a threat to an employee; the fact that he believes it does or fears it might is enough to make him feel insecure. Among the dangers he fears, the foremost is the possibility that his job may cease to exist and that he may be laid off or shunted into a less skilled position at lower pay. Even if he knows that his own job category is secure, however, he is likely to fear losing some of the important intangible advantages of his present position for instance, he may fear that he will be separated from his present companions and thrust in with a group of strangers, or that he will find himself in a lower position on the organizational ladder if a new position is created above his.

It is important that management recognize these natural fears and take them into account in planning any kind of major change. While there is no cut-and-dried formula for preventing employee resistance, there are several steps that can be taken to reduce employees' fears and gain their cooperation. First, unwarranted fears can be dispelled if employees are kept informed of the planning from the start and if they know exactly what to expect. Next, assurance on matters such as retraining, transfers, and placement help should be given as soon as it is clear what direction the reorganization will take. Finally, employees' participation in the planning should be actively sought. There is a great psychological difference between feeling that a change is being forced upon one from the outside, and feeling that one is an insider who is helping to bring about a change.

25. According to the above passage, employees who are not in real danger of losing their jobs because of a proposed reorganization
    A. will be eager to assist in the reorganization
    B. will pay little attention to the reorganization
    C. should not be taken into account in planning the reorganization
    D. are nonetheless likely to feel threatened by the reorganization

26. The above passage mentions the *intangible advantages* of a position. Which of the following BEST describes the kind of advantages alluded to in the passage?
    A. Benefits such as paid holidays and vacations
    B. Satisfaction of human needs for things like friendship and status
    C. Qualities such as leadership and responsibility
    D. A work environment that meets satisfactory standards of health and safety

27. According to the above passage, an employee's fear that a reorganization may separate him from his present companions is a(n)
    A. childish and immature reaction to change
    B. unrealistic feeling, since this is not going to happen
    C. possible reaction that the planners should be aware of
    D. incentive to employees to participate in the planning

28. On the basis of the above passage, it would be *desirable*, when planning a departmental reorganization, to
    A. be governed by employee feelings and attitudes
    B. give some employees lower positions
    C. keep employees informed
    D. lay off those who are less skilled

29. What does the above passage say can be done to help gain employees' cooperation in a reorganization?
    A. Making sure that the change is technically sound, that it is economically practical, and that the human factor is taken into account
    B. Keeping employees fully informed, offering help in fitting them into new positions, and seeking their participation in the planning
    C. Assuring employees that they will not be laid off, that they will not be reassigned to a group of strangers, and that no new positions will be created on the organization ladder
    D. Reducing employees' fears, arranging a retraining program, and providing for transfers

30. Which of the following suggested title would be MOST appropriate for this passage? 30._____
    A. Planning a Departmental Reorganization
    B. Why Employees are Afraid
    C. Looking Ahead to the Future
    D. Planning for Change: The Human Factor

KEY (CORRECT ANSWERS)

1.	C	11.	A	21.	D
2.	A	12.	D	22.	B
3.	D	13.	D	23.	D
4.	B	14.	B	24.	C
5.	C	15.	A	25.	D
6.	A	16.	C	26.	B
7.	C	17.	B	27.	C
8.	B	18.	A	28.	C
9.	A	19.	B	29.	B
10.	D	20.	D	30.	D

EXAMINATION SECTION
TEST 1

DIRECTIONS: Each question or incomplete statement is followed by several suggested answers or completions. Select the one that BEST answers the question or completes the statement. *PRINT THE LETTER OF THE CORRECT ANSWER IN THE SPACE AT THE RIGHT.*

1. You are operating the switchboard and you receive an outside call for an extension line which is busy.
   The one of the following which you should do FIRST is to
   A. ask the caller to try again later
   B. ask the caller to wait and inform him every thirty seconds about the status of the extension line
   C. tell the caller the line is busy and ask him if he wishes to wait
   D. tell the caller the line is busy and that you will connect him as soon as possible

   1.____

2. A person comes to your work area. He makes comments which make no sense, gives foolish opinions, and tells you that he has enemies who are after him. He appears to be mentally ill.
   Of the following, the FIRST action to take is to
   A. humor him by agreeing and sympathize with him
   B. try to reason with him and point out that his fears or opinions are unfounded
   C. have him arrested immediately
   D. tell him to leave at once

   2.____

3. You are speaking with someone on the telephone who asks you a question which you cannot answer. You estimate that you can probably obtain the requested information in about five minutes.
   Of the following, the MOST appropriate course of action would be to tell the caller that
   A. the information will take a short while to obtain, and then ask her for her name and number so that you can call her back when you have the information
   B. the information is available now, but she should call back later
   C. you do not know the answer and refer her to another division you think might be of service
   D. she is being placed on *hold* and that you will be with her in about five minutes

   3.____

4. A person with a very heavy foreign accent comes to your work area and starts talking to you. He is very excited and is speaking too rapidly for you to understand what he is saying.
   Of the following, the FIRST action for you to take is to

   4.____

A. refer the person to your supervisor
B. continue your work and ignore the person in the hope that he will be discouraged and leave the building
C. ask or motion to the person to speak more slowly and have him repeat what he is trying to communicate
D. assume that the person is making a complaint, tell him that his problem will be taken care of, and then go back to your work

5. Assume that you are responsible for handling supplies. You notice that you are running low on a particular type of manila file folder exceptionally fast. You believe that someone in the precinct is taking the folders for other than official use.
   In this situation, the one of the following that you should do FIRST is to
   A. put up a notice stating that supplies have been disappearing and ask for the staff's cooperation in eliminating the problem
   B. speak to your supervisor about the matter and let him decide on a course of action
   C. watch the supply cabinet to determine who is taking the folders
   D. ignore the situation and put in a requisition for additional folders

5.____

6. One afternoon, several of the officers ask you to perform different tasks. Each task requires a half day of work. Each officer tells you that his assignment must be finished by 4 P.M. the next day.
   Of the following, the BEST way to handle this situation is to
   A. do the assignments as quickly as you can, in the order in which the officers handed them to you
   B. do some work on each assignment in the order of the ranks of the assigning officers and hand in as much as you are able to finish
   C. speak to your immediate supervisor in order to determine the priority of assignments
   D. accept all four assignments but explain to the last officer that you may not be able to finish his job

6.____

7. Every morning, several officers congregate around your work station during their breaks. You find their conversations very distracting.
   The one of the following which you should do FIRST is to
   A. ask them to cooperate with you by taking their breaks somewhere else
   B. concentrate as best you can because their breaks do not last very long
   C. reschedule your break to coincide with theirs
   D. tell your supervisor that the officers are very uncooperative

7.____

8. One evening when you are very busy, you answer the phone and find that you are speaking with one of the neighborhood cranks, an elderly man who constantly complains that his neighbors are noisy.
   In this situation, the MOST appropriate action for you to take is to
   A. hang up and go on with your work
   B. note the complaint and process it in the usual way
   C. tell the man that his complaint will be investigated and then forget about it
   D. tell the man that you are very buy and ask him to call back later

8.____

9. One morning you answer a telephone call for Lieutenant Jones, who is busy on another line. You inform the caller that Lieutenant Jones is on another line and this party says he will hold. After two minutes, Lieutenant Jones is still speaking on the first call.
Of the following, the FIRST thing for you to do is to
   A. ask the second caller whether it is an emergency
   B. signal Lieutenant Jones to let him know there is another call waiting for him
   C. request that the second caller try again later
   D. inform the second caller that Lieutenant Jones' line is still busy

10. The files in your office have been overcrowded and difficult to work with since you started working there. One day your supervisor is transferred and another aide in your office decides to discard three drawers of the oldest materials.
For him to take this action is
   A. *desirable*; it will facilitate handling the more active materials
   B. *undesirable*; no file should be removed from its point of origin
   C. *desirable*; there is no need to burden a new supervisor with unnecessary information
   D. *undesirable*; no file should be discarded without first noting what material has been discarded

11. You have been criticized by the lieutenant-in-charge because of spelling errors in some of your typing. You have only copied the reports as written, and you realize that the errors occurred in work given to you by Sergeant X.
Of the following, the BEST way for you to handle this situation is to
   A. tell the lieutenant that the spelling errors are Sergeant X's, not yours, because they occur only when you type his reports
   B. tell the lieutenant that you only type the reports as given to you, without implicating anyone
   C. inform Sergeant X that you have been unjustly criticized because of his spelling errors and politely request that he be more careful in the future
   D. use a dictionary whenever you have doubt regarding spelling

12. You have recently found several items misfiled. You believe that this occurred because a new administrative aide in your section has been making mistakes.
The BEST course of action for you to take is to
   A. refile the material and say nothing about it
   B. send your supervisor an anonymous note of complaint about the filing errors
   C. show the errors to the new administrative aide and tell him why they are errors in filing
   D. tell your supervisor that the new administrative aide makes a lot of errors in filing

13. One of your duties is to record information on a standard printed form regarding missing cars. One call you receive concerns a custom-built auto which has apparently been stolen. There seems to be no place on the form for many of the details which the owner gives you.

Of the following, the BEST way for you to obtain an adequate description of this car would be to
- A. complete the form as best you can and attach another sheet containing the additional information the owner gives you
- B. complete the form as best you can and request that the owner submit a photograph of the missing car
- C. scrap the form since it is inadequate in this case and make out a report based on the information the owner gives you
- D. complete the form as best you can and ignore extraneous information that the form does not call for

14. One weekend, you develop a painful infection in one hand. You know that your typing speed will be much slower than normal, and the likelihood of your making mistakes will be increased.
Of the following, the BEST course of action for you to take in this situation is to
- A. report to work as scheduled and do your typing assignments as best you can without complaining
- B. report to work as scheduled and ask your co-workers to divide your typing assignments until your hand heals
- C. report to work as scheduled and ask your supervisor for non-typing assignments until your hand heals
- D. call in sick and remain on medical leave until your hand is completely healed so that you can perform your normal duties

14.____

15. When filling out a departmental form during an interview concerning a citizen complaint, an administrative aide should know the purpose of each question that he asks the citizen.
For such information to be supplied by the department is
- A. *advisable*, because the aide may lose interest in the job if he is not fully informed about the questions he has to ask
- B. *inadvisable*, because the aide may reveal the true purpose of the questions to the citizens
- C. *advisable*, because the aide might otherwise record superficial or inadequate answers if he does not fully understand the questions
- D. *inadvisable*, because the information obtained through the form may be of little importance to the aide

15.____

16. Which one of the following is NOT a general accepted rule of telephone etiquette for an administrative aide?
- A. Answer the telephone as soon as possible after the first ring
- B. Speak in a louder than normal tone of voice, on the assumption that the caller is hard-of-hearing
- C. Have a pencil and paper ready at all times with which to make notes and take messages
- D. Use the tone of your voice to give the caller the impression of cooperativeness and willingness to be of service

16.____

17. The one of the following which is the BEST reason for placing the date and time of receipt of incoming mail is that this procedure
    A. aids the filing of correspondence in alphabetical order
    B. fixes responsibility for promptness in answering correspondence
    C. indicates that the mail has been checked for the presence of a return address
    D. makes it easier to distribute the mail in sequence

17.____

18. Which one of the following is the FIRST step that you should take when filing a document by subject?
    A. Arrange related documents by date with the latest date in front
    B. Check whether the document has been released for filing
    C. Cross-reference the document if necessary
    D. Determine the category under which the document will be filed

18.____

19. The one of the following which is NOT generally employed to keep tract of frequently used material requiring future attention is a
    A. card tickler file   B. dated follow-up folder
    C. periodic transferral of records   D. signal folder

19.____

20. Assume that a newly appointed administrative aide arrives 15 minutes late for the start of his tour of duty. One of his co-workers tells him not to worry because he has signed him in on time. The co-worker assures him that he would be willing to over for him anytime he is late and hopes the aide will do the same for him. The aide agrees to do so.
    This arrangement is
    A. *desirable*; it prevents both men from getting a record for tardiness
    B. *undesirable*; signing in for each other is dishonest
    C. *desirable*; cooperation among co-workers is an important factor in morale
    D. *undesirable*; they will get caught if one is held up in a lengthy delay

20.____

21. An administrative aide takes great pains to help a citizen who approaches him with a problem. The citizen thanks the aide curtly and without enthusiasm. Under these circumstances, it would be MOST courteous for the aide to
    A. tell the citizen he was glad to be of service
    B. ask the citizen to put the compliment into writing and send it to his supervisor
    C. tell the citizen just what pains he took to render this service so that the citizen will be fully aware of his efforts
    D. make no reply and ignore the citizen's remarks

21.____

22. Assume that your supervisor spends a week training you, a newly appointed administrative aide, to sort fingerprint for filing purposes. After doing this type of filing for several day, you get an idea which you believe would improve upon the method in use.
    Of the following, the BEST action for you to take in this situation is to
    A. wait to see whether your idea still look good after you have had more experience
    B. try your idea out before bringing it up with your supervisor

22.____

C. discuss your idea with your supervisor
D. forget about this idea since the fingerprint sorting system was devised by experts

23. Which one of the following is NOT a useful filing practice?
    A. Filing active records in the most accessible parts of the file cabinet
    B. Filling a file drawer to capacity in order to save space
    C. Gluing small documents to standard-size paper before filing
    D. Using different colored tab for various filing categories

24. A citizen comes in to make a complaint to an administrative aide.
    The one of the following action which would be the MOST serious example of discourtesy would be for the aide to
    A. refuse to look up from his desk even though he knows someone is waiting to speak to him
    B. not use the citizen's name when addressing him once his identity has been ascertained
    C. interrupt the citizen's story to ask questions
    D. listen to the complaint and refer the citizen to a special office

25. Suppose that one of your neighbors walks into the precinct where you are an administrative aide and asks you to make 100 copies of a letter on the office duplicating machine for his personal use.
    Of the following, what action should you take FIRST in this situation?
    A. Pretend that you do not know the person and order him to leave the building
    B. Call a police officer and report the person for attempting to make illegal use of police equipment
    C. Tell the person that you will copy the letter but only when you are off-duty
    D. Explain to the person that you cannot use police equipment for non-police work

KEY (CORRECT ANSWERS)

1.	C	11.	D
2.	A	12.	C
3.	A	13.	A
4.	C	14.	C
5.	B	15.	C
6.	C	16.	B
7.	A	17.	B
8.	B	18.	B
9.	D	19.	C
10.	D	20.	B

21. A
22. C
23. B
24. A
25. D

TEST 2

DIRECTIONS: Each question or incomplete statement is followed by several suggested answers or completions. Select the one that BEST answers the question or completes the statement. *PRINT THE LETTER OF THE CORRECT ANSWER IN THE SPACE AT THE RIGHT.*

Questions 1-6.

DIRECTIONS: Questions 1 through 6 are to be answered on the basis of the information supplied in the chart below.

LAW ENFORCEMENT OFFICERS KILLED
(By Type of Activity)
2012-2021

2012-2016
2017-2021

Activity	2012-2016	2017-2021
RESPONDING TO DISTURBANCE CALLS	48	50
BURGLARIES IN PROGRESS OR PURSUING BURGLARY SUSPECT	28	25
ROBBERIES IN PROGRESS OR PURSUING ROBBERY SUSPECT	48	74
ATTEMPTING OTHER ARRESTS	56	112
CIVIL DISORDERS	2	8
HANDLING, TRANSPORTING, CUSTODY OF PRISONERS	12	17
INVESTIGATING SUSPICIOUS PERSONS AND CIRCUMSTANCES	28	29
AMBUSH	13	29
UNPROVOKED MENTALLY DERANGED	5	20
TRAFFIC STOPS	10	19

1. According to the above chart, the percent of the total number of law enforcement officers killed from 2012-2021 in activities related to burglaries and robberies is MOST NEARLY _____ percent.
    A. 8.4   B. 19.3   C. 27.6   D. 36.2

1._____

2 (#2)

2. According to the above chart, the two of the following categories which increased from 2012–16 to 2017–21 by the same percent are
   A. ambush and traffic stops
   B. attempting other arrests and ambush
   C. civil disorders and unprovoked mentally deranged
   D. response to disturbance calls and investigating suspicious persons and circumstances

2.____

3. According to the above chart, the percentage increase in law enforcement officers killed from the 2012-16 period to the 2017-21 period is MOST NEARLY _____ percent.
   A. 34   B. 53   C. 65   D. 100

3.____

4. According to the above chart, in which one of the following activities did the number of law enforcement officers killed increase by 100 percent?
   A. Ambush
   B. Attempting other arrests
   C. Robberies in progress or pursuing robbery suspect
   D. Traffic stops

4.____

5. According to the above chart, the two of the following activities during which the total number of law enforcement officers killed from 2012 to 2021 was the same are
   A. burglaries in progress or pursuing burglary suspect and investigating suspicious persons and circumstances
   B. handling, transporting, custody of prisoner and traffic stops
   C. investigating suspicious persons and circumstances and ambush
   D. responding to disturbance calls and robberies in progress or pursuing robbery suspect

5.____

6. According to the categories in the above chart, the one of the following statements which can be made about law enforcement officers killed from 2012 to 2016 is that
   A. the number of law enforcement officers killed during civil disorders equals one-sixth of the number killed responding to disturbance calls
   B. the number of law enforcement officers killed during robberies in progress or pursuing robbery suspect equals 25 percent of the number killed while handling or transporting prisoners
   C. the number of law enforcement officers killed during traffic stops equals one-half the number killed for unprovoked reasons or by the mentally deranged
   D. twice as many law enforcement officers were killed attempting other arrests as were killed during burglaries in progress or pursuing burglary suspect

6.____

Questions 7-10.

DIRECTIONS: Assume that all arrests fall into two mutually exclusive categories, felonies and misdemeanors. Last week 620 arrests were made in Precinct A, of which 403 were for felonies. Questions 7 through 10 are to be answered on the basis of this information.

7. The percent of all arrests made in Precinct A last week which were for felonies was _____ percent.
   A. 55   B. 60   C. 65   D. 70

8. If 3/5 of all persons arrested for felonies and 1/4 of all persons arrested for misdemeanors were carrying weapons, then the number of arrests involving persons carrying weapons in Precinct A last week was MOST NEARLY
   A. 135   B. 295   C. 415   D. 525

9. If five times as many men as women were arrested for felonies, and half as many women as men were arrested for misdemeanors, then the number of women arrested in Precinct A last week was APPROXIMATELY
   A. 90   B. 120   C. 175   D. 210

10. If the ratio of arrests made on weekends (Friday through Sunday) to arrests made on weekdays (Monday through Thursday) is 2:1, then the number of arrests made in Precinct A last weekend was
    A. 308   B. 340   C. 372   D. 413

11. The police precincts covering the county receive calls at the average rate of two per minute during the 8 A.M. to 4 P.M. tour, but this rate increases by 50 percent during the 4 P.M. to 12 A.M. tour. However, the initial rate decreases by 50 percent during the 12 A.M. to 8 A.M. tour.
    The number of calls received by the precincts covering the county on this basis is one 24-hour day is
    A. 960   B. 1,440   C. 2,880   D. 3,360

12. If an administrative aide is expected to handle 15 calls per hour and Precinct C averages 840 calls during the 4 P.M. to 12 A.M. tour, then the number of aides needed in Precinct C to handle calls during this tour is
    A. 4   B. 5   C. 6   D. 7

13. If in a group of ten administrative aides, four type 40 words per minute, one types 45, two type 50, two type 60, and one types 65, then the average speed in the group is
    A. 49   B. 50   C. 51   D. 52

14. An administrative aide works from midnight to 8 A.M. on a certain day and then is off for 64 hours.
    He is due back at work at
    A. 8 A.M.   B. 12 noon   C. 4 P.M.   D. 12 midnight

4 (#2)

15. If a certain aide take one hour to type 2 accident reports or 6 missing person reports, then the length of time he will require to finish 7 accident reports and 15 missing persons reports is _____ hours _____ minutes.
    A. 6; 0   B. 6; 30   C. 8; 0   D. 8; 40

    15._____

16. If one administrative aide can alphabetize 320 reports per hour and another can do 280 per hour, then the number of reports that both could alphabetize during an 8-hour tour is
    A. 4,800   B. 5,200   C. 5,400   D. 5,700

    16._____

17. If 1,000 candidates applied for administrative aide, and out of those applying 7/8 appear for the written test, and out of those who take the written test 66 2/4 percent pass it, and out of those who pass the written test 85 percent pass the medical exam, then the number of candidates still eligible to become administrative aides will be about
    A. 245   B. 495   C. 585   D. 745

    17._____

18. If the number of murders in the city in 2018 was 415, and the number of murders has increased by 8 percent each year since that year, then in 2021 we would expect the number of murders to be about
    A. 484   B. 523   C. 548   D. 565

    18._____

19. If a person reported missing on April 15 was found murdered on July 4, how many days was he missing? (Include April 15 but NOT July 4 in the total.)
    A. 76   B. 80   C. 82   D. 84

    19._____

20. Suppose that a pile of 96 file cards measures one inch in height and that it takes you ½ hour to file these cards away.
    If you are given three piles of cards which measure 2½ inches high, 1¾ inches high, and 3³/₈ inches high, respectfully, the time it would take to file the cards is MOST NEARLY _____ hours and _____ minutes.
    A. 2; 30   B. 3; 50   C. 6; 45   D. 8; 15

    20._____

Questions 21-30.

DIRECTIONS: Questions 21 through 30 test how good you are at catching mistakes in typing or printing. In each question, the name and addresses in Column II should be an exact copy of the name and address in Column I.
Mark your answer:
A. if there is no mistake in either name or address
B. if there is a mistake in both name and address
C. if there is a mistake only in the name
D. if there is a mistake only in the address

COLUMN I   COLUMN II

21. Milos Yanocek   Milos Yanocek   21._____
    33-60 14 Street   33-60 14 Street
    Long Island City, NY 11011   Long Island City, NY 11001

49

5 (#2)

22. Alphonse Sabattelo   Alphonse Sabbattelo   22.____
    24 Minnetta Lane   24 Minetta Lane
    New York, NY 10006   New York, NY 10006

23. Helen Stearn   Helene Steam   23.____
    5 Metroplitan Oval   5 Metropolitan Oval
    Bronx, NY 10462   Bronx, NY 10462

24. Jacob Weisman   Jacob Weisman   24.____
    231 Francis Lewis Boulevard   231 Francis Lewis Boulevard
    Forest Hills, NY 11325   Forest Hill, NY 11325

25. Riccardo Fuente   Riccardo Fuentes   25.____
    135 West 83 Street   134 West 88 Street
    New York, NY 10024   New York, NY 10024

26. Dennis Lauber   Dennis Lauder   26.____
    52 Avenue D   52 Avenue D
    Brooklyn, NY 11216   Brooklyn, NY 11216

27. Paul Cutter   Paul Cutter   27.____
    195 Galloway Avenue   175 Galloway Avenue
    Staten Island, NY 10356   Staten Island, NY 10365

28. Sean Donnelly   Sean Donnelly   28.____
    45-58 41 Avenue   45-58 41 Avenue
    Woodside, NY 11168   Woodside, NY 11168

29. Clyde Willot   Clyde Willat   29.____
    1483 Rockaway Avenue   1483 Rockaway Avenue
    Brooklyn, NY 11238   Brooklyn, NY 11238

30. Michael Stanakis   Michael Stanakis   30.____
    419 Sheriden Avenue   419 Sheraden Avenue
    Staten Island, NY 10363   Staten Island, NY 10363

Questions 31-40.

DIRECTIONS: Questions 31 through 40 are to be answered SOLELY on the basis of the following information.

Column I consists of serial numbers of dollar bills. Column II shows different ways of arranging the corresponding serial numbers.

The serial numbers of dollar bills in Column I begin and end with a capital letter and have an eight-digit number in between. The serial numbers in Column I are to be arranged according to the following rules:

First: In alphabetical order according to the first letter.
Second: When two or more serial numbers have the same first letter, in alphabetical order according to the last letter.
Third: When two or more serial numbers have the same first and last letters, in numerical order, beginning with the lowest number.

The serial numbers in Column I are numbered (1) through (5) in the order in which they are listed. In Column II, the numbers (1) through (5) are arranged in four different ways to show different arrangements of the corresponding serial numbers. Choose the answer in Column II in which the serial numbers are arranged according to the above rules.
SAMPLE QUESTION:

	COLUMN I		COLUMN II
(1)	E75044127B	(A)	4, 1, 3, 2, 5
(2)	B96399104A	(B)	4, 1 2, 3, 5
(3)	B93939086A	(C)	4, 3, 2 5, 1
(4)	B47064465H	(D)	3, 2, 5, 4, 1
(5)	B99040922A		

In the sample question, the four serial numbers starting with B should be put before the serial numbers starting with E. The serial numbers starting with B and ending with A should be put before the serial number starting with B and ending with H. The three serial numbers starting with B and ending with A should be listed in numerical order, beginning with the lowest number. The correct way to arrange the serial numbers, therefore, is

(3) B93939086A
(2) B96399104A
(5) B99040922A
(4) B47064465H
(1) B75044127B

Since the order of arrangement is 3, 2, 5, 4, 1, the answer to the sample question is (D).

		COLUMN I		COLUMN II
31.	(1)	P44343324Y	A.	2, 3, 1, 4, 5
	(2)	P44141341S	B.	1, 5, 3, 2, 4
	(3)	P44141431L	C.	4, 2, 3, 5, 1
	(4)	P41143413W	D.	5, 3, 2, 4, 1
	(5)	P44313433H		
32.	(1)	D89077275M	A.	3, 2, 5, 3, 1
	(2)	D98073724N	B.	1, 4, 3, 2, 5
	(3)	D90877274N	C.	4, 1, 5, 2, 3
	(4)	D98877275M	D.	1, 3, 2, 5, 3
	(5)	D98873725N		

31.____

32.____

7 (#2)

33. (1) H32548137E   A. 2, 4, 5, 1, 3   33._____
    (2) H35243178A   B. 1, 5, 2, 3, 4
    (3) H35284378F   C. 1, 5, 2, 4, 3
    (4) H35288337A   D. 2, 1, 5, 3, 4
    (5) H32883173B

34. (1) K24165039H   A. 4, 2, 5, 3, 1   34._____
    (2) F24106599A   B. 2, 3, 4, 1, 5
    (3) L21406639G   C. 4, 2, 5, 1, 3
    (4) C24156093A   D. 1, 3, 4, 5, 2
    (5) K24165593D

35. (1) H79110642E   A. 2, 1, 3, 5, 4   35._____
    (2) H79101928E   B. 2, 1, 4, 5, 3
    (3) A79111567F   C. 3, 5, 2, 1, 4
    (4) H79111796E   D. 4, 3, 5, 1, 2
    (5) A79111618F

36. (1) P16388385W   A. 3, 4, 5, 2, 1   36._____
    (2) R16388335V   B. 2, 3, 4, 5, 1
    (3) P16383835W   C. 2, 4, 3, 1, 5
    (4) R18386865V   D. 3, 1, 5, 2, 4
    (5) P18686865W

37. (1) B42271749G   A. 4, 1, 5, 2, 3   37._____
    (2) B42271779G   B. 4, 1, 2, 5, 3
    (3) E43217779G   C. 1, 2, 4, 5, 3
    (4) B42874119C   D. 5, 3, 1, 2, 4
    (5) E42817749G

38. (1) M57906455S   A. 4, 1, 5, 3, 2   38._____
    (2) N87077758S   B. 3, 4, 1, 5, 2
    (3) N87707757B   C. 4, 1, 5, 2, 3
    (4) M57877759B   D. 1, 5, 3, 2, 4
    (5) M57906555S

39. (1) C69336894Y   A. 2, 5, 3, 1, 4   39._____
    (2) C69336684V   B. 3, 2, 5, 1, 4
    (3) C69366887W   C. 3, 1, 4, 5, 2
    (4) C69366994Y   D. 2, 5, 1, 3, 4
    (5) C69336865V

40. (1) A56247181D   A. 1, 5, 3, 2, 4   40._____
    (2) A56272128P   B. 3, 1, 5, 2, 4
    (3) H56247128D   C. 3, 2, 1, 5, 4
    (4) H56272288P   D. 1, 5, 2, 3, 4
    (5) A56247188D

Questions 41-48.

DIRECTIONS: Questions 41 through 48 are to be answered SOLELY on the basis of the following passage.

Auto theft is prevalent and costly. In 2020, 486,000 autos valued at over $500 million were stolen. About 28 percent of the inhabitants of federal prisons are there as a result of conviction of interstate auto theft under the Dyer Act. In California alone, auto thefts cost the criminal justice system approximately $60 million yearly.

The great majority of auto theft is for temporary use rather than resale, as evidenced by the fact that 88 percent of autos stolen in 2020 were recovered. In Los Angeles, 64 percent of stolen autos that were recovered were found within two days and about 80 percent within a week. Chicago reports that 71 percent of the recovered autos were found within four miles of the point of theft. The FBI estimates that 8 percent of stolen cars are taken for the purpose of stripping them for parts, 12 percent for resale, and 5 percent for use in another crime. Auto thefts are primarily juvenile acts. Although only 21 percent of all arrests for nontraffic offenses in 2020 were of individuals under 18 years of age, 63 percent of auto theft arrests were of persons under 18. Auto theft represents the start of many criminal careers; in an FBI sample of juvenile auto theft offenders, 41 percent had no prior arrest record.

41. In the above passage, the discussion of the reasons for auto theft does NOT include the percent of
    A. autos stolen by prior offenders
    B. recovered stolen autos found close to the point of theft
    C. stolen autos recovered within a week
    D. stolen autos which were recovered

42. Assuming the figures in the above passage remain constant, you may logically estimate the cost of auto thefts to the California criminal justice system over a five-year period beginning in 2020 to have been about _____ million.
    A. $200   B. $300   C. $440   D. $500

43. According to the above passage, the percent of stolen autos in Los Angeles which were not recovered within a week was _____ percent.
    A. 12   B. 20   C. 29   D. 36

44. According to the above passage, MOST auto thefts are committed by
    A. former inmates of federal prisons
    B. juveniles
    C. persons with a prior arrest record
    D. residents of large cities

45. According to the above passage, MOST autos are stolen for
    A. resale
    B. stripping of parts
    C. temporary use
    D. use in another crime

46. According to the above passage, the percent of persons arrested for auto theft who were under 18
    A. equals nearly the same percent of stolen autos which were recovered
    B. equals nearly two-thirds of the total number of persons arrested for nontraffic offenses
    C. is the same as the percent of persons arrested for nontraffic offenses who were under 18
    D. is three times the percent of persons arrested for nontraffic offenses who were under 18

47. An APPROPRIATE title for the above passage is
    A. How Criminal Careers Begin   B. Recovery of Stolen Cars
    C. Some Statistics on Auto Theft D. The Costs of Auto Theft

48. Based on the above passage, the number of cars taken for use in another crime in 2020 was
    A. 24,300   B. 38,880   C. 48,600   D. 58,320

Questions 49-55.

DIRECTIONS: Questions 49 through 55 are to be answered SOLELY on the basis of the following passage.

Burglar alarms are designed to detect intrusion automatically. Robbery alarms enable a victim of a robbery or an attack to signal for help. Such devices can be located in elevators, hallways, homes and apartments, businesses and factories, and subways, as well as on the street in high-crime areas. Alarms could deter some potential criminals from attacking targets so protected. If alarms were prevalent and not visible, then they might serve to suppress crime generally. In addition, of course, the alarms can summon the police when they are needed.

All alarms must perform three functions: sensing or initiation of the signal, transmission of the signal, and annunciation of the alarm. A burglar alarm needs a sensor to detect human presence or activity in an unoccupied enclosed area like a building or a room. A robbery victim would initiate the alarm by closing a foot or wall switch, or by triggering a portable transmitter which would send the alarm signal to a remote receiver. The signal can sound locally as a loud noise to frighten away a criminal, or it can be sent silently by wire to a central agency. A centralized annunciator requires either private lines from each alarmed point, or the transmission of some information on the location of the signal.

49. A conclusion which follows LOGICALLY from the above passage is that
    A. burglar alarms employ sensor devices; robbery alarms make use of initiation devices
    B. robbery alarms signal intrusion without the help of the victim; burglar alarms require the victim to trigger a switch
    C. robbery alarms sound locally; burglar alarms are transmitted to a central agency
    D. the mechanisms for a burglar alarm and a robbery alarm are alike

50. According to the above passage, alarms can be located
    A. in a wide variety of settings
    B. only in enclosed areas
    C. at low cost in high-crime areas
    D. only in places where potential criminal will be deterred

51. According to the above passage, which of the following is ESSENTIAL if a signal is to be received in a central office?
    A. A foot or wall switch
    B. A noise producing mechanism
    C. A portable reception device
    D. Information regarding the location of the source

52. According to the above passage, an alarm system can function WITHOUT a
    A. centralized annunciating device
    B. device to stop the alarm
    C. sensing or initiating device
    D. transmission device

53. According to the above passage, the purpose of robbery alarms is to
    A. find out automatically whether a robbery has taken place
    B. lower the crime rate in high-crime areas
    C. make a loud noise to frighten away the criminal
    D. provide a victim with the means to signal for help

54. According to the above passage, alarms might aid in lessening crime if they were
    A. answered promptly by police
    B. completely automatic
    C. easily accessible to victims
    D. hidden and widespread

55. Of the following, the BEST title for the above passage is
    A. Detection of Crime By Alarms
    B. Lowering the Crime Rate
    C. Suppression of Crime
    D. The Prevention of Robbery

KEY (CORRECT ANSWERS)

1. C	11. C	21. D	31. D	41. A	51. D
2. C	12. D	22. B	32. B	42. B	52. A
3. B	13. A	23. C	33. A	43. B	53. D
4. B	14. D	24. A	34. C	44. B	54. D
5. B	15. A	25. B	35. C	45. C	55. A
6. D	16. A	26. C	36. D	46. D	
7. C	17. B	27. D	37. B	47. C	
8. B	18. B	28. A	38. A	48. A	
9. C	19. B	29. B	39. A	49. A	
10. D	20. B	30. D	40. D	50. A	

EXAMINATION SECTION
TEST 1

DIRECTIONS: Each question or incomplete statement is followed by several suggested answers or completions. Select the one that BEST answers the question or completes the statement. *PRINT THE LETTER OF THE CORRECT ANSWER IN THE SPACE AT THE RIGHT.*

1. You answer a phone complaint from a person concerning an improper labeling practice in a shop in his neighborhood. Upon listening to the complaint, you get the impression that the person is exaggerating and may be too excited to view the matter clearly.
   Of the following, your BEST course would be to
   A. tell the man that you can understand his anger but think it is not a really serious problem
   B. suggest to the man that he file a complaint with the Department of Consumer Affairs
   C. tell the man to stay away from the shop and have his friends do the same
   D. take down the information that the man offers so that he will see that the Police Department is concerned

   1.____

2. Suppose that late at night you receive a call on 911. The caller turns out to be an elderly man who is not able to get out much and who is calling you not because he needs help but because he wants to talk with someone.
   The BEST way to handle such a situation is to
   A. explain to him that the number is for emergencies and his call may prevent others from getting the help they need
   B. talk to him if not many calls are coming in but excuse yourself and cut him off if you are busy
   C. cut him off immediately when you find out he does not need help because this will be the most effective way of discouraging him
   D. suggest that he call train or bus information as the clerks there are often not busy at night

   2.____

3. While you are on duty, you receive a call from a person whose name your recognize to be that of a person who calls frequently about matters of no importance. The caller requests your name and your supervisor's name so that she can report you for being impolite to her.
   You should
   A. ask her when and how you were impolite to her
   B. tell her that she should not call about such minor matters
   C. make a report about her complaint for your superior
   D. give her the information that she requests

   3.____

4. Of the following, the MOST important reason for requiring each employ of the Police Department to be responsible for good public relations is that
   A. the Police Department has better morale when employees join in an effort to improve public relations
   B. the public judges the Department according to impressions received at every level in the Department
   C. most employees will not behave well toward the public unless required to do so
   D. employees who improve public relations will receive commendations from superiors

5. Assume that you are in the Bureau of Public Relations. You receive a telephone call from a citizen who asks if a study has been made of the advisability of combining the city's police and fire departments. Assume that you have no information on the subject.
   Of the following, your BEST course would be to
   A. tell the caller that undoubtedly the subject has been studied but that you do not have the information available
   B. suggest to the caller that he telephone the Fire Department's Community Relations section for further information
   C. explain to the caller that the functions of the two departments are distinct and that combining them would be inefficient
   D. take the caller's number in order to call back, and then find information or referrals to give him

6. Suppose that Police Department officials have discouraged representatives of the press from contacting police administrative aides (except aides in the Public Relations Bureau) for information.
   Of the following, the BEST reason for such a policy would be to
   A. assure proper control over information released to the press by the Department
   B. increase the value of official press releases of the Department
   C. make press representatives realize that the Department is not seeking publicity
   D. reduce the chance of crimes being committed in imitation of those reported in the press

7. People who phone the Police Department often use excited, emotional, and sometimes angry speech.
   The BEST policy for you to take when speaking to this type of caller is to
   A. tell the person directly that he must speak in a more civil way
   B. tell the caller to call back when he is in a better mood
   C. give the person time to settle down, by doing most of the talking yourself
   D. speak calmly yourself to help the caller to gradually become more relaxed

8. On a particularly busy evening, the police administrative aide assigned to the telephones had answered a tremendous number of inquiries and complaints by irate citizens. His patience was exhausted when he received a call from a citizen who reported, *Officer, a bird just flew into my bedroom. What should I do?* In a release of tension, the aide responded, *Keep it for seven days; and if no one claims it, it is yours.*
This response by the aide would usually be considered
   A. *advisable*, because the person should see how unusual his question was
   B. *advisable*, because he avoided offering police services that were unavailable
   C. *not advisable*, because such a remark might be regarded as insulting rather than humorous
   D. *not advisable*, because the person might not want a bird for a pet

9. While temporarily assigned to switchboard duty, you receive a call from a man who says his uncle in Pittsburgh has just called him and threatened to commit suicide. The man is convinced his uncle intends to carry out his threat.
Of the following, you should
   A. advise the man to have neighbors of the uncle check to see if the uncle is all right
   B. politely inform the man that such out-of-town incidents are beyond the authority of the local precinct
   C. take the uncle's name, address, and telephone number and immediately contact police authorities in Pittsburgh
   D. get the man's name, address, and telephone number so that you can determine whether the call is a hoax

10. Assume that in the course of your assigned duties you have just taken a necessary action which you feel has angered a citizen. After he has gone, you suddenly realize that the incident might result in an unjustified complaint.
The MOST advisable action for you to take now would be to
   A. contact the person and apologize to him
   B. make complete notes on the incident and on any witnesses who might be helpful
   C. ask your superior what you might expect in case of such a complaint, without giving any hint of the actual occurrence
   D. accept the situation as one of the hazards of your job

11. Your job may bring you in contact with people from the community who are confronted with emergencies,, and are experiencing feelings of tension, anxiety, or even hostility. It is good to keep in mind what attitude is most helpful to people who, in such situations like these.
Which of the following would be BEST to do?
   A. Present similar examples of your own problems to make the person feel that his problems are not unusual.
   B. Recognize the person's feelings, present information on available services, and make suggestions as to proper procedures

C. Expect that some of the information is exaggerated and encourage the person to let some time pass before seeking further help.
D. Have the person wait while you try to make arrangements for his problem to be solved.

12. Suppose that while on duty you receive a call from the owner of a gas station which is located within the precinct. The owner is annoyed with a certain rule made by the Police Department which concerns the operation of such stations. You agree with him.
Of the following, the BEST action for you to take is to
    A. make a report on the call and suggest to the owner that he write a letter to the Department about the rule
    B. tell the owner that there is little that can be done since such rules are departmental policy
    C. tell the owner that you agree with his complaint and that you will write a memo of his call
    D. establish good relations with the owner by suggesting how to word a letter that will get action from the department

12._____

13. Suppose that you are working at the switchboard when a call comes in late at night from a woman who reports that her neighbors are having a very noisy party. She gives you her first name, surname, and address, and you ask her title is *Miss* or *Mrs.* She replies that her title is irrelevant to her complaint, and wants to know why you ask.
Of the following possible ways of handling this, which is BEST?
    A. Insist that the title is necessary for identification purposes
    B. Tell her that it is merely to find out what her marital status is
    C. Agree that the information is not necessary and ask her how she wants to be referred to
    D. Find out why she shows such a peculiar reaction to a request for harmless information

13._____

14. While covering an assignment on the switchboard, you receive a call from a young girl who tells you of rumored plans for a gang fight in her neighborhood. You should
    A. take down the information so that a patrol squad can investigate the area and possibly keep the fight from starting
    B. discourage the girl from becoming alarmed by reminding her that it is only a rumor
    C. realize that this is a teenager looking for attention, humor her, and dismiss the matter
    D. take down the information but tell the girl that you need concrete information, and not just rumors, to take any action on her call

14._____

15. The one of the following which would MOST likely lead to friction among police administrative aides in a unit would be for the supervisor in charge of the unit to
    A. defend the actions of the aides he supervises when discussing them with his own supervisor

15._____

5 (#1)

    B. get his men to work together as a team in completing the work of the unit
    C. praise each of the aides he supervises *in confidence* as the best aide in the unit
    D. consider the point of view of the aides he supervises when assigning unpleasant tasks

16. Suppose that a police administrative aide who had been transferred to your office from another unit in your Department because of difficulties with his supervisor has been placed under your supervision.
The BEST course of action for you to take FIRST is to
    A. analyze the aide's past grievance to determine if the transfer was the best settlement of the problem
    B. advise him of the difficulties his former supervisor had with other employees and encourage him not to feel bad about the transfer
    C. warn him that you will not tolerate any nonsense and that he will be watched carefully while assigned to your unit
    D. instruct him in the duties he will be performing in your unit and make him feel *wanted* in his new position

16.____

17. In which of the following circumstances would it be MOST appropriate for you to use an impersonal style of writing rather than a personal style, which relies on the use of personal pronouns and other personal references?
When writing a memorandum to
    A. give your opinion to an associate on the advisability of holding a weekly staff meeting
    B. furnish your superior with data justifying a proposed outlay of funds for new equipment
    C. give your version of an incident which resulted in a complaint by a citizen about your behavior
    D. support your request for a transfer to another division

17.____

18. A newly appointed supervisor should learn as much as possible about the backgrounds of his subordinates.
The statement is generally CORRECT because
    A. effective handling of subordinates is based upon knowledge of their individual differences
    B. knowing their backgrounds assures they will be treated objectively, equally, and without favor
    C. some subordinates perform more efficiently under one supervisor than under another
    D subordinates have confidence in a supervisor who knows all about them

18.____

19. You have found it necessary, for valid reasons, to criticize the work of one of the female police administrative aides. She later comes to your desk and accuses you of criticizing her work because she is a woman.
The BEST way for you to deal with this employee is to
    A. ask her to apologize, since you would never allow yourself to be guilty of his kind of discrimination

19.____

B. discuss her complaint with her, explaining again and at greater length the reason for your criticism
C. assure her you wish to be fair, and ask her to submit a written report to you on her complaint
D. apologize for hurting her feelings and promise that she will be left alone in the future

20. The following steps are recognized steps in teaching an employee a new skill:
    I. Demonstrate how to do the work
    II. Let the learner do the work himself
    III. Explain the nature and purpose of the work
    IV. Correct poor procedures by suggestion and demonstration
    The CORRECT order for these steps is
    A. III, II, IV, I   B. II, I, III, IV   C. III, I, II, IV   D. I, III, II, IV

21. Suppose you have arranged an interview with a subordinate to try to help him overcome a serious shortcoming in his technical work. While you do not intend to talk to him about his attitude, you have noticed that he seems to be suspicious and resentful of people in authority. You need a record of the points covered in the discussion since further interviews are likely to be necessary.
    Your BEST course would be to
    A. write a checklist of points you wish to discuss and carefully check the points off as the interview progresses
    B. know exactly how you wish to proceed, and then make written notes during the interview of your subordinate's comments
    C. frankly tell your subordinate that you are recording the talk on tape but place the recorder where it will not hinder discussion
    D. keep in mind what you wish to accomplish and make notes on the interview immediately after it is over

22. A police administrative aide has explained a complicated procedure to several subordinates. He has been talking clearly, allowing time for information to sink in. He has also encouraged questions. Yet, he still questions his subordinates after his explanation, with the obvious objective of finding out whether they completely understand the procedure.
    Under these circumstances, the action of the police administrative aide, in asking questions about the procedure, is
    A. *not advisable*, because subordinates who do not now know the procedure which has been explained so carefully can read and study it
    B. *not advisable*, because he endangers his relationship with his subordinates by insulting their intelligence
    C. *advisable*, because subordinate basically resent instructions and seldom give their full attention in a group situation
    D. *advisable*, because the answers to his questions help him to determine whether he has gained his objective

23. The most competent of the police administrative aides is a pleasant, intelligent young woman who breaks the rules of the Department by occasionally making long personal telephone calls during working hours. You have not talked to her up until now about this fault. However, the calls are beginning to increase, and you decide to deal directly with the problem.
The BEST way to approach the subject with her would be to
    A. review with her the history of her infractions of the rules
    B. point out that her conduct is not fair to the other workers
    C. tell her that her personal calls are excessive and discuss it with her
    D. warn her quietly that you intend to apply penalties if necessary

24. Assume that you are supervising eight male police administrative aides who do similar clerical work. A group of four of them work on each side of a row of files which can be moved without much trouble. You notice that in each group there is a clique of three aides, leaving one member isolated. The two isolated members are relative newcomers.
Your BEST course in such a case would be to
    A. ignore the situation because to concern yourself with informal social arrangements of your subordinates would distract you from more important matters
    B. ask each of the cliques to invite the isolated member in their working group to lunch with them from time to time
    C. tell each group that you cannot allow cliques to form as it is bad for the morale of the unit
    D. find an excuse to move the file cabinet to the side of the room and then move the desks of the two isolated members close together

25. Suppose that your supervisor, who has recently been promoted and transferred to your division, asks you to review a certain procedure with a view to its possible revision. You know that several years ago a sergeant made a lengthy and intensive report based on a similar review.
Which of the following would it be BEST for you to do FIRST?
    A. Ask your supervisor if he is aware of the previous report
    B. Read the sergeant's report before you begin work to see what bearing it has on your assignment
    C. Begin work on the review without reading his report so that you will have a fresh point of view
    D. Ask the sergeant to assist you in your review

26. Using form letters in business correspondence is LEAST effective when
    A. answering letters on a frequently recurring subject
    B. giving the same information to many addresses
    C. the recipient is only interested in the routing information contained in the form letter
    D. a reply must be keyed to the individual requirements of the intended reader

27. From the viewpoint of an office administrator, the BEST of the following reasons for distributing the incoming mail before the beginning of the regular work day is that
    A. distribution can be handled quickly and most efficiently at that time
    B. distribution later in the day may be distracting to or interfering with other employees
    C. the employees who distribute the mail can then perform other tasks during the rest of the day
    D. office activities for the day based on the mail may then be started promptly

27.____

28. Suppose you have had difficulty locating a document in the files because you could not decide where it should have been filed. You learn that other people in the office have had the same problem. You know that the document will be needed from time to time in the future.
    Your BEST course, when refiling the document, would be to
    A. make a written note of where you found it so that you will find it more easily the next time
    B. reclassify it and file it in the file where you first looked for it
    C. file it where you found it and put cross-reference sheets in the other likely files
    D. make a mental association to help you find it the next time and put it back where you found it

28.____

29. Suppose that your supervisor is attending a series of meetings of police captains in Philadelphia and will not be back until next Wednesday. He has left no instructions with you as to how you should handle telephone calls for him.
    In most instances, your BEST course of action would be to say:
    A. He isn't here just now.
    B. He is out of town and won't be back until next Wednesday.
    C. He won't be in today.
    D. He is in Philadelphia attending a meeting of police captains.

29.____

30. The one of the following which is USUALLY an important by-product of the preparation of a procedure manual is that
    A. information uncovered in the process of preparation may lead to improvement of procedures
    B. workers refer to the manual instead of bothering their supervisors for information
    C. supervisors use the manual for training stenographers
    D. employees have equal access to information needed to do their jobs

30.____

31. You have been asked to organize a clerical job and supervise police administrative aides who will do the actual work. The job consists of removing, from several boxes of data processing cards which are arranged in alphabetical order, the cards of those whose names appear on certain lists. The person removing the card then notes a date on the card. Assume that the work will be done accurately whatever system is used.

31.____

Which of the following statements describes both the MOST efficient method and the BEST reasons for using that method? Have
- A. two aides work together, one calling names and the other extracting cards, and dating them, because the average production of any two aides working together should be higher, under these circumstances, than that of any two aides working alone
- B. each aide work alone, because it is easier to check spelling when reading the names than when listening to them
- C. two aides work together, one calling names and the other extracting cards and dating them, because social interaction tends to make work go faster
- D. each aide work alone, because the average production of any two aides, each working alone, should be higher, under these circumstances, than that of any two aides working together

32. The term *work flow*, when used in connection with office management or the activities in an office GENERALLY means the 32.____
- A. rate of speed at which work flows through a single section of an office
- B. use of charts in the analysis of various office functions
- C. number of individual work units which can be produced by the average employee
- D. step-by-step physical routing of work through its various procedures

Questions 33-40.

DIRECTIONS: Name of Offense   V A N D S B R U G H
Code Letter   c o m p l e x i t y
File Number   1 2 3 4 5 6 7 8 9 0

Assume that each of the above capital letters is the first letter of the name of an offense, that the small letter directly beneath each capita letter is the code letter for the offense, and that the number directly beneath each code letter is the file number for the offense.
In each of Questions 33 through 40, the code letters and file numbers should correspond to the capital letters.
If there is an error only in Column 2, mark your answer A.
If there is an error only in Column 3, mark your answer B.
If there is an error in both Column 2 and Column, mark your answer C.
If both Columns 2 and 3 are correct, mark your answer D.

Sample Questions:

COLUMN 1	COLUMN 2	COLUMN 3
BNARGHSVVU	emoxtylcci	6357905118

The code letters in Column 2 are correct, but the first 5 in Column 3 should be 2. Therefore, the answer is B.

	COLUMN 1	COLUMN 2	COLUMN 3	
33.	HGDSBNBSVR	ytplxmelcx	0945736517	33.____

34.	SDGUUNHVAH	lptiimycoy	5498830120	34.____
35.	BRSNAAVUDU	exlmooctpi	6753221848	35.____
36.	VSRUDNADUS	cleipmopil	1568432485	36.____
37.	NDSHVRBUAG	mplycxeiot	3450175829	37.____
38.	GHUSNVBRDA	tyilmcexpo	9805316742	38.____
39.	DBSHVURANG	pesycixomt	4650187239	39.____
40.	RHNNASBDGU	xymnolepti	7033256398	40.____

KEY (CORRECT ANSWERS)

1.	B	11.	B	21.	D	31.	D
2.	A	12.	A	22.	D	32.	D
3.	D	13.	C	23.	C	33.	C
4.	B	14.	A	24.	D	34.	D
5.	D	15.	C	25.	A	35.	A
6.	A	16.	D	26.	D	36.	C
7.	D	17.	B	27.	D	37.	B
8.	C	18.	A	28.	C	38.	D
9.	C	19.	B	29.	B	39.	A
10.	B	20.	C	30.	A	40.	C

READING COMPREHENSION
UNDERSTANDING AND INTERPRETING WRITTEN MATERIAL
EXAMINATION SECTION
TEST 1

DIRECTIONS: Each question or incomplete statement is followed by several suggested answers or completions. Select the one that BEST answers the question or completes the statement. *PRINT THE LETTER OF THE CORRECT ANSWER IN THE SPACE AT THE RIGHT.*

Questions 1-6.

DIRECTIONS: Questions 1 through 6 are to be answered SOLELY on the basis of the following passage.

An aide assigned to the Complaint Room must be familiar with the various forms used by that office. Some of these forms and their uses are:

Complaint Report: Used to record information on or information about crimes reported to the Police Department.

Complaint Report Follow-Up: Used to record additional information after the follow-up initial complaint report has been filed.

Aided Card: Used to record information pertaining to sick and injured persons aided by the police.

Accident Report: Used to record information on or information about injuries and/or property damage involving motorized vehicles.

Property Voucher: Used to record information on or information about property which comes into possession of the Police Department. (Motorized vehicles are not included.)

Auto Voucher: Used to record information on or information about a motorized vehicle which comes into possession of the Police Department.

1. Mr. Brown walks into the police precinct and informs the Administrative Aide that, while he was at work, someone broke into his apartment and removed property belonging to him. He does not know everything that was taken, but he wants to make a report now and will make a list of what was taken and bring it in later.
   According to the above passage, the CORRECT form to use in this situation should be the
   A. Property Voucher
   B. Complaint Report
   C. Complaint Report Follow-Up
   D. Aided Card

1.____

2. Mrs. Wilson telephones the precinct and informs the Administrative Aide she wishes to report additional property which was taken from her apartment. The Administrative Aide finds a Complaint Report had been previously filed for Mrs. Wilson.
According to the above passage, the CORRECT form to use in this situation should be the
   A. Property Voucher
   B. Complaint Report
   C. Complaint Report Follow-Up
   D. Aided Card

3. Police Officer Jones walks into the Complaint Room and informs he Administrative Aide that, while he was on patrol, he observed a woman fall to the sidewalk and remain there, apparently hurt. He comforted the injured woman and called for an ambulance, which came and brought the woman to the hospital.
According to the above passage, the CORRECT form on which to record this information should be the
   A. Accident Report
   B. Complaint Report
   C. Complaint Report Follow-Up
   D. Aided Card

4. Police Officer Smith informed the Administrative Aide assigned to the Complaint Room that Mr. Green, while crossing the street, was struck by a motorcycle and had to be taken to the hospital.
According to the above passage, the facts regarding this incident should be recorded on which one of the following forms?
   A. Accident Report
   B. Complaint Report
   C. Complaint Report Follow-Up
   D. Aided Card

5. Police Officer Williams reports to the Administrative Aide assigned to the Complaint Room that he and his partner, Police Officer Murphy, found an auto which was reported stolen and had the auto towed into the police garage.
Of the following forms listed in the above passage, which is the CORRECT one to use to record this information?
   A. Property Voucher
   B. Auto Voucher
   C. Complaint Report Follow-Up
   D. Complaint Report

6. Administrative Aide Lopez has been assigned to the Complaint Room. During her tour of duty, a person who does not identify herself hands Ms. Lopez a purse. The person states that she found the purse on the street. She then leaves the station house.
According to the information in the above passage, which is the CORRECT form to fill out to record the incident?
   A. Property Voucher
   B. Auto Voucher
   C. Complaint Report Follow-Up
   D. Complaint Report

Questions 7-9.

DIRECTIONS: Questions 7 through 9 are to be answered SOLELY on the basis of the following passage.

Traffic Enforcement Agent Lewis, while on patrol, received a radio call from Lieutenant Oliva instructing him to proceed to 34th Street, between Madison and Park Avenues, in order to report on the traffic condition in that area.

When Agent Lewis arrived at the assigned location, he discovered approximately 100 demonstrators on the sidewalk in front of the Bamlian Mission to the United Nations located at 135 E. 34th Street. Agent Lewis radioed Lt. Oliva and informed him that traffic was moving very slowly because the demonstration had spilled out onto the street. Lt. Oliva responded that he understood the situation and would contact the Police Department, as well as send an additional agent to the scene.

Police Sergeant Rodriguez arrived at the Bamlin Mission along with several police officers and informed Agent Lewis that he was going to seal off the street between Madison and Park Avenues to contain the demonstration and prevent any demonstrators from being injured.

Agent McMillian arrived at the scene shortly after the police. He and Agent Lewis decided that to divert traffic from 34th Street, which has east and westbound traffic, Agent McMillian would go to the intersection of 34th Street and Madison Avenue and direct eastbound traffic north onto Madison Avenue. Meanwhile, Agent Lewis would position himself at the intersection of 34th Street and Park Avenue and direct westbound traffic south onto Park Avenue.

7. Agent Lewis was sent to 34th Street to
   A. direct traffic at the Bamlin Mission
   B. keep demonstrators out of the street
   C. report on the traffic condition
   D. assist the police

8. Police Sergeant Rodriguez closed 34th Street because he wanted to
   A. prevent injuries and wait for additional police officers
   B. contain the demonstration and wait for instructions from Lt. Oliva
   C. divert traffic and wait for additional police officers
   D. prevent injuries and contain the demonstration

9. Agent McMillian directed
   A. eastbound traffic north onto Madison Avenue
   B. westbound traffic south onto Park Avenue
   C. eastbound traffic south onto Madison Avenue
   D. westbound traffic north onto Park Avenue

Questions 10-11.

DIRECTIONS: Questions 10 and 11 are to be answered SOLELY on the basis of the following passage.

Traffic Enforcement Agents who drive patrol cars are required to perform vehicle maintenance inspections twice a week. Maintenance inspections are conducted on Wednesdays and Saturdays under the direct supervision of a Traffic Enforcement Lieutenant. The main purpose of this program is to make sure that the vehicle fleet is working properly. The responsibility for vehicle maintenance lies first with the driver and then up through the supervisory chain within each command.

10. The MAIN purpose of the Vehicle Maintenance Inspections Program is to 10.____
    A. ensure that the vehicles operate properly
    B. assign responsibility for the operation of the vehicles
    C. reduce the amount of time between the initial reporting of defects and repairs
    D. set up a cost reduction policy whereby minor repairs are conducted at the command level

11. Who supervises maintenance inspections? 11.____
    A. Lieutenant   B. Agent
    C. Maintenance Specialist D. Captain

Questions 12-15.

DIRECTIONS: Questions 12 through 15 are to be answered SOLELY on the basis of the following passage.

Traffic Enforcement Agent Krieg is assigned to direct traffic at the intersection of Frame and Taylor Streets, which is the only way into or out of the Reese Tunnel in the Bronx. At 2:25 P.M., a motorist, driving a blue Cadillac, exits the tunnel and informs Agent Krieg that a U.P.S. truck is on fire in an eastbound lane of the tunnel. Agent Krieg notifies Traffic Control that he has received an unconfirmed report of a fire in the Reese Tunnel. Traffic Control replies that once they receive confirmation of the fire, they will notify the Fire Department and also the District Office so that they may send additional agents and a tow truck to the scene. At 2:30 P.M., a motorist in a gray Ford exits the tunnel and informs Agent Krieg that the tunnel is filled with smoke and that driving is dangerous. Agent Krieg again informs Traffic Control of the situation. Traffic control informs Agent Krieg that they have received confirmation of the fire from the Port Authority Police and that the Fire Department is on the way, as well as six Traffic Enforcement Agents and a tow truck. When the additional agents arrive, they close the tunnel to traffic in both directions in order to clear a path for the Fire Department and other emergency vehicles. Agent Krieg notifies Traffic Control that the Fire Department arrived at 2:45 P.M. and that the tunnel is closed. At 3:15 P.M., Lt. Backman of the Fire Department informs Agent Krieg that the fire has been extinguished, but that there are three vehicles in the tunnel that have to be towed, as well as the U.P.S. truck. At 3:20 P.M., the Fire Department leaves the scene, and the westbound lane is re-opened. At 3:40 P.M., the last vehicle is towed from the tunnel, and Agent Krieg notifies Traffic Control that all lanes in the tunnel are re-opened to traffic.

12. What vehicle was reported to be on fire?
    A. Blue Cadillac
    B. U.P.S. truck
    C. Gray Ford
    D. Tow truck

13. From whom did Traffic Control receive confirmation that there was a fire?
    A. Agent Krieg
    B. A motorist
    C. Lt. Backman
    D. Port Authority Police

14. At what time was Agent Krieg informed that the fire was extinguished?
    A. 2:25   B. 2:30   C. 3:15   D. 3:20

15. How many vehicles had to be towed out of the tunnel?
    A. 1   B. 2   C. 3   D. 4

Questions 16-17.

DIRECTIONS: Questions 16 and 17 are to be answered SOLELY on the basis of the following passage.

Traffic Enforcement Agents Benjamin and O'Brien are assigned to direct traffic at the entrance of the eastbound side of the Smithsonian Bridge. While the agents are directing traffic, Agent Benjamin notices that eastbound traffic going onto the bridge is at a standstill. While Agent O'Brien remains at the intersection to direct traffic, Agent Benjamin goes onto the eastbound side of the bridge's lower level and observes a tractor trailer stopped in a lane. When Agent Benjamin reaches the trailer, she observes that it exceeds the height limit for vehicles to safely use the bridge. Agent Benjamin radios Traffic Control about the situation, and Traffic Control replies that they will notify the Bureau of Bridges but that, in the meantime, Agents Benjamin and O'Brien should try to handle the situation themselves. Agent Benjamin radios Agent O'Brien and tells him to stop all eastbound traffic from coming onto the bridge. Once this is done, Agent Benjamin then stops all westbound traffic at the site of the trailer. She then directs the eastbound vehicles behind the trailer to go around the trailer by using the westbound lane. Once all the traffic behind the tractor trailer has passed, Agent Benjamin has the trailer back off the bridge.

16. The tractor trailer did not proceed across the bridge because it was
    A. too high   B. too heavy   C. too wide   D. out of fuel

17. Agent O'Brien was told to stop traffic heading in which direction?
    A. Northbound   B. Southbound   C. Eastbound   D. Westbound

Questions 18-20.

DIRECTIONS: Questions 18 through 20 are to be answered SOLELY on the basis of the following passage.

Traffic Enforcement Agents Miner and LaBatt are assigned to direct traffic at the intersection of 181st Street and Broadway. While directing traffic, Agent LaBatt is informed by a motorist that there is a brown Ford Escort partially blocking the 181st Street exit of the Cross-Bronx Expressway. While Agent LaBatt proceeds to investigate this report, Agent Minor radios Traffic Control and informs Traffic Lieutenant Wesley that Agent LaBatt has left the intersection in order to investigate the motorist's report.

When Agent LaBatt arrives at the scene, he sees the reported vehicle partially blocking the 181st Street exit ramp. Agent LaBatt inspects the vehicle and discovers that the right front fender is missing and the left rear fender is dented. Upon further inspection, he finds that the license plates are missing, as well as the car's registration sticker. Agent LaBatt, believing that the car is abandoned, follows the procedures for an abandoned vehicle by writing his District Office number and the date and time on both rear fenders. Agent LaBatt also believes that the vehicle creates a hazard to safe traffic flow. He radios Traffic Control with this information and informs Lt. Wesley that a tow truck will be necessary. Lt. Wesley instructs Agent LaBatt to remain with the vehicle and direct exiting traffic off the expressway until the tow truck arrives.

18. The vehicle blocking the exit was missing its
    A. left rear fender, front license plate, and car registration sticker
    B. right rear fender, left rear fender, and license plates
    C. right front fender, license plates, and car registration sticker
    D. left front fender, rear license plate, and car registration sticker

19. Agent LaBatt was directed to remain with the vehicle
    A. to prevent the vehicle from being stripped
    B. so the tow truck would know where to go
    C. because traffic at 181st Street and Broadway was light
    D. to direct traffic off the expressway

20. What are the procedures to be followed regarding an abandoned vehicle? Write the date, time,
    A. and the District Office number on the left and right rear fenders
    B. District Office number and registration sticker number on both rear fenders
    C. and the District Office number on both front fenders
    D. the District Office number, and the license plate number on both front fenders

Questions 21-23.

DIRECTIONS: Questions 21 through 23 are to be answered SOLELY on the basis of the following passage.

Traffic Lieutenant Seaver informs Traffic Enforcement Agent Roberts that his assignment for the day is to direct traffic at the intersection of 72nd Street and Madison Avenue. At 11:30 A.M., Agent Roberts observes that the westbound lane at the corner of 120 E. 72nd Street is crumbling and water is pouring out of a huge crack in the street. Mrs. Perry, a resident at 140 E. 72nd Street is looking out her window at the time and immediately dials 911 to report the incident. Agent Roberts radios Traffic Control and informs them of the situation. He requests additional agents to respond to the scene. Traffic Control informs Agent Roberts that they will contact the appropriate utilities and city agencies. However, Agent Roberts is told that until additional agents arrive, he should handle the situation. Fortunately for Agent Roberts, Mrs. Perry's call to 911 brought Police Officers Monroe and Lanier to the scene at 11:35 A.M. Since the crack is located in the westbound lane at 72nd Street and Madison Avenue, Police Officer Monroe proceeds to 72nd Street and 5th Avenue in order to divert westbound traffic before it reaches Madison Avenue. Police Officer Lanier proceeds to 71st Street and Madison Avenue to divert northbound traffic, while Agent Roberts diverts eastbound traffic at the 72nd Street and Madison Avenue intersection.

21. Police Officers Monroe and Lanier arrived at the scene at
    A. 11:00 P.M.   B. 11:15 A.M.   C. 11:30 P.M.   D. 11:35 A.M.

22. Who diverted traffic at 71st Street and Madison Avenue?
    A. Traffic Agent Roberts
    B. Police Officer Lanier
    C. Lieutenant Seaver
    D. Police Officer Monroe

23. The water is pouring out of the street at the corner of _____ 72nd Street.
    A. 120 W.   B. 140 E.   C. 120 E.   D. 140 W.

Questions 24-25.

DIRECTIONS: Questions 24 and 25 are to be answered SOLELY on the basis of the following passage.

Traffic Enforcement Agent Murray was on patrol in his vehicle at the corner of Chambers and Church Streets when he noticed an accident between a white van and a green station wagon at the intersection of Church and Duane Streets. The two drivers were involved in a heated argument when Agent Murray approached them. He advised them to move their vehicles out of the intersection and over to the curb. Once at the curb, Ms. Ambrose, the driver of the station wagon, informed Agent Murray that the van had cut her off. The driver of the fan, Mr. Hope, informed Agent Murray that he was simply trying to change lanes when the station wagon hit his van. Agent Murray asked both drivers for their drivers' licenses and registrations. He informed them that since no one was injured and the damage to the vehicles was minor, they should have driven their cars from the intersection before arguing as to who was at fault. Since they failed to do so, he was going to issue both drivers a summons for obstructing traffic. At this point, Mr. Hope jumped into his van and raced up Reade Street. Agent Murray completed two summonses, one for Ms. Ambrose and the other for Mr. Hope. He issued Ms. Ambrose her summons and at the end of the day returned to his District Office and prepared a Summons Refusal Form. He then attached Mr. Hope's summons to the Summons Refusal Form so that the summons could be mailed to Mr. Hope.

24. At what intersection did the accident occur?
    A. Chambers Street and Church Street
    B. Church Street and Duane Street
    C. Chambers Street and Reade Street
    D. Reade Street and Duane Street

25. When Agent Murray arrived at the scene, the drivers involved in the accident were 25._____
   A. moving their vehicles to a side street
   B. exchanging insurance information
   C. involved in an argument
   D. waiting for an ambulance

KEY (CORRECT ANSWERS)

1.	B		11.	A
2.	C		12.	B
3.	D		13.	D
4.	A		14.	C
5.	B		15.	D
6.	A		16.	A
7.	C		17.	C
8.	D		18.	C
9.	A		19.	D
10.	A		20.	A

21.	D
22.	B
23.	C
24.	B
25.	C

TEST 2

DIRECTIONS: Each question or incomplete statement is followed by several suggested answers or completions. Select the one that BEST answers the question or completes the statement. *PRINT THE LETTER OF THE CORRECT ANSWER IN THE SPACE AT THE RIGHT.*

Questions 1-2.

DIRECTIONS: Questions 1 and 2 are to be answered SOLELY on the basis of the following passage.

    At 2:00 P.M., Traffic Enforcement Agent Black was on foot patrol on Hack Avenue when Mrs. Herbet approached him about a faulty parking meter. She complained that for the two quarters she deposited she is supposed to get two hours of parking tie and not just the forty minutes that the meter shows. Agent Black accompanied Mrs. Herbet to her car which was parked at 243 Chief Street. He tested the meter by turning the knob and found that the meter was broken because any amount of money deposited in the meter would register forty minutes of parking time. He searched for the serial number of the meter which was P26601 and recorded it along with the location of the meter on his Daily Field Patrol Sheet. Agent Black informed Mrs. Herbet that she would have two hours of parking time, the maximum amount of time she would have received if the meter were working properly. He also informed her that he was starting this two hour limit as of 2:05 P.M. and recorded this time and her license plate number (DRE-927) on his Daily Field Patrol Sheet. The agent told Mrs. Herbet that if her car was parked at the meter past the two hour limit, he would have to issue her a summons. Mrs. Herbet thanked the agent and said she would be gone long before the limit was up.

    At 4:15 P.M., Agent Black was again on Chief Street when he saw that Mrs. Herbet's car was still parked at the meter. He issued her a summons for a meter violation and continued on his patrol.

1. Which of the following is recorded on Agent Black's Daily Field Patrol Sheet? 1.____
   A. 243 Hack Avenue, P26611, 2:05 P.M., DRE-927
   B. 243 Chief Street, P26601, 2:05 P.M., DRE-927
   C. 243 Hack Street, P26661, 2:05 P.M., DRE-927
   D. 243 Chief Avenue, P26601, 2:05 P.M., DRE-927

2. Agent Black allowed Mrs. Herbet to park at the meter for two hours because 2.____
   A. it is the maximum amount of parking time allowed if the meter were working properly
   B. he felt bad that she lost her money
   C. she was complaining to him
   D. she assured him she would be gone before the two hour limit was up

Questions 2-5.

DIRECTIONS: Questions 2 through 5 are to be answered SOLELY on the basis of the following passage.

At 10:35 A.M., Police Communications Technician Ross receives a second call from Mrs. Smith who is very upset because she has been waiting for the police and an ambulance since her first call, one hour ago. Mrs. Smith was mugged, and in resisting the attack, her nose was broken. The location of the incident is the uptown side of the subway station for the IND #2 train located at Jay Street and Borough Hall. Operator Ross advises Mrs. Smith to hold on and that she will check the status of her complaint. Operator Ross calls the Emergency Medical Service (EMS) and connects Mrs. Smith to the EMS operator. The EMS operator informs Mrs. Smith that an ambulance is coming from a far distance away and will be at the location at approximately 11:03 A.M. Operator Ross then calls the Transit Authority Police Department (TAPD). The TAPD received Mrs. Smith's call at 9:37 A.M., and police arrived at location at 9:46 A.M. However, the police arrived at the downtown side of the subway station for the IND #3 train. TAPD informs Operator Ross that a police car will arrive at the correct location as soon as possible.

3. What is the CLOSEST approximate time that Mrs. Smith made her first call for help?
   A. 9:35   B. 9:46   C. 10:35   D. 11:03

4. The ambulance was delayed because
   A. the ambulance responded to the downtown side of the subway station for the IND #2 train
   B. EMS never received Mrs. Smith's request for an ambulance
   C. a broken nose is not a priority request for an ambulance
   D. the ambulance was coming from a far distance

5. There was a delay in TAPD response to the crime scene because TAPD
   A. was coming from a far distance
   B. responded on the uptown side of the subway station for the IND #2 train
   C. was waiting for the Police Department to respond first
   D. responded on the downtown side of the subway station for the IND #3 train

Questions 6-8.

DIRECTIONS: Questions 6 through 8 are to be answered SOLELY on the basis of the following passage.

Police Communications Technician Robbins receives a call at 5:15 P.M. from Mr. Adams reporting he witnessed a shooting in front of 230 Eagle Road. Mr. Adams, who lives at 234 Eagle Road, states he overheard two white males arguing with a black man. He describes one white male as having blonde hair and wearing a black jacket with blue jeans, and the other white male as having brown hair and wearing a white jacket and blue jeans.

3 (#2)

Mr. Adams recognized the black man as John Rivers, the son of Mrs. Mary Rivers, who lives at 232 Eagle Road. At 5:10 P.M., the blonde male took a gun, shot John in the stomach, and dragged his body into the alleyway. The two males ran into the backyard of 240 Eagle Road and headed west on Randall Boulevard. Dispatcher Robbins connects Mr. Adams to the Emergency Medical Service. The Ambulance Receiving Operator processes the call at 5:25 P.M. and advises Mr. Adams that the next available ambulance will be sent.

6. Who was the witness to the shooting?
   A. Dispatcher Robbins
   B. Mr. Adams
   C. Mrs. Rivers
   D. John Rivers

7. In front of what address was John Rivers shot?
   _____ Eagle Road.
   A. 230
   B. 232
   C. 234
   D. 240

8. What is the description of the male who fired the gun?
   A _____ male wearing a _____ jacket, and blue jeans.
   A. white blonde-haired; white
   B. white brown-haired; black
   D. white blonde-haired; black
   D. black brown-haired; white

Questions 9-10.

DIRECTIONS: Questions 9 and 10 are to be answered SOLELY on the basis of the following passage.

At the beginning of their tours, Police Communications Technicians need to call the precinct to find out what patrol cars are covering which sections of the precinct and which special assignment cars are being used. Special assignment cars are used instead of regular patrol cars when certain situations arise. Special assignment cars should be assigned before a patrol car when a call comes in that is related to the car's special assignment, regardless of what section the incident is occurring in. Otherwise, a regular patrol car should be assigned.

Police Communications Technician Tanner is assigned to the 83rd Precinct. He calls the precinct and determines the following patrol cars and special assignment cars are being used:

Patrol cars are assigned as follows:
   Patrol Car 83A – Covers Sections A, B, C
   Patrol Car 83D – Covers Sections D, E, F
   Patrol Car 83G – Covers Sections G, H, I

Special assignment cars are assigned as follows:
   83SP1 – Burglary Car
   83SP2 – Religious Establishment
   83SP8 – Anti-Crime (plainclothes officers)

9. Dispatcher Tanner receives a call located in the 83rd Precinct in E Section Which car should be assigned?
   A. 83D
   B. 83A
   C. 83SP8
   D. 83SP2

10. Dispatcher Tanner receives a call concerning a burglary in B Section. Which is the CORRECT car to be assigned?
   A. 83A   B. 83G   C. 83SP1   D. 83SP2

Questions 11-13.

DIRECTIONS: Questions 11 through 13 are to be answered SOLELY on the basis of the following passage.

Mrs. Arroyo returns from work one evening to find her door open and loud noise coming from her apartment. She peeks through the crack of the door and sees a white male moving rapidly through her apartment wearing blue jeans and a pink T-shirt. She runs to the nearest public telephone and dials 911. Police Communications Technician Ms. Lopez takes the call. Mrs. Arroyo informs Operator Lopez that there is a strange man in her apartment. The operator asks the caller for her address, apartment number, name, and telephone number, and then puts Mrs. Arroyo on hold. Operator Lopez enters the address in the computer and, realizing it is a high priority call, tries to notify the Radio Dispatcher directly by depressing the *hotline* button. The Radio Dispatcher does not respond, and Operator Lopez realizes the *hotline* button is not working. The operator then continues to enter the rest of the information into the computer and notifies the caller that the police will respond. Operator Lopez then walks into the dispatcher's room to make sure the dispatcher received the information entered into the computer, and then notifies the supervisor of her malfunctioning equipment.

11. The operator notified her supervisor because
   A. the suspect was still in the apartment
   B. the *hotline* button was not working
   C. she could not enter the address in the computer
   D. it was a high priority call

12. What was the FIRST action the operator took after putting the complainant on hold?
   A. Entered the caller's telephone number and name in the computer
   B. Walked into the dispatcher's room
   C. Entered the caller's address into the computer
   D. Tried to notify the Radio Dispatcher by depressing the *hotline* button

13. Operator Lopez depressed the *hotline* button
   A. to check if the *hotline* button was working properly
   B. because it was a high priority call
   C. to make sure the dispatcher received the information entered into the computer
   D. because the computer was not working properly

Questions 14-16.

DIRECTIONS: Questions 14 through 16 are to be answered SOLELY on the basis of the following passage.

Police Communications Technician John Clove receives a call from a social worker, Mrs. Norma Harris of Presbyterian Hospital, who states there is a 16-year-old teenager on the other line speaking to Dr. Samuel Johnson, a psychologist at the hospital. The teenager is threatening suicide and claims that she is an out-patient, but refuses to give her name, address, or telephone number. She further states that the teenager took 100 pills of valium and is experiencing dizziness, numbness of the lips, and heart palpitations. The teenager tells Dr. Johnson that she wants to die because her boyfriend left her because she is pregnant.

Dr. Johnson is keeping her on the line persuading her to give her name, telephone number, and address. The social worker asks the dispatcher to trace the call. The dispatcher puts the caller on hold and informs his supervisor, Mrs. Ross, of the incident. The supervisor contacts Telephone Technician Mr. Ralph Taylor. Mr. Taylor contacts the telephone company and speaks to Supervisor Wallace, asking him to trace the call between Dr. Johnson and the teenager. After approximately 10 minutes, the dispatcher gets back to the social worker and informs her that the call is being traced.

14. Why did the social worker call Dispatcher Clove? 14.____
    A. A teenager is threatening suicide
    B. Mrs. Ross took 100 pills of valium
    C. Dr. Johnson felt dizzy, numbness of the lips, and heart palpitations
    D. An unmarried teenager is pregnant

15. Who did Mr. Clove notify FIRST? 15.____
    A. Mrs. Norma Harris   B. Dr. Samuel Johnson
    C. Mr. Wallace   D. Mrs. Ross

16. The conversation between which two individuals is being traced? 16.____
    A. Mrs. Norma Harris and the 16-year-old teenager
    B. The Telephone Technician and Telephone Company Supervisor
    C. Dr. Johnson and the 16-year-old teenager
    D. the dispatcher and the Hospital social worker

Questions 17-19.

DIRECTIONS: Questions 17 through 19 are to be answered SOLELY on the basis of the following passage.

Police Communications Technician Flood receives a call from Mr. Michael Watkins, Program Director for *Meals On Wheels*, a program that delivers food to elderly people who cannot leave their homes. Mr. Watkins states he received a call from Rochelle Berger, whose elderly aunt, Estelle Sims, is a client of his. Rochelle Berger informed Mr. Watkins that she had just received a call from her aunt's neighbor, Sally Bowles, who told her that her aunt has not eaten in several days and is in need of medical attention.

After questioning Mr. Watkins, Dispatcher Flood is informed that Estelle Sims lives at 300 79th Street in Apartment 6K, and her telephone number is 686-4527; Sally Bowles lives in Apartment 6H, and her telephone number is 678-2456. Mr. Watkins further advises that if there is difficulty getting into Estelle Sims' apartment, to ring Sally Bowles bell and she will let you in.

Mr. Watkins gives his phone number as 776-0451, and Rochelle Berger's phone number is 291-7287. Dispatcher Flood advises Mr. Watkins that the appropriate medical assistance will be sent.

17. Who did Sally Bowles notify that her neighbor needed medical attention? 17._____
    A. Dispatcher Flood B. Michael Watkins
    C. Rochelle Berger D. Estelle Sims

18. If the responding medical personnel are unable to get into Apartment 6K, they should speak to 18._____
    A. Rochelle Berger B. Sally Bowles
    C. Dispatcher Flood D. Michael Watkins

19. Whose telephone number is 686-4527? 19._____
    A. Michael Watkins B. Estelle Sims
    C. Sally Bowles D. Rochelle Berger

Questions 20-22.

DIRECTIONS: Questions 20 through 22 are to be answered SOLELY on the basis of the following passage.

On May 15, 2020, at 10:15 A.M., Mr. Price was returning to his home at 220 Kings Walk when he discovered two of his neighbors' apartment doors slightly opened. One neighbor, Mrs. Kagan, who lives alone in Apartment 1C, was away on vacation. The other apartment, 1B, is occupied by Martin and Ruth Stone, an elderly couple, who usually take a walk everyday at 10:00 A.M. Fearing a robbery might be taking place, Mr. Price runs downstairs to Mr. White in Apartment B1 to call the police. Police Communications Technician Johnson received the call at 10:20 A.M. Mr. Price gave his address and stated that two apartments were possibly being burglarized. Communications Technician Johnson verified the address in the computer and then asked Mr. Price for descriptions of the suspects. He explained that he had not seen anyone, but he believed that they were still inside the building. Communications Technician Johnson immediately notified the dispatcher ho assigned two patrol cars at 10:25 A.M., while Mr. Price was still on the phone. Communications technician Johnson told Mr. Price that the police were responding to the location.

20. Who called Communications Technician Johnson? 20._____
    A. Mrs. Kagan B. Mr. White C. Mrs. Stone D. Mr. Price

21. What time did Communications Technician Johnson receive the call? 21._____
    _____ A.M.
    A. 10:00 B. 10:15 C. 10:20 D. 10:25

22. Which tenant was away on vacation? 22._____
    The tenant in Apartment
    A. 1C B. 1B C. B1 D. 1D

Questions 23-25.

DIRECTIONS: Questions 23 through 25 are to be answered SOLELY on the basis of the following passage.

On Tuesday, March 20, 2020, at 11:55 P.M., Dispatcher Uzel receives a call from a female stating that she immediately needs the police. The dispatcher asks the caller for her address. The excited female answers, *I cannot think of it right now*. The dispatcher tries to calm down the caller. At this point, the female caller tells the dispatcher that her address is 1934 Bedford Avenue. The caller then realizes that 1934 Bedford Avenue is her mother's address and gives her address as 3455 Bedford Avenue. Dispatcher Uzel enters the address into the computer and tells the caller that the cross streets are Myrtle and Willoughby Avenues. The caller answers, *I don't live near Willoughby Avenue*. The dispatcher repeats her address at 3455 Bedford Avenue. Then the female states that her name is Linda Harris and her correct address is 5534 Bedford Avenue. Dispatcher Uzel enters the new address into the computer and determines the cross streets to be Utica Avenue and Kings Highway. The caller agrees that these are the cross streets where she lives.

23. What is the caller's CORRECT address?
    A. Unknown
    B. 1934 Bedford Avenue
    C. 3455 Bedford Avenue
    D. 5534 Bedford Avenue

24. What are the cross streets of the correct answer?
    A. Myrtle Avenue and Willoughby Avenue
    B. Utica Avenue and Kings Highway
    C. Bedford Avenue and Myrtle Avenue
    D. Utica Avenue and Willoughby Avenue

25. Why did the female caller telephone Dispatcher Uzel?
    A. She needed the cross streets for her address
    B. Her mother needed assistance
    C. The purpose of the call was not mentioned
    D. She did not know where she lived

KEY (CORRECT ANSWERS)

1. B
2. A
3. A
4. D
5. D
6. B
7. A
8. C
9. A
10. C

11. B
12. C
13. B
14. A
15. D
16. C
17. C
18. B
19. B
20. D

21. C
22. A
23. D
24. B
25. C

TEST 3

DIRECTIONS: Each question or incomplete statement is followed by several suggested answers or completions. Select the one that BEST answers the question or completes the statement. *PRINT THE LETTER OF THE CORRECT ANSWER IN THE SPACE AT THE RIGHT.*

Questions 1-3.

DIRECTIONS: Questions 1 through 3 are to be answered SOLELY on the basis of the following passage.

    Dispatcher Clark, who is performing a 7:30 A.M. to 3:30 P.M. tour of duty, receives a call from Mrs. Gold. Mrs. Gold states there are four people selling drugs in front of Joe's Cleaners, located at the intersection of Main Street and Broadway. After checking the location in the computer, Dispatcher Clark asks the caller to give a description of each person. She gives the following descriptions: one white male wearing a yellow shirt, green pants, and red sneakers; one Hispanic male wearing a red and white shirt, black pants, and white sneakers; one black female wearing a green and red striped dress and red sandals; and one black male wearing a green shirt, yellow pants, and green sneakers. She also states that the Hispanic male, who is standing near a blue van, has the drugs inside a small black shoulder bag. She further states that she saw the black female hide a gun inside a brown paper bag and place it under a black car parked in front of Joe's Cleaners. The drug selling goes on everyday at various times. During the week, it occurs from 7 A.M. to 1 P.M. and from 5 P.M. to 12 A.M., but on weekends it occurs from 3 P.M. until 7 A.M.

1. Which person was wearing red sneakers?
   A. Black male
   B. Hispanic male
   C. Black female
   D. White male

2. Mrs. Gold stated the drugs were located
   A. under the blue van
   B. inside the black shoulder bag
   C. under the black car
   D. inside the brown paper bag

3. At what time does Mrs. Gold state the drugs are sold on weekends?
   A. 7:30 A.M. – 3:30 P.M.
   B. 7:00 A.M. – 1:00 P.M.
   C. 5:00 P.M. – 12:00 A.M.
   D. 3:00 P.M. – 7:00 A.M.

1._____

2._____

3._____

Questions 4-6.

DIRECTIONS: Questions 4 through 6 are to be answered SOLELY on the basis of the following passage.

    911 Operator Gordon receives a call from a male stating there is a bomb set to explode in the gym of Public School 85 in two hours. Realizing the urgency of the call, the Operator calls the radio dispatcher, who assigns Patrol Car 43A to the scene. Operator Gordon then notifies her supervisor, Miss Smith, who first reviews the tape of the call, then calls the Operations Unit, which is notified of all serious incidents, and she reports the facts. The Operations Unit notifies the Mayor's Information Agency and Borough Headquarters of the emergency situation.

2 (#3)

4. Who did Operator Gordon notify FIRST? 4.____
   A. Supervisor Smith
   B. Operations Unit
   C. Patrol Car 43A
   D. Radio dispatcher

5. The Operations Unit was notified 5.____
   A. to inform school personnel of the bomb
   B. so they can arrive at the scene before the bomb is scheduled to go off
   C. to evacuate the school
   D. due to the seriousness of the incident

6. Who did Miss Smith notify? 6.____
   A. Patrol Car 43A
   B. Operations Unit
   C. Mayor's Information Agency
   D. Borough Headquarters

Questions 7-9.

DIRECTIONS: Questions 7 through 9 are to be answered SOLELY on the basis of the following passage.

Communications Operator Harris receives a call from Mrs. Stein who reports that a car accident occurred in front of her home. She states that one of the cars belongs to her neighbor, Mrs. Brown, and the other car belongs to Mrs. Stein's son, Joseph Stein. Communications Operator Harris enters Mrs. Stein's address into the computer and receives information that no such address exists. She asks Mrs. Stein to repeat her address. Mrs. Stein repeats her address and states that gasoline is leaking from the cars and that smoke is coming from their engines. She further states that people are trapped in the cars and then hangs up.

Communications Operator Harris notifies her supervisor, Jones, that she received a call but was unable to verify the address and that the caller hung up. Mrs. Jones listens to the tape of the call and finds that the caller stated 450 Park Place, not 415 Park Place. She advises Communications Operator Harris to enter the correct address, then notify Emergency Service Unit to respond to the individuals trapped in the cars, the Fire Department for the smoke condition, and Emergency Medical Service for any possible injuries.

7. Who did Communications Operator Harris notify concerning the problem with the caller's address? 7.____
   A. Mrs. Brown
   B. Joseph Stein
   C. Joseph Brown
   D. Mrs. Jones

8. Which agency was Communications Operator Harris advised to notify concerning individuals trapped in the cars? 8.____
   A. Emergency Medical Service
   B. Fire Department
   C. Emergency Service Unit
   D. NYC Police Department

9. Which agency did Supervisor Jones advise Communications Operator Harris to notify for the smoke condition? 9.____
   A. NYC Police Department
   B. Emergency Medical Service
   C. Fire Department
   D. Emergency Service Unit

Questions 10-12.

DIRECTIONS: Questions 10 through 12 are to be answered SOLELY on the basis of the following passage.

On May 12, at 3:35 P.M., Police Communications Technician Connor receives a call from a child caller requesting an ambulance for her mother, whom she cannot wake. The child did not know her address, but gave Communications Technician Connor her apartment number and telephone number. Communications Technician Connor's supervisor, Ms. Bendel, is advised of the situation and consults Cole's Director, a listing published by the Bell Telephone Company to obtain an address when only the telephone number is known. The telephone number is unlisted. Ms. Bendel asks Communications Technician Taylor to call Telco Security to obtain an address from their telephone number listing. Communications Technician Taylor speaks to Ms. Morris of Telco Security and obtains the address. Communications Technician Connor, who is still talking with the child, is given the address by Communications Technician Taylor. She enters the information into the computer system and transfers the caller to the Emergency Medical Service.

10. What information did Communications Technician Connor obtain from the child caller?
    A. Telephone number and apartment number
    B. Name and address
    C. Address and telephone number
    D. Apartment number and address

11. Communications Technician Taylor obtained the address from
    A. Communications Technician Connor
    B. Ms. Morris
    C. Supervisor Bendel
    D. the child caller

12. The caller's address was obtained by calling
    A. Cole's Directory
    B. Telco Security
    C. Emergency Medical Service
    D. the Telephone Company

Questions 13-15.

DIRECTIONS: Questions 13 through 15 are to be answered SOLELY on the basis of the following passage.

Bridge and Tunnel Officer Frankel is assigned to Post 33 inside the Main Street Tunnel. All posts in the northbound tunnel are numbered using odd numbers. All posts in the southbound tunnel are numbered with even numbers. The sergeant on duty, Sgt. Hanks, drives through the northbound tunnel at 10:30 P.M. to check on the tunnel posts before taking his meal break. When he reaches Officer Frankel, Sgt. Hanks stops the patrol car and exits from his car in order to speak with Frankel. He informs the officer that at 11:05 P.M. a truck with a wide load is expected to pass through the tunnel. Officer Frankel states he will be prepared for the vehicle and will watch for it.

Sgt. Hanks gets back into his patrol car and continues on his way to inform the other three officers in the northbound tunnel. At 10:50 P.M., Sgt. Hanks is heading to the facility building when his patrol car stalls in front of Post 44. Bridge and Tunnel Officer Torrey, stationed at the post, observes the disabled patrol car and leave his post in order to assist the sergeant. Sgt. Hanks orders Officer Torrey to call for a wrecker to remove the patrol car from the tunnel.

13. At what post did Sgt. Hanks' patrol car break down? 13.____
    A. 34, Northbound
    B. 44, Southbound
    C. 43, Northbound
    D. 33, Southbound

14. How many Bridge and Tunnel Officers were posted in the northbound tunnel? 14.____
    A. 2   B. 3   C. 4   D. 5

15. Sgt. Hanks was driving through the northbound tunnel in order to 15.____
    A. inform the posts of the *wide load* truck
    B. find where Bridge and Tunnel Officer Frankel was stationed
    C. check on the tunnel posts
    D. return to the facility building

Questions 16-18.

DIRECTIONS: Questions 16 through 18 are to be answered SOLELY on the basis of the following passage.

At 6:45 P.M., two motorists were involved in a minor accident on the toll plaza at the Cross-Bay Bridge. Tempers became short, and soon the two motorists were involved in a heated argument.

Bridge and Tunnel Officers Bender and Rourke, who were to start their tour at 6:50 P.M., arrived and broke up the altercation. The two drivers were separated and calmed. Each began to describe the accident to the officers.

Nicholas Warren informed Officer Rourke that he paid his toll in Lane 1, which is the extreme right lane. He wanted to go into the left lane on the bridge and began to move his vehicle to the left when his vehicle was struck in the rear by a vehicle leaving Toll Lane 2.

Olga Miller informed Officer Bender that she had paid her toll and was leaving Lane 2 when Mr. Warren's vehicle cut directly in front of her vehicle and caused the accident.

Ten minutes after the accident occurred, Bridge and Tunnel Officers Pena and Bickford rang their supervisor and asked when they were to be relieved since their tours were scheduled to end at 7:00 P.M. Sergeant White explained to the two officers that their relief officers were taking information on an accident. Officers Pena and Bickford told the Sergeant that they would take over for Bender and Rourke and finish taking the information. Sgt. White approved the switch. Twenty-five minutes after the accident, all information was taken, and all parties left the scene.

16. Ms. Miller FIRST spoke to Officer 16.____
    A. Bender   B. Bickford   C. White   D. Pena

17. Officer Pena was due to end his tour at _____ P.M. 17.____
    A. 6:45   B. 6:50   C. 7:00   D. 7:10

18. In what toll lane did Mr. Warren pay the toll? 18.____
    A. 1   B. 2   C. 3   D. 4

Questions 19-20.

DIRECTIONS: Questions 19 through 20 are to be answered SOLELY on the basis of the following passage.

Bridge and Tunnel Officer Wendell is assigned to a toll plaza at the Wilson Bridge. At about 2:15 P.M., he observes John Edwards drive into the toll lane without throwing any money into the Exact Coin Machine. As Officer Wendell approaches the vehicle, Mr. Edwards starts to blow his horn. Officer Wendell instructs Mr. Edwards to place the proper toll into the machine, but Mr. Edwards refuses, stating that the bridge toll is unfair. When Officer Wendell requests Mr. Edwards' drivers license and car registration, Mr. Edwards starts to yell and use abusive language. Officer Wendell warns Mr. Edwards that he will be arrested if he continues to block the toll lane. Mr. Edwards continues to yell, refuses to leave the lane, and is arrested by Officer Wendell.

19. Officer Wendell FIRST observed Mr. Edwards when he 19.____
    A. started blowing his horn
    B. refused to leave the toll lane
    C. entered the toll lane
    D. began yelling and using abusive language

20. Officer Wendell arrested Mr. Edwards because he 20.____
    A. refused to pay the toll
    B. was yelling and using abusive language
    C. refused to give his license and registration to Officer Wendell
    D. was blocking the toll lane

KEY (CORRECT ANSWERS)

1.	D	11.	B
2.	B	12.	B
3.	D	13.	B
4.	D	14.	C
5.	D	15.	A/C
6.	B	16.	A
7.	D	17.	C
8.	C	18.	A
9.	C	19.	C
10.	A	20.	D

REPORT WRITING
EXAMINATION SECTION
TEST 1

DIRECTIONS: Each question or incomplete statement is followed by several suggested answers or completions. Select the one that BEST answers the question or completes the statement. *PRINT THE LETTER OF THE CORRECT ANSWER IN THE SPACE AT THE RIGHT.*

Questions 1-10.

DIRECTIONS: Questions 1 through 10 are to be answered SOLELY on the basis of the following passage and Stolen Vehicle Report Form, which appears on the following page. The form contains 43 numbered boxes. Read the passage and look at the form before answering the questions.

Police Officers Walton and Wright, patrolling in their radio patrol car in the industrial area of the 29th Precinct, were dispatched to 523 Johnson Boulevard at 10:30 A.M. on October 30, 2020 by the Police Radio Dispatcher. The Dispatcher had received a telephone call from a Ms. Ann Graham at 10:28 A.M. that her friend's car was being stolen from in front of her house.

Officers Walton and Wright arrived at 523 Johnson Boulevard at 10:32 A.M. Ms. Graham was waiting outside and informed them that the car had already been stolen. She stated that her friend, Samantha Merlin, had gone on vacation to California three days before and had left her car in Ms. Graham's care. Ms. Graham had parked the car in front of her own house the night before.

Ms. Graham stated that she looked out of her window at 10:25 A.M. that day and saw a strange man breaking into the car using a wire coat hanger. The car's hood was raised. She ran to her telephone to call the police. When she returned to her window, she saw the man doing something under the hood and, within a minute, he drove the car away. She had been too frightened to try to stop him, and there was no one else on the street.

Ms. Graham described the car as a black 2002 Buick 2-door sedan, New York license plate number 113-ABT, Vehicle Identification Number 7641239877. She stated that her friend, Ms. Merlin, lives at 1905 Junis Road, her telephone number is 978-4123, she is unmarried, 30 years old, and will return from vacation on November 13. Until then, she can be reached by telephone at 213-804-9112. She is employed at the law firm of Adams and Adams, 360 Park Avenue, as an office manager.

Ms. Graham described the man who stole the car as white, in his early twenties, about 5'7", 155 lbs., and wearing blue pants, a black jacket, and an earring in his left ear. He had dark brown, short curly hair.

Ms. Graham gave her telephone number as 275-8722 and stated that she is divorced, employed as a securities analyst at F.G. Sutton and Company, 125 Wall Street, and is 32 years old. Her birth date is June 13, 1976. Her telephone number at work is 217-7273.

2 (#1)

STOLEN VEHICLE REPORT FORM

COMPLAINT INFORMATION	Complaint Number (1)	Precinct (2)	Date Complaint Reported (3)	Time Reported (4)	Place Complaint Taken (5)
VEHICLE DESCRIPTION	Year (6)	Make (7)	Color (8)		License Number (9)
	I.D. Number (10)		Type (11)		Location of Theft (122)
OWNER INFORMATION	Name (13)		Address (14)		Home Telephone (15)
	Age (16)		Marital Status (17)		Occupation (18)
	Business Address (19)			Business Telephone (20)	
WITNESS INFORMATION	Name (21)		Address (22)		Home Telephone (23)
	Age (24)		Marital Status (25)		Occupation (26)
	Business Address (27)			Business Telephone (28)	
	Witness' Description of Incident (29)				
DESCRIPTION OF SUSPECT	Name (If Known) (30)	Age (31)	Race (32)	Sex (33)	Height (34)	Weight (35)	Hair (36
	Eyes (37)		Clothing (38)		Distinctive Marks (39)
	Other (40)				
OFFICER INFORMATION	Name (41)			Date (42)	
	Shield Number (43)				

1. Which one of the following should be entered in Box 3?   1._____
   A. June 13   B. October 13
   C. October 30   D. November 13

2. Which one of the following should be entered in Box 31? 2.____
   A. Late teens   B. Early twenties   C. 30   D. 32

3. Which one of the following should be entered in Box 12? 3.____
   In front of
   A. 1905 Junis Road   B. 523 Johnson Boulevard
   C. 125 Wall Street   D. 360 Park Avenue

4. Which one of the following should be entered in Box 8? 4.____
   A. Blue   B. Brown   C. Black   D. Red

5. Which one of the following should be entered in Box 11? 5.____
   A. 2-door sedan   B. 4-door sedan
   C. 4-door station wagon   D. 2-door sportscar

6. Which one of the following should be entered in Box 15? 6.____
   A. 804-9112   B. 217-7273   C. 275-8722   D. 978-4123

7. Which one of the following should be entered in Box 17? 7.____
   A. Married   B. Legally separated
   C. Single   D. Divorced

8. Which one of the following should be entered in Box 21? 8.____
   A. Samantha Merlin   B. Samantha Graham
   C. Ann Merlin   D. Ann Graham

9. Which one of the following should be entered in Box 26? 9.____
   A. Securities analyst   B. Housewife
   C. Office Manager   D. Secretary

10. Which one of the following should be entered in Box 40? 10.____
    A. Scar on left cheek   B. Earring in left ear
    C. Short curly brown hair   D. Blue pants, black jacket

Questions 11-20.

DIRECTIONS: Questions 11 through 20 are to be answered SOLELY on the basis of the following story and Complaint Report Form.

Officers Fred Johnson and Carl Adams, patrolling in their radio car in the Riverfront section of Precinct #8, were dispatched to 124 Selwyn Lane at 3:23 P.M. on April 26 by the dispatcher. The dispatcher had received a telephone call at 3:20 P.M. from a Mrs. Green who said that her house had been burglarized and all of the contents of her house had been stolen.

Officers Johnson and Adams arrived at 124 Selwyn Lane at 3:28 P.M. Mrs. Green and two neighbors were waiting for them on the front steps. The Officers parked their patrol car in front of the house and locked the doors. Mrs. Green explained that she is a schoolteacher and her husband is a lawyer. They usually leave the house around 8:00 A.M. each morning. She is the first to arrive home since school lets out at 3:00 P.M. She tells the Officers that today, when she arrived home, she found the door to her house slightly open. She was frightened and went to her neighbor's house. Both women then returned to 124 Selwyn and, upon entering the house, found that the contents of the house had been removed. At that point, Mrs. Green called the Police Department.

While Officer Johnson took statements from Mrs. Green and Mrs. Walters, her neighbor, Officer Adams questioned other residents of the street. Most of the other residents were standing outside of the Green's house.

Mrs. Schneider, age 56, who lives 5 doors down at 138 Selwyn, told Officer Adams that she arrived home at 2:45 P.M. She then told Adams that she saw a large truck parked near 124 Selwyn and remembers wondering if anyone new was moving into the neighborhood. She remembers the truck was dented, painted bright blue with a white top, and it had New Jersey plates. Also she was able to describe one of the suspects. She saw him get into the truck before it pulled away. The man was white, about 6'2" tall, about 220 lbs., and thinning brown hair. He was wearing a pair of dirty white overalls and brown work boots. He appeared to walk with a limp. There was another man already in the truck, and Mrs. Schneider described him as a very short Black man wearing a white hat. Mrs. Schneider said the truck turned left on Second Street as it pulled away.

Mrs. Jones, Mrs. Dartnell, and Mrs. Leopold, when questioned by Officer Adams, said that they saw nothing. They were all at Mrs. Leopold's house playing cards and didn't come outside until they heard Mrs. Green screaming.

Officer Adams found that Mrs. Schneider's home phone number was 683-2291 and that she lives alone. Officer Johnson found that both Mrs. Green and her neighbor were 48 years of age and that the school's telephone number was 925-6394. Mrs. Walters' home telephone number is 683-7642, and she lives with her husband at 126 Selwyn Lane. Mr. Green's office number is 238-4296. It is located at 555 Fifth Avenue, Suite 816.

Officers Johnson and Adams then completed the complaint form. The complaint number assigned by the dispatcher was 479638G.

5 (#1)

COMPLAINT REPORT					
COMPLAINT INFORMATION	Complaint Number (1)	Precinct (2)	Date of Complaint (3)	Time of Complaint (4)	Place Complaint Taken (5)
INFORMATION ABOUT PERSON MAKING COMPLAINT	Name of Person Making Complaint (6) Last Name First Name Middle			Address of Person Making Complaint (7) Street City State	
	Age (8)	Marriage (9) Married ☐ Not-Married ☐		Occupation (If Any) (10)	
	Spouse's Occupation (If Any) (11)			Spouse's Business Address (12) Street City State	
WITNESS INFORMATION	Name of Witness (If Any) (13) Last Name First Name Middle			Address of Witness (If Any) (14) Street City State	
	Age (15)	Occupation (If Any) (16)			
	Spouse's Occupation (If Any) (17)			Spouse's Business Address (18) Street City State	
DESCRIPTION OF INCIDENT	Description (19)				

DESCRIPTION OF SUSPECTS (if Any)	Suspect #1	Name (20)	Age (21)	Race (22) *white*	Sex (23) *male*	Height (24)	Weight (25)	Hair (26)	Eyes (27)
	Suspect #2	Name (28)	Age (29)	Race (30) *black*	Sex (31) *male*	Height (32)	Weight (33)	Hair (34)	Eyes (35)
	Suspect #3	Name (36)	Age (37)	Race (38)	Sex (39)	Height (40)	Weight (41)	Hair (42)	Eyes (43)
	Special Suspect Description (44) Suspect Number _____				Description (45) *Walked with limp*				
SUSPECT VEHICLE DESCRIPTION (If Any)	Year (46)			Make (47)		Color (48)			License Number 49)
OFFICER INFORMATION	Name (50) Shield No. (52)				Date (51)				

11. Which one of the following should be entered in Box 4?   11.____
     A. 8:00 AM   B. 2:45 PM   C. 3:20 PM   D. Not known

12. Which one of the following should be entered in Box 6?   12.____
     A. Mrs. Schneider   B. Mrs. Green
     C. Officer Johnson   D. Not known

13. Which one of the following should be entered in Box 7?   13.____
     A. 138 Selwyn Lane   B. 125 Selwyn Lane
     C. 124 Selwyn Lane   D. Not known

14. Which one of the following should be entered in Box 8? 14._____
    A. 48   B. 52   C. 46   D. Not known

15. Which one of the following should be entered in Box 10? 15._____
    A. Lawyer   B. Widow   C. Teacher   D. Not known

16. Which one of the following should be entered in Box 11? 16._____
    A. Lawyer   B. Widow   C. Teacher   D. Not known

17. Which one of the following should be entered in Box 13? 17._____
    A. Mrs. Green   B. Mrs. Schneider
    C. Mrs. Leopold   D. Not known

18. Which one of the following should be entered in Box 16? 18._____
    A. Lawyer   B. Teacher   C. Widow   D. Not known

19. Which one of the following should be entered in Box 26? 19._____
    A. Black   B. Brown   C. Blonde   D. Not known

20. Which one of the following should be entered in Box 44? 20._____
    A. 1   B. 2   C. 3   D. Not known

KEY (CORRECT ANSWERS)

1.	C	11.	C
2.	B	12.	B
3.	B	13.	C
4.	C	14.	A
5.	A	15.	C
6.	D	16.	A
7.	C	17.	B
8.	D	18.	D
9.	A	19.	B
10.	B	20.	A

TEST 2

DIRECTIONS: Each question or incomplete statement is followed by several suggested answers or completions. Select the one that BEST answers the question or completes the statement. *PRINT THE LETTER OF THE CORRECT ANSWER IN THE SPACE AT THE RIGHT.*

Questions 1-10.

DIRECTIONS: Questions 1 through 10 are to be answered SOLELY on the basis of the following story and Complaint Report Form.

    Officers Hunt and Torry respond to a suspected burglary-in-process call at 285 E. Reed Street. They arrive there at 2:32 P.M. A man wearing gray slacks, white dress shirt, and red tie is standing in front of the store yelling, *Stop, robbers!* He is pointing east. Officer Hunt sees three men running about one hundred and fifty feet away. He immediately starts to chase after them. One suspect is 5'9" and weighs about 140 lbs. He has black hair in an Afro cut and is wearing tan pants with a blue work shirt. He is wearing white tennis shoes with blue stripes. He turns the corner and runs south on Elm Street. Another one is 6'2" and weighs about 200 lbs. He has long dark brown hair and is wearing a green headband, white jacket, and blue jeans. He is carrying a brown paper bag in his left hand. He also turns south on Elm. The third man is 5'9" and weighs about 180 lbs. He has long dark brown hair and is wearing a white cap. He is wearing blue jeans and a light blue jacket with a white stripe around it. He continues running east on Reed.

    Officer Torry questions the man in the red tie and finds he is the manager of the Elite Jewelry Store and that he has just been robbed by the men running away. Torry radios in the information and continues his questioning. The manager, Mr. Oscar Freehold, says that he was showing a ruby and diamond necklace to Mrs. Mandt, a customer, when these men entered the store. One of them, the tallest one, pointed a gun at Freehold and grabbed the necklace. He put the necklace in the pocket of his white jacket. The other two men were shorter and the same height. The heaver one of the two opened the cash register and emptied the money into a brown paper bag.

    The thinner short man opened a display case and put several sapphire and emerald rings in his pants pocket. He then took a knife from his pocket and held it on Mrs. Mandt. The tall one forced Mr. Freehold to open the safe. The tall one took jewels and money from the safe and put them in another brown paper bag. The three men ran out.

    Officer Hunt chased the two suspects who turned south on Elm Street. At the next corner, they turned east on Maple. They ran one block to the corner of Beech, where the one with the Afro cut turned south. The other suspect got into a car and drove east on Maple. It was a dark blue 2018 Ford sedan with New York license number 677-HKL. As he drove east on Maple, he sideswiped a 2016 red Dodge and a 2019 tan Volvo.

    Officer Hunt returns to the jewelry store and radios in the additional information. Officer Torry completes the Complaint Report.

2 (#2)

COMPLAINT REPORT					
COMPLAINT INFORMATION	Complaint Number (1)	Precinct (2)	Date of Complaint (3)	Time of Complaint (4)	Place Complaint Taken (5)
INFORMATION ABOUT PERSON MAKING COMPLAINT	Name of Person Making Complaint (6) Last Name First Name Middle			Address of Person Making Complaint (7) Street City State	
	Age (8)	Marriage (9) Married ☐ Not-Married ☐		Occupation (If Any) (10)	
	Spouse's Occupation (If Any) (11)			Spouse's Business Address (12) Street City State	
WITNESS INFORMATION	Name of Witness (If Any) (13) Last Name First Name Middle			Address of Witness (If Any) (14) Street City State	
	Age (15)	Occupation (If Any) (16)			
	Spouse's Occupation (If Any) (17)			Spouse's Business Address (18) Street City State	
DESCRIPTION OF INCIDENT	Description (19)				

DESCRIPTION OF SUSPECTS (if Any)		Name	Age	Race	Sex	Height	Weight	Hair	Eyes
	Suspect #1	(20)	(21)	(22)	(23) male	(24) 5'9"	(25) 140	(26)	(27)
	Suspect #2	(28)	(29)	(30) black	(31) male	(32) 6'2"	(33) 200	(34)	(35)
	Suspect #3	(36)	(37)	(38)	(39) male	(40) 5'9"	(41) 180	(42)	(43)
	Special Suspect Description (44) Suspect Number _____				Description (45) Walked with limp				

SUSPECT VEHICLE DESCRIPTION (If Any)	Year (46)	Make (47)	Color (48)	License Number 49)
OFFICER INFORMATION	Name (50)		Date (51)	
	Shield No. (52)			

1. Which of the following should be entered in Box 6?   1._____
   - A. Officer Hunt
   - B. Mr. Oscar Freehold
   - C. Mrs. Mandt
   - D. Not known

2. Which of the following should be entered in Box 10?   2._____
   - A. Jewelry store manager
   - B. Police officer
   - C. Clerk
   - D. Not known

3. Which of the following should be entered in Box 13?   3._____
   - A. Mr. Oscar Freehold
   - B. Mrs. Mandt
   - C. Officer Hunt
   - D. Not known

4. Which of the following should be entered in Box 14? 4.____
   A. East Reed Street   B. East Elm Street
   C. South Beech Street   D. Not known

5. Which of the following should be entered in Box 26? 5.____
   A. Blonde   B. Brown   C. Black   D. Not known

6. Which of the following should be entered in Box 34? 6.____
   A. Blonde   B. Brown   C. Black   D. Not known

7. Which of the following should be entered in Box 42? 7.____
   A. Blonde   B. Brown   C. Black   D. Not known

8. Which of the following should be entered in Box 46? 8.____
   A. 2016   B. 2018   C. 2019   D. Not known

9. Which of the following should be entered in Box 48? 9.____
   A. Green   B. Tan   C. Blue   D. Not known

10. Which of the following should be entered in Box 50? 10.____
    A. Officer Hunt   B. Officer Freehold
    C. Officer Torry   D. Not known

Questions 11-20.

DIRECTIONS: Questions 11 through 20 are to be answered SOLELY on the basis of the following story and Arrest Form.

Officer John Smith, on foot patrol near a delicatessen, heard a man's cry for help. When he reached the man, Peter Laxalt Green, Green told him that he had just been robbed by a young white male who could be seen running down the street. The officer ran after the youth and saw him jump into a 2019 two-door white Buick, New York plate number 761-QCV. While the youth was trying to start the car, the officer caught up with him and arrested him in front of 49 Second Avenue, Brooklyn. The arrest took place ten minutes after the robbery occurred. The officer brought his prisoner to the 65th Precinct station house at 57 Second Avenue, Brooklyn. At the station house, thirty minutes after the robbery, it was determined that the prisoner's legal name was John Wright Doman and his nickname was *Beefy*. Mr. Doman lives at 914 East 140th Street, Brooklyn, Apartment 3G, telephone number 737-1392. He was born in Calgary, Canada, on February 3, 2005. He became a U.S. citizen on February 3, 2012. His Social Security number is 056-46-7056. Doman is not married. He is employed at the Bollero Wine Company, 213 Fourth Avenue, Brooklyn. An arrest report was prepared at the Precinct. The number assigned to the report was 17460.

At the station house, Mr. Green described the incident in detail. Mr. Green stated that at 11:55 P.M. on July 18, 2023, a young, heavy-set white male, 5'11" tall, weighing 220 pounds, with brown hair and blue eyes, entered Mr. Green's delicatessen, at 141 Second Avenue, Brooklyn, New York. Green, who lives in the apartment above the delicatessen, asked him if he could help him. The male replied, *Yes, you can*, and then immediately pulled out a knife. Mr.

4 (#2)

Green then noticed that the male had a red tattoo of an ax on his right arm. The male demanded that Mr. Green give him all the money from the cash register or else Mr. Green would get hurt. Mr. Green picked up a bottle that was on the counter and threw it at the male, striking him in the chest. The male fled from the delicatessen and headed south on Second Avenue. Mr. Green then ran out of the delicatessen and yelled for the police.

Mr. Green was born on March 17, 1969. His business phone number is 871-3113; his home phone number is 330-5286.

ARREST REPORT					
ARREST INFORMATION	Arrest Number (1)	Precinct (2)	Date of Arrest (3)	Time of Arrest (4)	Place of Arrest (5)
DESCRIPTION OF INCIDENT	Date & Time (6)			Prisoner's Weapon (Description) (7)	
	Prisoner's Auto (color, year, make, model, license plate number, state) (8)				
	Location of Incident (be specific) (9)			Type of Business (10)	
DESCRIPTION OF PRISONER	Last Name First Name Middle (11)			Date of Birth (12)	
	Age (13)	Sex (14)	Race (15)	Eyes (16)	Hair (17)	Weight (18)	Height (19)
	Address City State			Apt. No. (21)	Home Phone Number (22)
	Place of Birth (23)		Citizenship (24) Citizen ☐ Non-citizen ☐		Marital Status (25)
	Social Security Number (26)		Where Employed (Company and Address) (27)		
	Nickname (28)	Scars, Tattoos (Describe fully and give location) (29)			
DESCRIPTION OF COMPLAINANT	Last Name First Name Middle (30)			Date of Birth (31)	
	Address City State (32)			Telephone Numbers Business: (33)	Home: (34)

11. Which of the following should be entered in Box 3? _____, 2018 11.____
    A. February 3   B. March 17   C. July 18   D. July 19

12. Which of the following should be entered in Box 4? 12.____
    A. 11:55 P.M.   B. 12:05 A.M.   C. 12:25 A.M.   D. 12:35 A.M.

13. Which of the following should be entered in Box 6? 13.____
    A. 7/18/23, 11:55 P.M.   B. 7/18/23, 11:55 A.M.
    C. 7/19/23, 11:55 P.M.   D. 7/19/23, 11:55 A.M.

14. Which of the following should be entered in Box 7? 14.____
    A. Ax   B. Gun   C. Bottle   D. Knife

15. Which of the following should be entered in Box 8? 15.____
    White _____ Buick, _____, New York
    A. 2019; two-door; 761-QCV   B. 2020; four-door; 762-QCV
    C. 2019; two-door; 761-VCQ   D. 2020; four-door; 167-QCV

16. Which of the following should be entered in Box 12? 16.____
    A. 3/17/69   B. 2/3/05   C. 7/18/05   D. 2/3/12

17. Which of the following should be entered in Box 27? 17.____
    Bollero _____, Brooklyn, N.Y.
    A. Beer Company, 213 Fourth Avenue
    B. Wine Company, 213 Fourth Avenue
    C. Beer & Wine Company, 213 Second Avenue
    D. Wine Company, 213 Fourth Street

18. Which of the following should be entered in Box 32? _____, Brooklyn. 18.____
    A. 49 Second Avenue   B. 57 Second Avenue
    C. 141 Second Avenue   D. 914 East 140th Street

19. Which of the following should be entered in Box 33? 19.____
    A. 330-1392   B. 330-5286   C. 737-1392   D. 871-3113

20. Which of the following should be entered in Box 28? 20.____
    A. Doman   B. Axe   C. Beefy   D. Maniac

KEY (CORRECT ANSWERS)

1.	B	11.	D
2.	A	12.	B
3.	B	13.	A
4.	D	14.	D
5.	C	15.	A
6.	B	16.	B
7.	B	17.	B
8.	B	18.	C
9.	C	19.	D
10.	C	20.	C

PREPARING WRITTEN MATERIAL

PARAGRAPH REARRANGEMENT
COMMENTARY

The sentences that follow are in scrambled order. You are to rearrange them in proper order and indicate the letter choice containing the correct answer at the space at the right.

Each group of sentences in this section is actually a paragraph presented in scrambled order. Each sentence in the group has a place in that paragraph; no sentence is to be left out. You are to read each group of sentences and decide upon the best order in which to put the sentences so as to form a well-organized paragraph.

The questions in this section measure the ability to solve a problem when all the facts relevant to its solution are not given.

More specifically, certain positions of responsibility and authority require the employee to discover connection between events sometimes, apparently, unrelated. In order to do this, the employee will find it necessary to correctly infer that unspecified events have probably occurred or are likely to occur. This ability becomes especially important when action must be taken on incomplete information.

Accordingly, these questions require competitors to choose among several suggested alternatives, each of which presents a different sequential arrangement of the events. Competitors must choose the MOST logical of the suggested sequences.

In order to do so, they may be required to draw on general knowledge to infer missing concepts or events that are essential to sequencing the given events. Competitors should be careful to infer only what is essential to the sequence. The plausibility of the wrong alternatives will always require the inclusion of unlikely events or of additional chains of events which are NOT essential to sequencing the given events.

It's very important to remember that you are looking for the best of the four possible choices, and that the best choice of all may not even be one of the answers you're given to choose from.

There is no one right way to solve these problems. Many people have found it helpful to first write out the order of the sentences, as they would have arranged them, on their scrap paper before looking at the possible answers. If their optimum answer is there, this can save them some time. If it isn't, this method can still give insight into solving the problem. Others find it most helpful to just go through each of the possible choices, contrasting each as they go along. You should use whatever method feels comfortable and works for you.

While most of these types of questions are not that difficult, we've added a higher percentage of the difficult type, just to give you more practice. Usually there are only one or two questions on this section that contain such subtle distinctions that you're unable to answer confidently. And you then may find yourself stuck deciding between two possible choices, neither of which you're sure about.

PREPARING WRITTEN MATERIAL
PARAGRAPH REARRANGEMENT
EXAMINATION SECTION
TEST 1

DIRECTIONS: The sentences that follow are in scrambled order. You are to rearrange them in proper order and indicate the letter choice containing the CORRECT answer. *PRINT THE LETTER OF THE CORRECT ANSWER IN THE SPACE AT THE RIGHT.*

1. Police Officer Jenner responds to the scene of a burglary at 2106 La Vista Boulevard. He is approached by an elderly man named Richard Jenkins, whose account of the incident includes the following five sentences:
    I. I saw that the lock on my apartment door had been smashed and the door was open.
    II. My apartment was a shambles; my belongings were everywhere and my television set was missing.
    III. As I walked down the hallway toward the bedroom, I heard someone opening a window.
    IV. I left work at 5:30 P.M. and took the bus home.
    V. At that time, I called the police.
    The MOST logical order for the above sentence to appear in the report is
    A. I, V, IV, II, III   B. IV, I, II, III, V   C. I, V, II, III, IV   D. IV, III, II, V, I

1.____

2. Police Officer LaJolla is writing an Incident Report in which back-up assistance was required. The report will contain the following five sentences:
    I. The radio dispatcher asked what my location was and he then dispatched patrol cars for back-up assistance.
    II. At approximately 9:30 P.M., while I was walking my assigned footpost, a gunman fired three shots at me.
    III. I quickly turned around and saw a white male, approximately 5'10", with black hair, wearing blue jeans, a yellow T-shirt, and white sneaker, running across the avenue carrying a handgun.
    IV. When the back-up officers arrived, we searched the area but could not find the suspect.
    V. I advised the radio dispatcher that a gunman had just fired a gun at me, and then I gave the dispatcher a description of the man
    The MOST logical order for the above sentences to appear in the report is:
    A. III, V, II, IV, I   B. II, III, V, I, IV   C. III, II, IV, I, V   D. II, V, I, III, IV

2.____

3. Police Officer Durant is completing a report of a robbery and assault. The report will contain the following five sentences:
    I. I went to Mount Snow Hospital to interview a man who was attacked and robbed of his wallet earlier that night.
    II. An ambulance arrived at 82nd Street and 3rd Avenue and took an intoxicated, wounded man to Mount Snow Hospital
    III. Two youths attacked the man and stole his wallet.

3.____

IV. A well-dressed man left Hanratty's Bar very drunk, with his wallet hanging out of his back pocket.
V. A passerby dialed 911 and requested police and ambulance assistance.

The MOST logical order for the above sentences to appear in the report is

A. I, II, IV, III, V B. IV, III, V, II, I C. IV, V, II, III, I D. V, IV, III, II, I

4. Police Officer Boswell is preparing a report of an armed robbery and assault which will contain the following five sentences:
   I. Both men approached the bartender and one of them drew a gun.
   II. The bartender immediately went to grab the phone at the bar.
   III. One of the men leaped over the counter and smashed a bottle over the bartender's head.
   IV. Two men in a blue Buick drove up to the bar and went inside.
   V. I found the cash register empty and the bartender unconscious on the floor, with the phone still dangling off the hook.

   The MOST logical order for the above sentences to appear in the report is

   A. IV, I, II, III, V B. V, IV, III, I, II C. IV, III, II, V, I D. II, I, III, IV, V

5. Police Officer Mitzler is preparing a report of a bank robbery, which will contain the following five sentences:
   I. The teller complied with the instructions on the note, but also hit the silent alarm.
   II. The perpetrator then fled south on Broadway.
   III. A suspicious male entered the bank at approximately 10:45 A.M.
   IV. At this time, an undetermined amount of money has been taken.
   V. He approached the teller on the far right side and handed her a note.

   The MOST logical order for the above sentences to appear in the report is:

   A. III, V, I, II, IV B. I, III, V, II, IV C. III, V, IV, I, II D. III, V, II, IV, I

6. A Police Officer is preparing an Accident Report for an accident which occurred at the intersection of East 119th Street and Lexington Avenue. The report will include the following five sentences:
   I. On September 18, while driving ten children to school, a school bus driver passed out.
   II. Upon arriving at the scene, I notified the dispatcher to send an ambulance.
   III. I notified the parents of each child once I got to the station house.
   IV. He said the school bus, while traveling west on East 119th Street, struck a parked Ford which was on the southwest corner of East 119th Street.
   V. A witness by the name of John Ramos came up to me to describe what happened.

   The MOST logical order for the above sentences to appear in the Accident Report is:

   A. I, II, V, III, IV B. I, II, V, IV, III C. II, V, I, III, IV D. II, V, I, IV, III

7. A Police Officer is preparing a report concerning a dispute. The report will contain the following five sentences:
   I. The passenger got out of the back of the taxi and leaned through the front window to complain to the driver about the fare.

II. The driver of the taxi caught up with the passenger and knocked him to the ground; the passenger then kicked the driver and a scuffle ensued.
III. The taxi drew up in front of the high-rise building and stopped.
IV. The driver got out of the taxi and followed the passenger into the lobby of the apartment building.
V. The doorman tried but was unable to break up the fight, at which point he called the precinct.

The MOST logical order for the above sentences to appear in the report is
   A. III, I, IV, II, V   B. III, IV, I, II, V   C. III, IV, II, V, I   D. V, I, III, IV, II

8. Police Officer Morrow is writing an Incident Report. The report will include the following four sentences:
   I. The man reached into his pocket and pulled out a gun.
   II. While on foot patrol, I identified a suspect, who was wanted for six robberies in the area, from a wanted picture I was carrying.
   III. I drew my weapon and fired six rounds at the suspect, killing him instantly.
   IV. I called for back-up assistance and told the man to put his hands up.

   The MOST logical order for the above sentences to appear in the report is
      A. II, III, IV, I   B. IV, I, III, II   C. IV, I, II, III   D. II, IV, I, III

9. Sergeant Allen responds to a call at 16 Grove Street regarding a missing child. At the scene, the Sergeant is met by Police Officer Samuels, who gives a brief account of the incident consisting of the following five sentences:
   I. I transmitted the description and waited for you to arrive before I began searching the area.
   II. Mrs. Banks, the mother, reports that she last saw her daughter Julie about 7:30 A.M. when she took her to school.
   III. About 6 P.M., my partner and I arrived at this location to investigate a report of a missing 8-year-old girl.
   IV. When Mrs. Banks left her, Julie was wearing a red and white striped T-shirt, blue jeans, and white sneakers.
   V. Mrs. Banks dropped her off in front of the playground of P.S. 11.

   The MOST logical order for the above sentences to appear in the report is
      A. III, V, IV, II, I   B. III, II, V, IV, I   C. III, IV, I, II, V   D. III, II, IV, I, V

10. Police Officer Franco is completing a report of an assault. The report will contain the following five sentences:
    I. In the park I observed an elderly man lying on the ground, bleeding from a back wound.
    II. I applied first aid to control the bleeding and radioed for an ambulance to respond.
    III. The elderly man stated that he was sitting on the park bench when he was attacked from behind by two males.
    IV. I received a report of a man's screams coming from inside the park, and I went to investigate.
    V. The old man could not give a description of his attackers.

    The MOST logical order for the above sentences to appear in the report is
       A. IV, I, II, III, V   B. V, III, I, IV, II   C. IV, III, V, II, I   D. II, I, V, IV, III

11. Police Officer Williams is completing a Crime Report. The report contains the following five sentences:
    I. As Police Officer Hanson and I approached the store, we noticed that the front door was broken.
    II. After determining that the burglars had fled, we notified the precinct of the burglary.
    III. I walked through the front door as Police Officer Hanson walked around to the back.
    IV. At approximately midnight, an alarm was heard at the Apex Jewelry Store.
    V. We searched the store and found no one.
    The MOST logical order for the above sentences to appear in the report is
    A. I, IV, II, III, V   B. I, IV, III, V, II   C. IV, I, III, II, V   D. IV, I, III, V, II

12. Police Officer Clay is giving a report to the news media regarding someone who has jumped from the Empire State Building. His report will include the following five sentences:
    I. I responded to the 86th floor, where I found the person at the edge of the roof.
    II. A security guard at the building had reported that a man was on the roof at the 86th floor.
    III. At 5:30 P.M., the person jumped from the building.
    IV. I received a call from the radio dispatcher at 4:50 P.M. to respond to the Empire State Building.
    V. I tried to talk to the person and convince him not to jump.
    The MOST logical order for the above sentences to appear in the report is
    A. I, II, IV, III, V   B. III, IV, I, II, V   C. II, IV, I, III, V   D. IV, II, I, V, III

13. The following five sentences are part of a report of a burglary written by Police Officer Reed:
    I. When I arrived at 2400 1st Avenue, I noticed that the door was slightly open.
    II. I yelled out, Police, don't move!
    III. As I entered the apartment, I saw a man with a TV set passing through a window to another man standing on a fire escape.
    IV. While on foot patrol, I was informed by the radio dispatcher that a burglary was in progress at 2400 1st Avenue.
    V. However, the burglars quickly ran down the fire escape.
    The MOST logical order for the above sentences to appear in the report is
    A. I, III, IV, V, II   B. IV, I, III, V, II   C. IV, I, III, II, V   D. I, IV, III, II, V

14. Police Officer Jenkins is preparing a report for Lost or Stolen Property. The report will include the following five sentences:
    I. On the stairs, Mr. Harris slipped on a wet leaf and fell on the landing.
    II. It wasn't until he got to the token booth that Mr. Harris realized his wallet was no longer in his back pants pocket.
    III. A boy wearing a football jersey helped him up and brushed off the back of Mr. Harris' pants.
    IV. Mr. Harris states he was walking up the stairs to the elevated subway at Queensborough Plaza.
    V. Before Mr. Harris could thank him, the boy was running down the stairs to the street.

The MOST logical order for the above sentences to appear in the report is
A. IV, III, V, I, II   B. IV, I, III, V, II   C. I, IV, II, III, V   D. I, II, IV, III, V

15. Police Officer Hubbard is completing a report of a missing person. The report will contain the following five sentences:
   I. I visited the store at 7:55 P.M. and asked the employees if they had seen a girl fitting the description I had been given.
   II. She gave me a description and said she had gone into the local grocery store at about 6:15 P.M.
   III. I asked the woman for a description of her daughter.
   IV. The distraught woman called the precinct to report that her daughter, aged 12, had not returned from an errand.
   V. The storekeeper said a girl matching the description had been in the store earlier, but he could not give an exact time.
   The MOST logical order for the above sentences to appear in the report is
   A. I, III, II, V, IV   B. IV, III, II, I, V   C. V, I, II, III, IV   D. III, I, II, IV, V

16. A police officer is completing an entry in his Daily Activity Log regarding traffic summonses which he issued. The following five sentences will be included in the entry:
   I. I was on routine patrol parked 16 yards west of 170th Street and Clay Avenue.
   II. The summonses were issued for unlicensed operator and disobeying a steady red light.
   III. At 8 A.M. hours, I observed an auto traveling westbound on 170th Street not stop for a steady red light at the intersection of Clay Avenue and 170th Street.
   IV. I stopped the driver of the auto and determined that he did not have a valid driver's license.
   V. After a brief conversation, I informed the motorist that he was receiving two summonses.
   The MOST logical order for the above sentences to appear in the report is
   A. I, III, IV, V, II   B. III, IV, II, V, I   C. V, II, I, III, IV   D. IV, V, II, I, III

17. The following sentences appeared on an Incident Report:
   I. Three teenagers who had been ejected from the theater were yelling at patrons who were now entering.
   II. Police Officer Dixon told the teenagers to leave the area.
   III. The teenager said that they were told by the manager to leave the theater because they were talking during the movie.
   IV. The theater manager called the precinct at 10:20 P.M. to report a disturbance outside the theater.
   V. A patrol car responded to the theater at 10:42 P.M. and two police officers went over to the teenagers.
   The MOST logical order for the above sentences to appear in the Incident Report is
   A. I, V, IV, III, II   B. IV, I, V, III, II   C. IV, I, III, V, II   D. IV, III, I, V, II

18. Activity Log entries are completed by police officers. Police Officer Samuels has written an entry concerning vandalism and part of it contains the following five sentences:
    I. The man, in his early twenties, ran down the block and around the corner.
    II. A man passing the store threw a brick through a window of the store.
    III. I arrived on the scene and began to question the witnesses about the incident.
    IV. Malcolm Holmes, the owner of the Fast Service Shoe Repair Store, was working in the back of the store at approximately 3 P.M.
    V. After the man fled, Mr. Holmes called the police.
    The MOST logical order for the above sentences to appear in the Activity Log is
    A. IV, II, I, V, III   B. II, IV, I, III, V   C. II, I, IV, III, V   D. IV, II, V, III, I

19. Police Officer Buckley is preparing a report concerning a dispute in a restaurant. The report will contain the following five sentences:
    I. The manager, Charles Chin, and a customer, Edward Green, were standing near the register arguing over the bill.
    II. The manager refused to press any charges providing Green pay the check and leave.
    III. While on foot patrol, I was informed by a passerby of a disturbance in the Dragon Flame Restaurant.
    IV. Green paid the $15.00 check and left the restaurant.
    V. According to witnesses, the customer punched the owner in the face when Chin asked him for the amount due.
    The MOST logical order for the above sentences to appear in the report is
    A. III, I, V, II, IV   B. I, II, III, IV, V   C. V, I, III, II, IV   D. III, V, II, IV, I

20. Police Officer Wilkins is preparing a report for leaving the scene of an accident. The report will include the following five sentences:
    I. The Dodge struck the right rear fender of Mrs. Smith's 2010 Ford and continued on its way.
    II. Mrs. Smith stated she was making a left turn from 40th Street onto Third Avenue.
    III. As the car passed, Mrs. Smith noticed the dangling rear license plate #412AEJ.
    IV. Mrs. Smith complained to police of back pains and was removed by ambulance to Bellevue Hospital.
    V. An old green Dodge traveling up Third Avenue went through the red light at 40th Street and Third Avenue.
    The MOST logical order for the above sentences to appear in the report is
    A. V, III, I, II, IV   B. I, III, II, V, IV   C. IV, V, I, II, III   D. II, V, I, III, IV

21. Detective Simon is completing a Crime Report. The report contains the following five sentences:
    I. Police Officer Chin, while on foot patrol, heard the yelling and ran in the direction of the man.
    II. The man, carrying a large hunting knife, left the High Sierra Sporting Goods Store at approximately 10:30 A.M.

III. When the man heard Police Officer Chin, he stopped, dropped the knife, and began to cry.
IV. As Police Officer Chin approached the man, he drew his gun and yelled, *Police, freeze.*
V. After the man left the store, he began yelling, over and over, *I am going to kill myself!*

The MOST logical order for the above sentences to appear in the report is
A. V, II, I, IV, III   B. II, V, I, IV, III   C. II, V, IV, I, III   D. II, I, V, IV, III

22. Police Officer Miller is preparing a Complaint Report which will include the following five sentences:
    I. From across the lot, he yelled to the boys to get away from his car.
    II. When he came out of the store, he noticed two teenage boys trying to break into his car.
    III. The boys fled as Mr. Johnson ran to his car.
    IV. Mr. Johnson stated that he parked his car in the municipal lot behind Tams Department Store.
    V. Mr. Johnson saw that the door lock had been broken, but nothing was missing from inside the auto.

    The MOST logical order for the above sentences to appear in the report is
    A. IV, I, II, V, III   B. II, III, I, V, IV   C. IV, II, I, III, V   D. I, II, III, V, IV

23. Police Officer O'Hara completes a Universal Summons for a motorist who has just passed a red traffic light. The Universal Summons includes the following five sentences:
    I. As the car passed the light, I followed in the patrol car.
    II. After the driver stopped the car, he stated that the light was yellow, not red.
    III. A blue Cadillac sedan passed the red light on the corner of 79th Street and 3rd Avenue at 11:25 P.M.
    IV. As a result, the driver was informed that he did pass a red light and that his brake lights were not working.
    V. The driver in the Cadillac stopped his car as soon as he saw the patrol car, and I noticed that the brake lights were not working.

    The MOST logical order for the above sentences to appear in the Universal Summons is
    A. I, III, V, II, IV   B. III, I, V, II, IV   C. III, I, V, IV, II   D. I, III, IV, II, V

24. Detective Egan is preparing a follow-up report regarding a homicide on 170th Street and College Avenue. An unknown male was found at the scene. The report will contain the following five sentences:
    I. Police Officer Gregory wrote down the names, addresses, and phone numbers of the witnesses.
    II. A 911 operator received a call of a man shot and dispatched Police Officers Worth and Gregory to the scene.
    III. They discovered an unidentified male dead on the street.
    IV. Police Officer Worth notified the Precinct Detective Unit immediately.
    V. At approximately 9:00 A.M., an unidentified male shot another male in the chest during an argument.

The MOST logical order for the above sentences to appear in the report is
A. V, II, III, IV, I   B. II, III, V, IV, I   C. IV, I, V, II, III   D. V, III, II, IV, I

25. Police Officer Tracey is preparing a Robbery Report which will include the following five sentences:
   I. I ran around the corner and observe a man pointing a gun at a taxidriver.
   II. I informed the man I was a police officer and that he should not move.
   III. I was on the corner of 125th Street and Park Avenue when I heard a scream coming from around the corner.
   IV. The man turned around and fired one shot at me.
   V. I fired once, shooting him in the arm and causing him to fall to the ground.
   The MOST logical order for the above sentences to appear in the report is
   A. I, III, IV, II, V   B. IV, V, II, I, III   C. III, I, II, IV, V   D. III, I, V, II, IV

KEY (CORRECT ANSWERS)

1.	B		11.	D
2.	B		12.	D
3.	B		13.	C
4.	A		14.	B
5.	A		15.	B
6.	B		16.	A
7.	A		17.	B
8.	D		18.	A
9.	B		19.	A
10.	A		20.	D

21.	B
22.	C
23.	B
24.	A
25.	C

TEST 2

DIRECTIONS: The sentences that follow are in scrambled order. You are to rearrange them in proper order and indicate the letter choice containing the CORRECT answer. *PRINT THE LETTER OF THE CORRECT ANSWER IN THE SPACE AT THE RIGHT*

1. Police Officer Weiker is completing a Complaint Report which will contain the following five sentences:
   I. Mr. Texlor was informed that the owner of the van would receive a parking ticket and that the van would be towed away.
   II. The police tow truck arrived approximately one half hour after Mr. Texlor complained.
   III. While on foot patrol on West End Avenue, I saw the owner of Rand's Restaurant arrive to open his business.
   IV. Mr. Texlor, the owner, called to me and complained that he could not receive deliveries because a van was blocking his driveway.
   V. The van's owner later reported to the precinct that his van had been stolen, and he was then informed that it had been towed.
   The MOST logical order for the above sentences to appear in the report is
   A. III, V, I, II, IV   B. III, IV, I, II, V   C. IV, III, I, II, V   D. IV, III, II, I, V

   1.____

2. Police Officer Ames is completing an entry in his Activity Log. The entry contains the following five sentences:
   I. Mr. Sands gave me a complete description of the robber.
   II. Alvin Sands, owner of the Star Delicatessen, called the precinct to report he had just been robbed.
   III. I then notified all police patrol vehicles to look for a white male in his early twenties wearing brown pants and shirt, a black leather jacket, and black and white sneakers.
   IV. I arrived on the scene after being notified by the precinct that a robbery had just occurred at the Star Delicatessen.
   V. Twenty minutes later, a man fitting the description was arrested by a police officer on patrol six blocks from the delicatessen.
   The MOST logical order for the above sentences to appear in the Activity Log is
   A. II, I, IV, III, V   B. II IV, III, I, V   C. II, IV, I, III, V   D. II, IV, I, V, III

   2.____

3. Police Officer Benson is completing a Complaint Report concerning a stolen taxicab, which will include the following five sentences:
   I. Police Officer Benson noticed that a cab was parked next to a fire hydrant.
   II. Dawson *borrowed* the cab for transportation purposes since he was in a hurry.
   III. Ed Dawson got into his car and tried to start it, but the battery was dead.
   IV. When he reached his destination, he parked the cab by a fire hydrant and placed the keys under the seat.
   V. He looked around and saw an empty cab with the engine running.
   The MOST logical order for the above sentences to appear in the report is
   A. I, III, II, IV, V   B. III, I, II, V, IV   C. III, V, II, IV, I   D. V, II, IV, III, I

   3.____

111

4. Police Officer Hatfield is reviewing his Activity Log entry prior to completing a report. The entry contains the following five sentences:
   I. When I arrived at Zand's Jewelry Store, I noticed that the door was slightly open.
   II. I told the burglar I was a police officer and that he should stand still or he would be shot.
   III. As I entered the store, I saw a man wearing a ski mask attempting to open the safe in the back of the store.
   IV. On December 16, 2020, at 1:38 A.M., I was informed that a burglary was in progress at Zand's Jewelry Store on East 59th Street.
   V. The burglar quickly pulled a knife from his pocket when he saw me.
   The MOST logical order for the above sentences to appear in the report is
   A. IV, I, III, V, II   B. I, IV, III, V, II   C. IV, III, II, V, I   D. I, III, IV, V, II

4.____

5. Police Officer Lorenz is completing a report of a murder. The report will contain the following five statements made by a witness:
   I. I was awakened by the sound of a gunshot coming from the apartment next door and I decided to check.
   II. I entered the apartment and looked into the kitchen and the bathroom.
   III. I found Mr. Hubbard's body slumped in the bathtub.
   IV. The door to the apartment was open, but I didn't see anyone.
   V. He had been shot in the head.
   The MOST logical order for the above sentences to appear in the report is
   A. I, III, II, IV, V   B. I, IV, II, III, V   C. IV, II, I, III, V   D. III, I, II, IV, V

5.____

6. Police Officer Baldwin is preparing an accident report which will include the following five sentences:
   I. The old man lay on the ground for a few minutes, but was not physically hurt.
   II. Charlie Watson, a construction worker, was repairing some brick work at the top of a building at 54th Street and Madison Avenue.
   III. Steven Green, his partner, warned him that this could be dangerous, but Watson ignored him.
   IV. A few minutes later, one of the bricks thrown by Watson smashed to the ground in front of an old man, who fainted out of fright.
   V. Mr. Watson began throwing some of the bricks over the side of the building.
   The MOST logical order for the above sentences to appear in the report is
   A. II, V, III, IV, I   B. I, IV, II, V, III   C. III, II, IV, V, I   D. II, III, I, IV, V

6.____

7. Police Officer Porter is completing an Incident Report concerning her rescue of a woman being held hostage by a former boyfriend. Her report will contain the following five sentences:
   I. I saw a man holding .25 caliber gun to a woman's head, but he did not see me.
   II. I then broke a window and gained access to the house.
   III. As I approached the house on foot, a gunshot rang out and I heard a woman scream.
   IV. A decoy van brought me as close as possible to the house where the woman was being held hostage.

7.____

V. I ordered the man to drop his gun, and he released the woman and was taken into custody.
The MOST logical order for the above sentences to appear in the report is
   A. I, III, II, IV, V   B. IV, III, II, I, V   C. III, II, I, IV, V   D. V, I, II, III, IV

8. Police Officer Byrnes is preparing a crime report concerning a robbery. The report will consist of the following five sentences:
    I. Mr. White, following the man's instructions, opened the car's hood, at which time the man got out of the auto, drew a revolver, and ordered White to give him all the money in his pockets.
    II. Investigation has determined there were no witnesses to this incident.
    III. The man asked White to check the oil and fill the tank.
    IV. Mr. White, a gas attendant, states that he was working alone at the gas station when a black male pulled up to the gas pump in a white Mercury.
    V. White was then bound and gagged by the male and locked in the gas station's rest room.
    The MOST logical order for the above sentences to appear in the report is
       A. IV, I, III, II, V   B. III, I, II, V, IV   C. IV, III, I, V, II   D. I, III, IV, II, V

9. Police Officer Gale is preparing a report of a crime committed against Mr. Weston. The report will consist of the following five sentences:
    I. The man, who had a gun, told Mr. Weston not to scream for help and ordered him back into the apartment.
    II. With Mr. Weston disposed of in this fashion, the man proceeded to ransack the apartment.
    III. Opening the door to see who was there, Mr. Weston was confronted by a tall white male wearing a dark blue jacket and white pants.
    IV. Mr. Weston was at home alone in his living room when the doorbell rang.
    V. Once inside, the man bound and gagged Mr. Weston and locked him in the bathroom.
    The MOST logical order for the above sentences to appear in the report is
       A. III, V, II, I, IV   B. IV, III, I, V, II   C. III, V, IV, II, I   D. IV, III, V, I, II

10. A police officer is completing a report of a robbery, which will contain the following five sentences:
    I. Two police officers were about to enter the Red Rose Coffee Shop on 47th Street and 8th Avenue.
    II. They then noticed a male running up the street carrying a brown paper bag.
    III. They heard a woman standing outside the Broadway Boutique yelling that her store had just been robbed by a young man, and she was pointing up the street.
    IV. They caught up with him and made an arrest.
    V. The police officers pursued the male, who ran past them on 8th Avenue.
    The MOST logical order for the above sentences to appear in the report is
       A. I, III, II, V, IV   B. III, I, II, V, IV   C. IV, V, I, II, III   D. I, V, IV, III, II

11. Police Officer Capalbo is preparing a report of a bank robbery. The report will contain the following five statements made by a witness:
    I. Initialing, all I could see were two men, dressed in maintenance uniforms, sitting in the area reserved for bank officers.
    II. I was passing the bank at 8 P.M. and noticed that all the lights were out, except in the rear section.
    III. Then I noticed two other men in the bank, coming from the direction of the vault, carrying a large metal box.
    IV. At this point, I decided to call the police.
    V. I knocked on the window to get the attention of the men in the maintenance uniforms, and they chased the two men carrying the box down a flight of steps.
    The MOST logical order for the above sentences to appear in the report is
    A. IV, I, II, V, III   B. I, III, II, V, IV   C. II, I, III, V, IV   D. II, III, I, V, IV

12. Police Officer Roberts is preparing a crime report concerning an assault and a stolen car. The report will contain the following five sentences:
    I. Upon leaving the store to return to his car, Winters noticed that a male unknown to him was sitting in his car.
    II. The man then re-entered Winters' car and drove away, fleeing north on 2nd Avenue.
    III. Mr. Winters stated that he parked his car in front of 235 East 25th Street and left the engine running while he went into the butcher shop at that location.
    IV. Mr. Robert Gering, a witness, stated that the male is known in the neighborhood as Bobby Rae and is believed to reside at 323 East 114th Street.
    V. When Winters approached the car and ordered the man to get out, the man got out of the auto and struck Winters with his fists, knocking him to the ground.
    The MOST logical order for the above sentences to appear in the report is
    A. III, II, V, I, IV   B. III, I, V, II, IV   C. I, IV, V, II, III   D. III, II, I, V, IV

13. Police Officer Robinson is preparing a crime report concerning the robbery of Mr. Edwards' store. The report will consist of the following five sentences:
    I. When the last customer left the store, the two men drew revolvers and ordered Mr. Edwards to give them all the money in the cash register.
    II. The men proceeded to the back of the store as if they were going to do some shopping.
    III. Janet Morley, a neighborhood resident, later reported that she saw the men enter a green Ford station wagon and flee northbound on Albany Avenue.
    IV. Edwards complied after which the gunmen ran from the store.
    V. Mr. Edwards states that he was stocking merchandise behind the store counter when two white males entered the store.
    The MOST logical order for the above sentences to appear in the report is
    A. V, II, III, I, IV   B. V, II, I, IV, III   C. II, I, V, IV, III   D. III, V, II, I, IV

14. Police Officer Wendell is preparing an accident report for a 6-car accident that occurred at the intersection of Bath Avenue and Bay Parkway. The report will consist of the following five sentences:
   I. A 2016 Volkswagen Beetle, traveling east on Bath Avenue, swerved to the left to avoid the Impala, and struck a 2014 Ford station wagon which was traveling west on Bath Avenue.
   II. The Seville then mounted the curb on the northeast corner of Bath Avenue and Bay Parkway and struck a light pole.
   III. A 2013 Buick Lesabre, traveling northbound on Bay Parkway directly behind the Impala, struck the Impala, pushing it into the intersection of Bath Avenue and Bay Parkway.
   IV. A 2015 Chevy Impala, traveling northbound on Bay Parkway, had stopped for a red light at Bath Avenue.
   V. A 2017 Toyota, traveling westbound on Bath Avenue, swerved to the right to avoid hitting the Ford station wagon, and struck a 2017 Cadillac Seville double-parked near the corner.
   The MOST logical order for the above sentences to appear in the report is
   A. IV, III, V, II, I   B. III, IV, V, II, I   C. IV, III, I, V, II   D. III, IV, V, I, II

15. The following five sentences are part of an Activity Log entry Police Officer Rogers made regarding an explosion:
   I. I quickly treated the pedestrian for the injury.
   II. The explosion caused a glass window in an office building to shatter.
   III. After the pedestrian was treated, a call was placed to the precinct requesting additional police officers to evacuate the area.
   IV. After all the glass settled to the ground, I saw a pedestrian who was bleeding from the arm.
   V. While on foot patrol near 5th Avenue and 53rd Street, I heard a loud explosion.
   The MOST logical order for the above sentences to appear in the report is
   A. II, V, IV, I, III   B. V, II, IV, III, I   C. V, II, I, IV, III   D. V, II, IV, I, III

16. Police Officer David is completing a report regarding illegal activity near the entrance to Madison Square Garden during a recent rock concert. The report will obtain the following five sentences:
   I. As I came closer to the man, he placed what appeared to be tickets in his pocket and began to walk away.
   II. After the man stopped, I questioned him about *scalping* tickets.
   III. While on assignment near the Madison Square Garden entrance, I observed a man apparently selling tickets.
   IV. I stopped the man by stating that I was a police officer.
   V. The man was then given a summons, and he left the area.
   The MOST logical order for the above sentences to appear in the report is
   A. I, III, IV, II, V   B. III, I, IV, V, II   C. III, IV, I, II, V   D. III, I, IV, II, V

6 (#2)

17. Police Officer Sampson is preparing a report containing a dispute in a bar. The report will contain the following five sentences:
    I. John Evans, the bartender, ordered the two men out of the bar.
    II. Two men dressed in dungarees entered the C and D Bar at 5:30 P.M.
    III. The two men refused to leave and began to beat up Evans.
    IV. A customer in the bar saw me on patrol and yelled to me to come separate the three men.
    V. The two men became very drunk and loud within a short time.
    The MOST logical order for the above sentences to appear in the report is
    A. II, I, V, III, IV   B. II, III, IV, V, I   C. III, I, II, V, IV   D. II, V, I, III, IV

    17.____

18. A police officer is completing a report concerning the response to a crime in progress. The report will include the following five sentences:
    I. The officers saw two armed men run out of the liquor store and into a waiting car.
    II. Police Officers Lunty and Duren received the call and responded to the liquor store.
    III. The robbers gave up without a struggle.
    IV. Lunty and Duren blocked the getaway car with their patrol car.
    V. A call came into the precinct concerning a robbery in progress at Jane's Liquor Store.
    The MOST logical order for the above sentence to appear in the report is
    A. V, II, I, IV, III   B. II, V, I, III, IV   C. V, I, IV, II, III   D. I, V, II, III, IV

    18.____

19. Police Officers Jenkins is preparing a Crime Report which will consist of the following five sentences:
    I. After making inquirie in the vicinity, Smith found out that his next door neighbor, Viola Jones, had seen two local teenagers, Michael Heinz and Vincent Gaynor, smash his car's windshields with a crowbar.
    II. Jones told Smith that the teenagers live at 8700 19th Avenue.
    III. Mr. Smith heard a loud crash at approximately 11:00 P.M., looked out of his apartment window, and saw two white males running away from his car.
    IV. Smith then reported the incident to the precinct, and Heinz and Gaynor were arrested at the address given.
    V. Leaving his apartment to investigate further, Smith discovered that his car's front and rear windshields had been smashed.
    The MOST logical order for the above sentences to appear in the report is
    A. III, IV, V, I, II   B. III, V, I, II, IV   C. III, I, V, II, IV   D. V, III, I, II, IV

    19.____

20. Sergeant Nancy Winston is reviewing a Gun Control Report which will contain the following five sentences:
    I. The man fell to the floor when hit in the chest with three bullets from 22 caliber gun.
    II. Merriam's 22 caliber gun was seized, and he was given a summons for not having a pistol permit.
    III. Christopher Merriam, the owner of A-Z Grocery, shot a man who attempted to rob him.
    IV. Police Officer Franks responded and asked Merriam for his pistol permit, which he could not produce.

    20.____

V. Merriam phoned the police to report he had just shot a man who had attempted to rob him.

The MOST logical order for the above sentences to appear in the report is
A. III, I, V, IV, II   B. I, III, V, IV, II   C. III, I, V, II, IV   D. I, III, II, V, IV

21. Detective John Manville is completing a report for his superior regarding the murder of an unknown male who was shot in Central Park. The report will contain the following five sentences:
    I. Police Officers Langston and Cavers responded to the scene.
    II. I received the assignment to investigate the murder in Central Park from Detective Sergeant Rogers.
    III. Langston notified the Detective Bureau after questioning Jason.
    IV. An unknown male, apparently murdered, was discovered in Central Park by Howard Jason, a park employee, who immediately called the police.
    V. Langston and Cavers questioned Jason.

    The MOST logical order for the above sentences to appear in the report is
    A. I, IV, V, III, II   B. IV, I, V, II, III   C. IV, I, V, III, II   D. IV, V, I, III, II

22. A police officer is completing a report concerning the arrest of a juvenile. The report will contain the following five sentences:
    I. Sanders then telephoned Jay's parents from the precinct to inform them of their son's arrest.
    II. The store owner resisted, and Jay then shot him and ran from the store.
    III. Jay was transported directly to the precinct by Officer Sanders.
    IV. James Jay, a juvenile, walked into a candy store and announced a hold-up.
    V. Police Officer Sanders, while on patrol, arrested Jay a block from the candy store.

    The MOST logical order for the above sentences to appear in the report is
    A. IV, V, II, I, III   B. IV, II, V, III, I   C. II, IV, V, III, I   D. V, IV, II, I, III

23. Police Officer Olsen prepared a crime report for a robbery which contained the following five sentences:
    I. Mr. Gordon was approached by this individual who then produced a gun and demanded the money from the cash register.
    II. The man then fled from the scene on foot, southbound on 5th Avenue.
    III. Mr. Gordon was working at the deli counter when a white male, 5'6", 150-160 lbs., wearing a green jacket and blue pants, entered the store.
    IV. Mr. Gordon complied with the man's demands and handed him the daily receipts.
    V. Further investigation has determined there are no other witnesses to this robbery.

    The MOST logical order for the above sentences to appear in the report is
    A. I, III, IV, V, II   B. I, IV, II, III, V   C. III, IV, I, V, II   D. III, I, IV, II, V

24. Police Officer Bryant responded to 285 E. 31st Street to take a crime report of a burglary of Mr. Bond's home. The report will contain a brief description of the incident, consisting of the following five sentences:
    I. When Mr. Bond attempted to stop the burglar by grabbing him, he was pushed to the floor.
    II. The burglar had apparently gained access to the home by forcing open the 2nd floor bedroom window facing the fire escape.
    III. Mr. Bond sustained a head injury in the scuffle, and the burglar exited the home through the front door.
    IV. Finding nothing in the dresser, the burglar proceeded downstairs to the first floor, where he was confronted by Mr. Bond who was reading in the dining room.
    V. Once inside, he searched the drawers of the bedroom dresser.
    The MOST logical order for the above sentences to appear in the report is
       A. V, IV, I, II, III   B. II, V, IV, I, III   C. II, IV, V, III, I   D. III, II, I, V, IV

25. Police Officer Derringer responded to a call of a rape-homicide case in his patrol area and was ordered to prepare an incident report, which will contain the following five sentences:
    I. He pushed Miss Scott to the ground and forcibly raped her.
    II. Mary Scott was approached from behind by a white male, 5'7", 150-160 lbs. wearing dark pants and a white jacket.
    III. As Robinson approached the male, he ordered him to stop.
    IV. Screaming for help, Miss Scott alerted one John Robinson, a local grocer, who chased her assailant as he fled the scene.
    V. The male turned and fired two shots at Robinson, who fell to the ground mortally wounded.
    The MOST logical order for the above sentences to appear in the report is
       A. IV, III, I, II, V   B. II, IV, III, V, I   C. II, IV, I, V, III   D. II, I, IV, III, V

KEY (CORRECT ANSWERS)

1. B
2. C
3. C
4. A
5. B

6. A
7. B
8. C
9. B
10. A

11. C
12. B
13. B
14. C
15. D

16. D
17. D
18. A
19. B
20. A

21. C
22. B
23. D
24. B
25. D

PREPARING WRITTEN MATERIAL
EXAMINATION SECTION
TEST 1

DIRECTIONS: Each question or incomplete statement is followed by several suggested answers or completions. Select the one that BEST answers the question or completes the statement. *PRINT THE LETTER OF THE CORRECT ANSWER IN THE SPACE AT THE RIGHT.*

1. The one of the following sentences which is LEAST acceptable from the viewpoint of correct usage is:
   A. The police thought the fugitive to be him.
   B. The criminals set a trap for whoever would fall into it.
   C. It is ten years ago since the fugitive fled from the city.
   D. The lecturer argued that criminals are usually cowards.
   E. The police removed four bucketfuls of earth from the scene of the crime.

1._____

2. The one of the following sentences which is LEAST acceptable from the viewpoint of correct usage is:
   A. The patrolman scrutinized the report with great care.
   B. Approaching the victim of the assault, two bruises were noticed by the patrolman.
   C. As soon as I had broken down the door, I stepped into the room.
   D. I observed the accused loitering near the building, which was closed at the time.
   E. The storekeeper complained that his neighbor was guilty of violating a local ordinance.

2._____

3. The one of the following sentences which is LEAST acceptable from the viewpoint of correct usage is:
   A. I realized immediately that he intended to assault the woman, so I disarmed him.
   B. It was apparent that Mr. Smith's explanation contained many inconsistencies.
   C. Despite the slippery condition of the street, he managed to stop the vehicle before injuring the child.
   D. Not a single one of them wish, despite the damage to property, to make a formal complaint.
   E. The body was found lying on the floor.

3._____

4. The one of the following sentences which contains NO error in usage is:
   A. After the robbers left, the proprietor stood tied in his chair for about two hours before help arrived.
   B. In the cellar I found the watchman's hat and coat.
   C. The persons living in adjacent apartments stated that they had heard no unusual noises.

4._____

121

D. Neither a knife or any firearms were found in the room.
E. Walking down the street, the shouting of the crowd indicated that something was wrong.

5. The one of the following sentences which contains NO error in usage is:
   A. The policeman lay a firm hand on the suspect's shoulder.
   B. It is true that neither strength nor agility are the most important requirement for a good patrolman.
   C. Good citizens constantly strive to do more than merely comply the restraints imposed by society.
   D. No decision was made as to whom the prize should be awarded.
   E. Twenty years is considered a severe sentence for a felony.

6. Which of the following sentences is NOT expressed in standard English usage?
   A. The victim reached a pay-phone booth and manages to call police headquarters.
   B. By the time the call was received, the assailant had left the scene.
   C. The victim has been a respected member of the community for the past eleven years.
   D. Although the lighting was bad and the shadows were deep, the storekeeper caught sight of the attacker.
   E. Additional street lights have since been installed, and the patrols have been strengthened.

7. Which of the following sentences is NOT expressed in standard English usage?
   A. The judge upheld the attorney's right to question the witness about the missing glove.
   B. To be absolutely fair to all parties is the jury's chief responsibility.
   C. Having finished the report, a loud noise in the next room startled the sergeant.
   D. The witness obviously enjoyed having played a part in the proceedings.
   E. The sergeant planned to assign the case to whoever arrived first.

8. In which of the following sentences is a word misused?
   A. As a matter of principle, the captain insisted that the suspect's partner be brought for questioning.
   B. The principle suspect had been detained at the station house for most of the day.
   C. The principal in the crime had no previous criminal record, but his closest associate had been convicted of felonies on two occasions.
   D. The interest payments had been made promptly, but the firm had been drawing upon the principal for these payments.
   E. The accused insisted that his high school principal would furnish him a character reference.

9. Which of the following statements is ambiguous?
   A. Mr. Sullivan explained why Mr. Johnson had been dismissed from his job.
   B. The storekeeper told the patrolman he had made a mistake.
   C. After waiting three hours, the patients in the doctor's office were sent home.
   D. The janitor's duties were to maintain the building in good shape and to answer tenants' complaints.
   E. The speed limit should, in my opinion, be raised to sixty miles an hour on that stretch of road.

10. In which of the following is the punctuation or capitalization faulty?
   A. The accident occurred at an intersection in the Kew Gardens section of Queens, near the bus stop.
   B. The sedan, not the convertible, was struck in the side.
   C. Before any of the patrolmen had left the police car received an important message from headquarters.
   D. The dog that had been stolen was returned to his master, John Dempsey, who lived in East Village.
   E. The letter had been sent to 12 Hillside Terrace, Rutland, Vermont 05702.

Questions 11-25.

DIRECTIONS: Questions 11 through 25 are to be answered in accordance with correct English usage; that is, standard English rather than nonstandard or substandard. Nonstandard and substandard English includes words or expressions usually classified as slang, dialect, illiterate, etc., which are not generally accepted as correct in current written communication. Standard English also requires clarity, proper punctuation and capitalization and appropriate use of words. Write the letter of the sentence NOT expressed in standard English usage in the space at the right.

11. A. There were three witnesses to the accident.
    B. At least three witnesses were found to testify for the plaintiff.
    C. Three of the witnesses who took the stand was uncertain about the defendant's competence to drive.
    D. Only three witnesses came forward to testify for the plaintiff.
    E. The three witnesses to the accident were pedestrians.

12. A. The driver had obviously drunk too many martinis before leaving for home.
    B. The boy who drowned had swum in these same waters many times before.
    C. The petty thief had stolen a bicycle from a private driveway before he was apprehended.
    D. The detectives had brung in the heroin shipment they intercepted.
    E. The passengers had never ridden in a converted bus before.

13. A. Between you and me, the new platoon plan sounds like a good idea.
    B. Money from an aunt's estate was left to his wife and he.
    C. He and I were assigned to the same patrol for the first time in two months.
    D. Either you or he should check the front door of that store.
    E. The captain himself was not sure of the witness's reliability.

14. A. The alarm had scarcely begun to ring when the explosion occurred.
    B. Before the firemen arrived at the scene, the second story had been destroyed.
    C. Because of the dense smoke and heat, the firemen could hardly approach the now-blazing structure.
    D. According to the patrolman's report, there wasn't nobody in the store when the explosion occurred.
    E. The sergeant's suggestion was not at all unsound, but no one agreed with him.

15. A. The driver and the passenger they were both found to be intoxicated.
    B. The driver and the passenger talked slowly and not too clearly.
    C. Neither the driver nor his passengers were able to give a coherent account of the accident.
    D. In a corner of the room sat the passenger, quietly dozing.
    E. the driver finally told a strange and unbelievable story, which the passenger contradicted.

16. A. Under the circumstances I decided not to continue my examination of the premises.
    B. There are many difficulties now not comparable with those existing in 1960.
    C. Friends of the accused were heard to announce that the witness had better been away on the day of the trial.
    D. The two criminals escaped in the confusion that followed the explosion.
    E. The aged man was struck by the considerateness of the patrolman's offer.

17. A. An assemblage of miscellaneous weapons lay on the table.
    B. Ample opportunities were given to the defendant to obtain counsel.
    C. The speaker often alluded to his past experience with youthful offenders in the armed forces.
    D. The sudden appearance of the truck aroused my suspicions.
    E. Her studying had a good affect on her grades in high school.

18. A. He sat down in the theater and began to watch the movie.
    B. The girl had ridden horses since she was four years old.
    C. Application was made on behalf of the prosecutor to cite the witness for contempt.
    D. The bank robber, with his two accomplices, were caught in the act.
    E. His story is simply not credible.

19. A. The angry boy said that he did not like those kind of friends.
     B. The merchant's financial condition was so precarious that he felt he must avail himself of any offer of assistance.
     C. He is apt to promise more than he can perform.
     D. Looking at the messy kitchen, the housewife felt like crying.
     E. A clerk was left in charge of the stolen property.

20. A. His wounds were aggravated by prolonged exposure to sub-freezing temperatures.
     B. The prosecutor remarked that the witness was not averse to changing his story each time he was interviewed.
     C. The crime pattern indicated that the burglars were adapt in the handling of explosives.
     D. His rigid adherence to a fixed plan brought him into renewed conflict with his subordinates.
     E. He had anticipated that the sentence would be delivered by noon.

21. A. The whole arraignment procedure is badly in need of revision.
     B. After his glasses were broken in the fight, he would of gone to the optometrist if he could.
     C. Neither Tom nor Jack brought his lunch to work.
     D. He stood aside until the quarrel was over.
     E. A statement in the psychiatrist's report disclosed that the probationer vowed to have his revenge.

22. A. His fiery and intemperate speech to the striking employees fatally affected any chance of a future reconciliation.
     B. The wording of the statute has been variously construed.
     C. The defendant's attorney, speaking in the courtroom, called the official a demagogue who contempuously disregarded the judge's orders.
     D. The baseball game is likely to be the most exciting one this year.
     E. The mother divided the cookies among her two children.

23. A. There was only a bed and a dresser in the dingy room.
     B. John was one of the few students that have protested the new rule.
     C. It cannot be argued that the child's testimony is negligible; it is, on the contrary, of the greatest importance.
     D. The basic criterion for clearance was so general that officials resolved any doubts in favor of dismissal.
     E. Having just returned from a long vacation, the officer found the city unbearably hot.

24. A. The librarian ought to give more help to small children.
     B. The small boy was criticized by the teacher because he often wrote careless.
     C. It was generally doubted whether the women would permit the use of her apartment for intelligence operations.
     D. The probationer acts differently every time the officer visits him.
     E. Each of the newly appointed officers has 12 years of service.

25.
A. The North is the most industrialized region in the country.
B. L. Patrick Gray 3d, the bureau's acting director, stated that, while "rehabilitation is fine" for some convicted criminals, "it is a useless gesture for those who resist every such effort."
C. Careless driving, faulty mechanism, narrow or badly kept roads all play their part in causing accidents.
D. The childrens' books were left in the bus.
E. It was a matter of internal security; consequently, he felt no inclination to rescind his previous order.

25._____

KEY (CORRECT ANSWERS)

1.	C		11.	C
2.	B		12.	D
3.	D		13.	B
4.	C		14.	D
5.	E		15.	A
6.	A		16.	C
7.	C		17.	E
8.	B		18.	D
9.	B		19.	A
10.	C		20.	C

21. B
22. E
23. B
24. B
25. D

TEST 2

DIRECTIONS: Each question or incomplete statement is followed by several suggested answers or completions. Select the one that BEST answers the question or completes the statement. *PRINT THE LETTER OF THE CORRECT ANSWER IN THE SPACE AT THE RIGHT.*

Questions 1-6.

DIRECTIONS: Each of Questions 1 through 6 consists of a statement which contains a word (one of those underlined) that is either incorrectly used because it is not in keeping with the meaning the quotation is evidently intended to convey, or is misspelled. There is only one INCORRECT word in each quotation. Of the four underlined words, determine if the first one should be replaced by the word lettered A, the second replaced by the word lettered B, the third replaced by the word lettered C, or the fourth replaced by the word lettered D.

1. Whether one depends on <u>fluorescent</u> or artificial light or both, adequate <u>standards</u> should be <u>maintained</u> by means of <u>systematic</u> tests.
   A. natural   B. safeguards   C. established   D. routine

2. A police officer has to be <u>prepared</u> to assume his <u>knowledge</u> as a social <u>scientist</u> in the <u>community</u>.
   A. forced   B. role   C. philosopher   D. street

3. It is <u>practically</u> impossible to <u>indicate</u> whether a sentence is <u>too</u> long simply by <u>measuring</u> its length.
   A. almost   B. tell   C. very   D. guessing

4. Strong <u>leaders</u> are <u>required</u> to organize a community for delinquency prevention and for <u>dissemination</u> of organized <u>crime</u> and drug addiction.
   A. tactics   B. important   C. control   D. meetings

5. The <u>demonstrators</u> who were taken to the Criminal Courts building in <u>Manhattan</u> (because it was large enough to <u>accommodate</u> them), contended that the arrests were <u>unwarranted</u>.
   A. demonstraters   B. Manhatten
   C. accomodate   D. unwarranted

6. They were <u>guaranteed</u> a calm <u>atmosphere</u>, free from <u>harassment</u>, which would be conducive to quiet consideration of the <u>indictments</u>.
   A. guarenteed   B. atmspher
   C. harassment   D. inditements

1.____
2.____
3.____
4.____
5.____
6.____

127

Questions 7-11.

DIRECTIONS: Each of Questions 7 through 11 consists of a statement containing four words in capital letters. One of these words in capital letters is not in keeping with the meaning which the statement is evidently intended to carry. The four words in capital letters in each statement are reprinted after the statement. Print the capital letter preceding the one of the four words which does MOST to spoil the true meaning of the statement in the space at the right.

7. Retirement and pension systems are essential not only to provide employees with with a means of support in the future, but also to prevent longevity and CHARITABLE considerations from UPSETTING the PROMOTIONAL opportunities RETIRED members of the career service. 7.____
   A. charitable   B. upsetting   C. promotional   D. retired

8. Within each major DIVISION in a properly set up public or private organization, provision is made so that each NECESSARY activity is CARED for and lines of authority and responsibility are clear-cut and INFINITE. 8.____
   A. division   B. necessary   C. cared   D. infinite

9. In public service, the scale of salaries paid must be INCIDENTAL to the services rendered, with due CONSIDERATION for the attraction of the desired MANPOWER and for the maintenance of a standard of living COMMENSURATE with the work to be performed. 9.____
   A. incidental   B. consideration
   C. manpower   D. commensurate

10. An understanding of the AIMS of an organization by the staff will AID greatly in increasing the DEMAND of the correspondence work of the office, and will to a large extent DETERMINE the nature of the correspondence. 10.____
   A. aims   B. aid   C. demand   D. determine

11. BECAUSE the Civil Service Commission strongly feels that the MERIT system is a key factor in the MAINTENANCE of democratic government, it has adopted as one of its major DEFENSES the progressive democratization of its own procedures in dealing with candidates for positions in the public service. 11.____
   A. Because   B. merit   C. maintenance   D. defenses

Questions 12-14.

DIRECTIONS: Questions 12 through 14 consist of one sentence each. Each sentence contains an incorrectly used word. First, decide which is the incorrectly used word. Then, from among the options given, decide which word, when substituted for the incorrectly used word, makes the meaning of the sentence clear.
EXAMPLE:
The U.S. national income exhibits a pattern of long term deflection.
   A. reflection   B. subjection   C. rejoicing   D. growth

The word *deflection* in the sentence does not convey the meaning the sentence evidently intended to convey. The word *growth* (Answer D), when substituted for the word *deflection*, makes the meaning of the sentence clear. Accordingly, the answer to the question is D.

12. The study commissioned by the joint committee fell compassionately short of the mark and would have to be redone.
    A. successfully
    B. insignificantly
    C. experimentally
    D. woefully

    12.____

13. He will not idly exploit any violation of the provisions of the order.
    A. tolerate
    B. refuse
    C. construe
    D. guard

    13.____

14. The defendant refused to be virile and bitterly protested service.
    A. irked
    B. feasible
    C. docile
    D. credible

    14.____

Questions 15-25.

DIRECTIONS: Questions 15 through 25 consist of short paragraphs. Each paragraph contains one word which is INCORRECTLY used because it is NOT in keeping with the meaning of the paragraph. Find the word in each paragraph which is INCORRECTLY used and then select as the answer the suggested word which should be substituted for the incorrectly used word.

SAMPLE QUESTION:
In determining who is to do the work in your unit, you will have to decide just who does what from day to day. One of your lowest responsibilities is to assign work so that everybody gets a fair share and that everyone can do his part well.
A. new   B. old   C. important   D. performance

EXPLANATION:
The word which is NOT in keeping with the meaning of the paragraph is *lowest*. This is the INCORRECTLY used word. The suggested word *important* would be in keeping with the meaning of the paragraph and should be substituted for *lowest*. Therefore, the CORRECT answer is choice C.

15. If really good practice in the elimination of preventable injuries is to be achieved and held in any establishment, top management must refuse full and definite responsibility and must apply a good share of its attention to the task.
    A. accept   B. avoidable   C. duties   D. problem

    15.____

16. Recording the human face for identification is by no means the only service performed by the camera in the field of investigation. When the trial of any issue takes place, a word picture is sought to be distorted to the court of incidents, occurrences, or events which are in dispute.
    A. appeals   B. description   C. portrayed   D. deranged

    16.____

17. In the collection of physical evidence, it cannot be emphasized too strongly that a haphazard systematic search at the scene of the crime is vital. Nothing must be overlooked. Often the only leads in a case will come from the results of this search.
    A. important
    B. investigation
    C. proof
    D. thorough

17.____

18. If an investigator has reason to suspect that the witness is mentally stable, or a habitual drunkard, he should leave no stone unturned in his investigation to determine if the witness was under the influence of liquor or drugs, or was mentally unbalanced either at the time of the occurrence to which he testified or at the time of the trial.
    A. accused   B. clue   C. deranged   D. question

18.____

19. The use of records is a valuable step in crime investigation and is the main reason every department should maintain accurate reports. Crimes are not committed through the use of departmental records alone but from the use of all records, of almost every type, wherever they may be found and whenever they give any incidental information regarding the criminal.
    A. accidental   B. necessary   C. reported   D. solved

19.____

20. In the years since passage of the Harrison Narcotic Act of 1914, making the possession of opium amphetamines illegal in most circumstances, drug use has become a subject of considerable scientific interest and investigation. There is at present a voluminous literature on drug use of various kinds.
    A. ingestion   B. derivatives   C. addiction   D. opiates

20.____

21. Of course, the fact that criminal laws are extremely patterned in definition does not mean that the majority of persons who violate them are dealt with as criminals. Quite the contrary, for a great many forbidden acts are voluntarily engaged in within situations of privacy and go unobserved and unreported.
    A. symbolic   B. casual   C. scientific   D. broad-gauged

21.____

22. The most punitive way to study punishment is to focus attention on the pattern of punitive action: to study how a penalty is applied, too study what is done to or taken from an offender.
    A. characteristic   B. degrading   C. objective   D. distinguished

22.____

23. The most common forms of punishment in times past have been death, physical torture, mutilation, branding, public humiliation, fines, forfeits of property, banishment, transportation, and imprisonment. Although this list is by no means differentiated, practically every form of punishment has had several variations and applications.
    A. specific   B. simple   C. exhaustive   D. characteristic

23.____

24. There is another important line of inference between ordinary and professional criminals, and that is the source from which they are recruited. The professional criminal seems to be drawn from legitimate employment and, in many instances, from parallel vocations or pursuits.
    A. demarcation   B. justification   C. superiority   D. reference

    24.____

25. He took the position that the success of the program was insidious on getting additional revenue.
    A. reputed   B. contingent   C. failure   D. indeterminate

    25.____

KEY (CORRECT ANSWERS)

1.	A	11.	D
2.	B	12.	D
3.	B	13.	A
4.	C	14.	C
5.	D	15.	A
6.	C	16.	C
7.	D	17.	D
8.	D	18.	C
9.	A	19.	D
10.	C	20.	B

21.	D
22.	C
23.	C
24.	A
25.	B

TEST 3

DIRECTIONS: Each question or incomplete statement is followed by several suggested answers or completions. Select the one that BEST answers the question or completes the statement. *PRINT THE LETTER OF THE CORRECT ANSWER IN THE SPACE AT THE RIGHT.*

Questions 1-5.

DIRECTIONS: Questions 1 through 5 are to be answered on the basis of the following.

You are a supervising officer in an investigative unit. Earlier in the day, you directed Detectives Tom Dixon and Sal Mayo to investigate a reported assault and robbery in a liquor store within your area of jurisdiction.

Detective Dixon has submitted to you a preliminary investigative report containing the following information:

- At 1630 hours on 2/20, arrived at Joe's Liquor Store at 350 SW Avenue with Detective Mayo to investigate A & R.
- At store interviewed Rob Ladd, store manager, who stated that he and Joe Brown (store owner) had been stuck up about ten minutes prior to our arrival.
- Ladd described the robbers as male whites in their late teens or early twenties. Further stated that one of the robbers displayed what appeared to be an automatic pistol as he entered the store, and said, *Give us the money or we'll kill you.* Ladd stated that Brown then reached under the counter where he kept a loaded .38 caliber pistol. Several shots followed, and Ladd threw himself to the floor.
- The robbers fled, and Ladd didn't know if any money had been taken.
- At this point, Ladd realized that Brown was unconscious on the floor and bleeding from a head wound.
- Ambulance called by Ladd, and Brown was removed by same to General Hospital.
- Personally interviewed John White, 382 Dartmouth Place, who stated he was inside store at the time of occurrence. White states that he hid behind a wine display upon hearing someone say, *Give us the money*. He then heard shots and saw two young men run from the store to a yellow car parked at the curb. White was unable to further describe auto. States the taller of the two men drove the car away while the other sat on passenger side in front.
- Recovered three spent .38 caliber bullets from premises and delivered them to Crime Lab.
- To General Hospital at 1800 hours but unable to interview Brown, who was under sedation and suffering from shock and a laceration of the head.
- Alarm #12487 transmitted for car and occupants.
- Case Active.

Based solely on the contents of the preliminary investigation submitted by Detective Dixon, select one sentence from the following groups of sentences which is MOST accurate and is grammatically correct.

1. A. Both robbers were armed.
    B. Each of the robbers were described as a male white.
    C. Neither robber was armed.
    D. Mr. Ladd stated that one of the robbers was armed.

2. A. Mr. Brown fired three shots from his revolver.
    B. Mr. Brown was shot in the head by one of the robbers.
    C. Mr. Brown suffered a gunshot wound of the head during the course of the robbery.
    D. Mr. Brown was taken to General Hospital by ambulance.

3. A. Shots were fired after one of the robbers said, *Give us the money or we'll kill you.*
    B. After one of the robbers demanded the money from Mr. Brown, he fired a shot.
    C. The preliminary investigation indicated that although Mr. Brown did not have a license for the gun, he was justified in using deadly physical force.
    D. Mr. Brown was interviewed at General Hospital.

4. A. Each of the witnesses were customers in the store at the time of occurrence.
    B. Neither of the witnesses interviewed was the owner of the liquor store.
    C. Neither of the witnesses interviewed were the owner of the store.
    D. Neither of the witnesses was employed by Mr. Brown.

5. A. Mr. Brown arrived at General Hospital at about 5:00 P.M.
    B. Neither of the robbers was injured during the robbery.
    C. The robbery occurred at 3:30 P.M. on February 10.
    D. One of the witnesses called the ambulance.

Questions 6-10.

DIRECTIONS: Each of Questions 6 through 10 consists of information given in outline form and four sentences labeled A, B, C, and D. For each question, choose the one sentence which CORRECTLY expresses the information given in outline form and which also displays PROPER English usage.

6. Client's Name: Joanna Jones
    Number of Children: 3
    Client's Income: None
    Client's Marital Status: Single

    A. Joanna Jones is an unmarried client with three children who have no income.
    B. Joanna Jones, who is single and has no income, a client she has three children.
    C. Joanna Jones, whose three children are clients, is single and has no income.
    D. Joanna Jones, who has three children, is an unmarried client with no income.

7. Client's Name: Bertha Smith
   Number of Children: 2
   Client's Rent: $1050 per month
   Number of Rooms: 4

   A. Bertha Smith, a client, pays $1050 per month for her four rooms with two children.
   B. Client Bertha Smith has two children and pays $1050 per month for four rooms.
   C. Client Bertha Smith is paying $1050 per month for two children with four rooms.
   D. For four rooms and two children client Bertha Smith pays $1050 per month.

   7.____

8. Name of Employee: Cynthia Dawes
   Number of Cases Assigned: 9
   Date Cases were Assigned: 12/16
   Number of Assigned Cases Completed: 8

   A. On December 16, employee Cynthia Dawes was assigned nine cases; she has completed eight of these cases.
   B. Cynthia Dawes, employee on December 16, assigned nine cases, completed eight.
   C. Being employed on December 16, Cynthia Dawes completed eight of nine assigned cases.
   D. Employee Cynthia Dawes, she was assigned nine cases and completed eight, on December 16.

   8.____

9. Place of Audit: Broadway Center
   Names of Auditors: Paul Cahn, Raymond Perez
   Date of Audit: 11/20
   Number of Cases Audited: 41

   A. On November 20, at the Broadway Center 41 cases was audited by auditors Paul Cahn and Raymond Perez.
   B. Auditors Raymond Perez and Paul Cahn has audited 41 cases at the Broadway Center on November 20.
   C. At the Broadway Center, on November 20, auditors Paul Cahn and Raymond Perez audited 41 cases.
   D. Auditors Paul Cahn and Raymond Perez at the Broadway Center, on November 20, is auditing 41 cases.

   9.____

10. Name of Client: Barbra Levine
    Client's Monthly Income: $2100
    Client's Monthly Expenses: $4520

    A. Barbra Levine is a client, her monthly income is $2100 and her monthly expenses is $4520.
    B. Barbra Levine's monthly income is $2100 and she is a client, with whose monthly expenses are $4520.

    10.____

C. Barbra Levine is a client whose monthly income is $2100 and whose monthly expenses are $4520.
D. Barbra Levine, a client, is with a monthly income which is $2100 and monthly expenses which are $4520.

Questions 11-13.

DIRECTIONS: Questions 11 through 13 involve several statements of fact presented in a very simple way. These statements of fact are followed by 4 choices which attempt to incorporate all of the facts into one logical statement which is properly constructed and grammatically correct.

11. I. Mr. Brown was sweeping the sidewalk in front of his house.
    II. He was sweeping it because it was dirty.
    III. He swept the refuse into the street.
    IV. Police Officer gave him a ticket.

    Which one of the following BEST presents the information given above?
    A. Because his sidewalk was dirty, Mr. Brown received a ticket from Officer Green when he swept the refuse into the street.
    B. Police Officer Green gave Mr. Brown a ticket because his sidewalk was dirty and he swept the refuse into the street.
    C. Police Officer Green gave Mr. Brown a ticket for sweeping refuse into the street because his sidewalk was dirty.
    D. Mr. Brown, who was sweeping refuse from his dirty sidewalk into the street, was given a ticket by Police Officer Green.

12. I. Sergeant Smith radioed for help.
    II. The sergeant did so because the crowd was getting larger.
    III. It was 10:00 A.M. when he made his call.
    IV. Sergeant Smith was not in uniform at the time of occurrence.

    Which one of the following BEST presents the information given above?
    A. Sergeant Smith, although not on duty at the time, radioed for help at 10 o'clock because the crowd was getting uglier.
    B. Although not in uniform, Sergeant Smith called for help at 10:00 A.M. because the crowd was getting uglier.
    C. Sergeant Smith radioed for help at 10:00 A.M. because the crowd was getting larger.
    D. Although he was not in uniform, Sergeant Smith radioed for help at 10:00 A.M. because the crowd was getting larger.

13. I. The payroll office is open on Fridays.
    II. Paychecks are distributed from 9:00 A.M. to 12 Noon.
    III. The office is open on Fridays because that's the only day the payroll staff is available.
    IV. It is open for the specified hours in order to permit employees to cash checks at the bank during lunch hour.

The choice below which MOST clearly and accurately presents the above idea is:
  A. Because the payroll office is open on Fridays from 9:00 A.M. to 12 Noon, employees can cash their checks when the payroll staff is available.
  B. Because the payroll staff is only available on Fridays until noon, employees can cash their checks during their lunch hour.
  C. Because the payroll staff is available only on Fridays, the office is open from 9:00 A.M. to 12 Noon to allow employees to cash their checks.
  D. Because of payroll staff availability, the payroll office is open on Fridays. It is open from 9:00 A.M. to 12 Noon so that distributed paychecks can be cashed at the bank while employees are on their lunch hour.

Questions 14-16.

DIRECTIONS: In each of Questions 14 through 6, the four sentences are from a paragraph in a report. They are not in the right order. Which of the following arrangements is the BEST one?

14. I. An executive may answer a letter by writing his reply on the face of the letter itself instead of having a return letter typed.
     II. This procedure is efficient because it saves the executive's time, the typist's time, and saves office file space.
     III. Copying machines are used in small offices as well as large offices to save time and money in making brief replies to business letters.
     IV. A copy is made on a copy machine to go into the company files, while the original is mailed back to the sender.

     The CORRECT answer is:
       A. I, II, IV, III   B. I, IV, II, III   C. III, I, IV, II   D. III, IV, II, I

15. I. Most organizations favor one of the types but always include the others to a lesser degree.
     II. However, we can detect a definite trend toward greater use of symbolic control.
     III. We suggest that our local police agencies are today primarily utilizing material control.
     IV. Control can be classified into three types: physical, material, and symbolic.

     The CORRECT answer is:
       A. IV, II, III, I   B. II, I, IV, III   C. III, IV, II, I   D. IV, I, III, II

16. I. They can and do take advantage of ancient political and geographical boundaries, which often give them sanctuary from effective policy activity.
     II. This country is essentially a country of small police forces, each operating independently within the limits of its jurisdiction.
     III. The boundaries that define and limit police operations do not hinder the movement of criminals, of course.
     IV. The machinery of law enforcement in America is fragmented, complicated, and frequently overlapping.

The CORRECT answer is:
A. III, I, IV   B. II, IV, I, III   C. IV, II, III, I   D. IV, III, II, I

17. Examine the following sentence, and then choose from below the words which should be inserted in the blank spaces to produce the best sentence.
The unit has exceeded _____ goals and the employees are satisfied with _____ accomplishments.
A. their, it's   B. it's; it's   C. its, there   D. its, their

17.____

18. Examine the following sentence, and then choose from below the words which should be inserted in the blank spaces to produce the best sentence.
Research indicates that employees who _____ no opportunity for close social relationships often find their work unsatisfying, and this _____ of satisfaction often reflects itself in low production.
A. have; lack   B. have; excess   C. has; lack   D. has; excess

18.____

19. Words in a sentence must be arranged properly to make sure that the intended meaning of the sentence is clear.
The sentence below that does NOT make sense because a clause has been separated from the word on which its meaning depends is:
A. To be a good writer, clarity is necessary.
B. To be a good writer, you must write clearly.
C. You must write clearly to be a good writer.
D. Clarity is necessary to good writing.

19.____

Questions 20-21.

DIRECTIONS: Each of Questions 20 and 21 consists of a statement which contains a word (one of those underlined) that is either incorrectly used because it is not in keeping with the meaning the quotation is evidently intended to convey, or is misspelled. There is only one INCORRECT word in each quotation. Of the four underlined words, determine if the first one should be replaced by the word lettered A, the second one replaced by the word lettered B, the third one replaced by the word lettered C, or the fourth one replaced by the word lettered D.

20. The alleged killer was occasionally permitted to excercise in the corridor.
A. alledged   B. ocasionally   C. permited   D. exercise

20.____

21. Defense counsel stated, in affect, that their conduct was permissible under the First Amendment.
A. council   B. effect   C. there   D. permissable

21.____

Question 22.

DIRECTIONS: Question 22 consists of one sentence. This sentence contains an incorrectly used word. First, decide which is the incorrectly used word. Then, from among the options given, decide which word, when substituted for the incorrectly used word, makes the meaning of the sentence clear.

22. As today's violence has no single cause, so its causes have no single scheme. 22.____
    A. deference B. cure C. flaw D. relevance

23. In the sentence, *A man in a light-grey suit waited thirty-five minutes in the ante-room for the all-important document,* the word IMPROPERLY hyphenated is 23.____
    A. light-grey
    B. thirty-five
    C. ante-room
    D. all-important

24. In the sentence, *The candidate wants to file his application for preference before it is too late,* the word *before* is used as a(n) 24.____
    A. preposition
    B. subordinating conjunction
    C. pronoun
    D. adverb

25. In the sentence, *The perpetrators ran from the scene,* the word *from* is a 25.____
    A. preposition B. pronoun C. verb D. conjunction

KEY (CORRECT ANSWERS)

1.	D	11.	D
2.	D	12.	D
3.	A	13.	D
4.	B	14.	C
5.	D	15.	D
6.	D	16.	C
7.	B	17.	D
8.	A	18.	A
9.	C	19.	A
10.	C	20.	D

21.	B
22.	B
23.	C
24.	B
25.	A

CLERICAL ABILITIES
EXAMINATION SECTION
TEST 1

DIRECTIONS: Each question or incomplete statement is followed by several suggested answers or completions. Select the one that BEST answers the question or completes the statement. *PRINT THE LETTER OF THE CORRECT ANSWER IN THE SPACE AT THE RIGHT.*

Questions 1-4.

DIRECTIONS: Questions 1 through 4 are to be answered on the basis of the information given below.

The most commonly used filing system and the one that is easiest to learn is alphabetical filing. This involves putting records in an A to Z order, according to the letters of the alphabet. The name of a person is filed by using the following order: first, the surname or last name; second, the first name; third, the middle name or middle initial. For example, *Henry C. Young* is filed under *Y* and thereafter under *Young, Henry C.* The name of a company is filed in the same way. For example, *Long Cabinet Co.* is filed under *L* while *John T. Long Cabinet Co.* is filed under *L* and thereafter under *Long, John T. Cabinet Co.*

1. The one of the following which lists the names of persons in the CORRECT alphabetical order is:
   A. Mary Carrie, Helen Carrol, James Carson, John Carter
   B. James Carson, Mary Carrie, John Carter, Helen Carrol
   C. Helen Carrol, James Carson, John Carter, Mary Carrie
   D. John Carter, Helen Carrol, Mary Carrie, James Carson

   1.____

2. The one of the following which lists the names of persons in the CORRECT alphabetical order is:
   A. Jones, John C.; Jones, John A.; Jones, John P.; Jones, John K.
   B. Jones, John P.; Jones, John K.; Jones, John C.; Jones, John A.
   C. Jones, John A.; Jones, John C.; Jones, John K.; Jones, John P.
   D. Jones, John K.; Jones, John C.; Jones, John A.; Jones, John P.

   2.____

3. The one of the following which lists the names of the companies in the CORRECT alphabetical order is:
   A. Blane Co., Blake Co., Block Co., Blear Co.
   B. Blake Co., Blane Co., Blear Co., Block Co.
   C. Block Co., Blear Co., Blane Co., Blake Co.
   D. Blear Co., Blake Co., Blane Co., Block Co.

   3.____

4. You are to return to the file an index card on *Barry C. Wayne Materials and Supplies Co.*
   Of the following, the CORRECT alphabetical group that you should return the index card to is
   A. A to G   B. H to M   C. N to S   D. T to Z

   4.____

Questions 5-10.

DIRECTIONS: In each of Questions 5 through 10, the names of four people are given. For each question, choose as your answer the one of the four names given which should be filed FIRST according to the usual system of alphabetical filing of names, as described in the following paragraph.

In filing names, you must start with the last name. Names are filed in order of the first letter of the last name, then the second letter, etc. Therefore, BAILY would be filed before BROWN, which would be filed before COLT. A name with fewer letters of the same type comes first, i.e., Smith before Smithe. If the last names are the same, the names are filed alphabetically by the first name. If the first name is an initial, a name with an initial would come before a first name that starts with the same letter as the initial. Therefore, I. BROWN would come before IRA BROWN. Finally, if both last name and first name are the same, the name would be filed alphabetically by the middle name, once again an initial coming before a middle name which starts with the same letter as the initial. If there is no middle name at all, the name would come before those with middle initials or names.

SAMPLE QUESTION:
A. Lester Daniels
B. William Dancer
C. Nathan Danzig
D. Dan Lester

The last names beginning with D are filed before the last name beginning with L. Since DANIELS, DANCER, and DANZIG all begin with the same three letters, you must look at the fourth letter of the last name to determine which name should be filed first. C comes before I or Z in the alphabet, so DANCER is filed before DANIELS or DANZIG. Therefore, the answer to the above sample question is B.

5. A. Scott Biala
    B. Mary Byala
    C. Martin Baylor
    D. Francis Bauer

    5.____

6. A. Howard J. Black
    B. Howard Black
    C. J. Howard Black
    D. John H. Black

    6.____

7. A. Theodora Garth Kingston
    B. Theadore Barth Kingston
    C. Thomas Kingston
    D. Thomas T. Kingston

    7.____

8.
- A. Paulette Mary Huerta
- B. Paul M. Huerta
- C. Paulette L. Huerta
- D. Peter A. Huerta

9.
- A. Martha Hunt Morgan
- B. Martin Hunt Morgan
- C. Mary H. Morgan
- D. Martine H. Morgan

10.
- A. James T. Meerschaum
- B. James M. Mershum
- C. James F. Mearshaum
- D. James N. Meshum

Questions 11-14.

DIRECTIONS: Questions 11 through 14 are to be answered SOLELY on the basis of the following information.

You are required to file various documents in file drawers which are labeled according to the following pattern:

DOCUMENTS

MEMOS		LETTERS	
File	Subject	File	Subject
84PM1	(A-L)	84PC1	(A-L)
84PM2	(M-Z)	84PC2	(M-Z)

REPORTS		INQUIRIES	
File	Subject	File	Subject
84PR1	(A-L)	84PQ1	(A-L)
84PR2	(M-Z)	84PQ2	(M-Z)

11. A letter dealing with a burglary should be filed in the drawer labeled
    A. 84PM1   B. 84PC1   C. 84PR1   D. 84PQ2

12. A report on Statistics should be found in the drawer labeled
    A. 84PM1   B. 84PC2   C. 84PR2   D. 84PQS

13. An inquiry is received about parade permit procedures. It should be filed in the drawer labeled
    A. 84PM2   B. 84PC1   C. 84PR1   D. 84PQ2

14. A police officer has a question about a robbery report you filed. You should pull this file from the drawer labeled
    A. 84PM1   B. 84PM2   C. 84PR1   D. 84PR2

Questions 15-22.

DIRECTIONS: Each of Questions 15 through 22 consists of four or six numbered names. For each question, choose the option (A, B, C, or D) which indicates the order in which the names should be filed in accordance with the following filing instructions:
- File alphabetically according to last name, then first name, then middle initial.
- File according to each successive letter within a name.
- When comparing two names in which the letters in the longer name are identical to the corresponding letters in the shorter name, the shorter name is filed first.
- When the last names are the same, initials are always filed before names beginning with the same letter.

15. I.   Ralph Robinson
     II. Alfred Ross
     III. Luis Robles
     IV. James Roberts

The CORRECT filing sequence for the above names should be
A. IV, II, I, III   B. I, IV, III, II   C. III, IV, I, II   D. IV, I, III, II

16. I.   Irwin Goodwin
     II. Inez Gonzalez
     III. Irene Goodman
     IV. Ira S. Goodwin
     V.   Ruth I. Goldstein
     VI. M.B. Goodman

The CORRECT filing sequence for the above names should be
A. V, II, I, IV, III, VI
B. V, II, VI, III, IV, I
C. V, II, III, VI, IV, I
D. V, II, III, VI, I, IV

17. I.   George Allan
     II. Gregory Allen
     III. Gary Allen
     IV. George Allen

The CORRECT filing sequence for the above names should be
A. IV, III, I, II   B. I, IV, II, III   C. III, IV, I, II   D. I, III, IV, II

18. I.   Simon Kauffman
     II. Leo Kaufman
     III. Robert Kaufmann
     IV. Paul Kauffmann

     The CORRECT filing sequence for the above names should be
     A. I, IV, II, III   B. II, IV, III, I   C. III, II, IV, I   D. I, II, III, IV

19. I.   Roberta Williams
     II. Robin Wilson
     III. Roberta Wilson
     IV. Robin Williams

     The CORRECT filing sequence for the above names should be
     A. III, II, IV, I   B. I, IV, III, II   C. I, II, III, IV   D. III, I, II, IV

20. I.   Lawrence Shultz
     II. Albert Schultz
     III. Theodore Schwartz
     IV. Thomas Schwarz
     V.   Alvin Schultz
     VI. Leonard Shultz

     The CORRECT filing sequence for the above names should be
     A. II, V, III, IV, I, VI
     B. IV, III, V, I, II, VI
     C. II, V, I, VI, III, IV
     D. I, VI, II, V, III, IV

21. I.   McArdle
     II. Mayer
     III. Maletz
     IV. McNiff
     V.   Meyer
     VI. MacMahon

     The CORRECT filing sequence for the above names should be
     A. I, IV, VI, III, II, V
     B. II, I, IV, VI, III, V
     C. VI, III, II, I, IV, V
     D. VI, III, II, V, I, IV

22. I.   Jack E. Johnson
     II. R.H. Jackson
     III. Bertha Jackson
     IV. J.T. Johnson
     V.   Ann Johns
     VI. John Jacobs

     The CORRECT filing sequence for the above names should be
     A. II, III, VI, V, IV, I
     B. III, II, VI, V, IV, I
     C. VI, II, III, I, V, IV
     D. III, II, VI, IV, V, I

Questions 23-30.

DIRECTIONS: The code table below shows 10 letters with matching numbers. For each question, there are three sets of letters. Each set of letters is followed by a set of numbers which may or may not match their correct letter according to the code table. For each question, check all three sets of letters and numbers and mark your answer:
    A. if no pairs are correctly matched
    B. if only one pair is correctly matched
    C. if only two pairs are correctly matched
    D. if all three pairs are correctly matched

CODE TABLE

T	M	V	D	S	P	R	G	B	H
1	2	3	4	5	6	7	8	9	0

SAMPLE QUESTION: TMVDSP – 123456
                              RGBHTM – 789011
                              DSPRGB – 256789

In the sample question above, the first set of numbers correctly match its set of letters. But the second and third pairs contain mistakes. In the second pair, M is correctly matched with number 1. According to the code table, letter M should be correctly matched with number 2. In the third pair, the letter D is incorrectly matched with number 2. According to the code table, letter D should be correctly matched with number 4. Since only one of the pairs is correctly matched, the answer to this sample question is B.

23.   RSBMRM – 759262
        GDSRVH – 845730
        VDBRTM - 349713

24.   TGVSDR – 183247
        SMHRDP – 520647
        TRMHSR – 172057

25.   DSPRGM – 456782
        MVDBHT – 234902
        HPMDBT – 062491

26.   BVPTRD – 936184
        GDPHMB – 807029
        GMRHMV – 827032

27.   MGVRSH – 283750
        TRDMBS – 174295
        SPRMGV - 567283

28. SGBSDM – 489542
    MGHPTM – 290612
    MPBMHT - 269301

    28.____

29. TDPBHM – 146902
    VPBMRS – 369275
    GDMBHM - 842902

    29.____

30. MVPTBV – 236194
    PDRTMB – 47128
    BGTMSM - 981232

    30.____

KEY (CORRECT ANSWERS)

1.	A	11.	B	21.	C
2.	C	12.	C	22.	B
3.	B	13.	D	23.	B
4.	D	14.	D	24.	B
5.	D	15.	D	25.	C
6.	B	16.	C	26.	A
7.	B	17.	D	27.	D
8.	B	18.	A	28.	A
9.	A	19.	B	29.	D
10.	C	20.	A	30.	A

TEST 2

DIRECTIONS: Each question or incomplete statement is followed by several suggested answers or completions. Select the one that BEST answers the question or completes the statement. *PRINT THE LETTER OF THE CORRECT ANSWER IN THE SPACE AT THE RIGHT.*

Questions 1-10.

DIRECTIONS: Questions 1 through 10 each consists of two columns, each containing four lines of names, numbers and/or addresses. For each question, compare the lines in Column I with the lines in Column II to see if they match exactly, and mark your answer A, B, C, or D, according to the following instructions:
    A. all four lines match exactly
    B. only three lines match exactly
    C. only two lines match exactly
    D. only one line matches exactly

	COLUMN I	COLUMN II	
1.	I. Earl Hodgson II. 1409870 III. Shore Ave. IV. Macon Rd.	Earl Hodgson 1408970 Schore Ave. Macon Rd.	1.____
2.	I. 9671485 II. 470 Astor Court III. Halprin, Phillip IV. Frank D. Poliseo	9671485 470 Astor Court Halperin, Phillip Frank D. Poliseo	2.____
3.	I. Tandem Associates II. 144-17 Northern Blvd. III. Alberta Forchi IV. Kings Park, NY 10751	Tandom Associates 144-17 Northern Blvd. Albert Forchi Kings Point, NY 10751	3.____
4.	I. Bertha C. McCormack II. Clayton, MO III. 976-4242 IV. New City, NY 10951	Bertha C. McCormack Clayton, MO 976-4242 New City, NY 10951	4.____
5.	I. George C. Morill II. Columbia, SC 29201 III. Louis Ingham IV. 3406 Forest Ave.	George C. Morrill Columbia, SD 29201 Louis Ingham 3406 Forest Ave.	5.____
6.	I. 506 S. Elliott Pl. II. Herbert Hall III. 4712 Rockaway Pkway IV. 169 E. 7 St.	506 S. Elliott Pl. Hurbert Hall 4712 Rockaway Pkway 169 E. 7 St.	6.____

7. I.   345 Park Ave.   345 Park Pl.   7.____
    II. Colman Oven Corp.   Coleman Oven Corp.
    III. Robert Conte   Robert Conti
    IV. 6179846   6179846

8. I.   Grigori Schierber   Grigori Schierber   8.____
    II. Des Moines, Iowa   Des Moines, Iowa
    III. Gouverneur Hospital   Gouverneur Hospital
    IV. 91-35 Cresskill Pl.   91-35 Cresskill Pl.

9. I.   Jeffery Janssen   Jeffrey Janssen   9.____
    II. 8041071   8041071
    III. 40 Rockefeller Plaza   40 Rockafeller Plaza
    IV. 407 6 St.   406 7 St.

10. I.   5971996   5871996   10.____
    II. 3113 Knickerbocker Ave.   31123 Knickerbocker Ave.
    III. 8434 Boston Post Rd.   8424 Boston Post Rd.
    IV. Penn Station   Penn Station

Questions 11-14.

DIRECTIONS: Questions 11 through 14 are to be answered by looking at the four groups of names and addresses listed below (I, II, III, and IV), and then finding out the number of groups that have their corresponding numbered lies exactly the same.

	GROUP I	GROUP II
Line 1.	Richmond General Hospital	Richman General Hospital
Line 2.	Geriatric Clinic	Geriatric Clinic
Line 3.	3975 Paerdegat St.	3975 Peardegat St.
Line 4.	Loudonville, New York 11538	Londonville, New York 11538

	GROUP III	GROUP IV
Line 1.	Richmond General Hospital	Richmend General Hospital
Line 2.	Geriatric Clinic	Geriatric Clinic
Line 3.	3795 Paerdegat St.	3975 Paerdegat St.
Line 4.	Loudonville, New York 11358	Loudonville, New York 11538

1. In how many groups is line one exactly the same?   11.____
    A. Two   B. Three   C. Four   D. None

12. In how many groups is line two exactly the same?   12.____
    A. Two   B. Three   C. Four   D. None

13. In how many groups is line three exactly the same?   13.____
    A. Two   B. Three   C. Four   D. None

14. In how many groups is line four exactly the same? 14.____
    A. Two   B. Three   C. Four   D. None

Questions 15-18.

DIRECTIONS: Each of Questions 15 through 18 has two lists of names and addresses. Each list contains three sets of names and addresses. Check each of the three sets in the list on the right to see if they are the same as the corresponding set in the list on the left. Mark your answers:
   A. if none of the sets in the right list are the same as those in the left list
   B. if only one of the sets in the right list is the same as those in the left list
   C. if only two of the sets in the right list are the same as those in the left list
   D. if all three sets in the right list are the same as those in the left list

15. Mary T. Berlinger   Mary T. Berlinger   15.____
    2351 Hampton St.   2351 Hampton St.
    Monsey, N.Y. 20117   Monsey, N.Y. 20117

    Eduardo Benes   Eduardo Benes
    483 Kingston Avenue   473 Kingston Avenue
    Central Islip, N.Y. 11734   Central Islip, N.Y. 11734

    Alan Carrington Fuchs   Alan Carrington Fuchs
    17 Gnarled Hollow Road   17 Gnarled Hollow Road
    Los Angeles, CA 91635   Los Angeles, CA 91685

16. David John Jacobson   David John Jacobson   16.____
    178 34 St. Apt. 4C   178 53 St. Apt. 4C
    New York, N.Y. 00927   New York, N.Y. 00927

    Ann-Marie Calonella   Ann-Marie Calonella
    7243 South Ridge Blvd.   7243 South Ridge Blvd.
    Bakersfield, CA 96714   Bakersfield, CA 96714

    Pauline M. Thompson   Pauline M. Thomson
    872 Linden Ave.   872 Linden Ave.
    Houston, Texas 70321   Houston, Texas 70321

17. Chester LeRoy Masterton   Chester LeRoy Masterson   17.____
    152 Lacy Rd.   152 Lacy Rd.
    Kankakee, Ill. 54532   Kankakee, Ill. 54532

    William Maloney   William Maloney
    S. LaCrosse Pla.   S. LaCross Pla.
    Wausau, Wisconsin 52136   Wausau, Wisconsin 52146

    Cynthia V. Barnes   Cynthia V. Barnes
    16 Pines Rd.   16 Pines Rd.
    Greenpoint, Miss. 20376   Greenpoint,, Miss. 20376

4 (#2)

18.
| Marcel Jean Frontenac | Marcel Jean Frontenac | 18._____ |
8 Burton On The Water 6 Burton On The Water
Calender, Me. 01471   Calender, Me. 01471

J. Scott Marsden   J. Scott Marsden
174 S. Tipton St.   174 Tipton St.
Cleveland, Ohio   Cleveland, Ohio

Lawrence T. Haney   Lawrence T. Haney
171 McDonough St.   171 McDonough St.
Decatur, Ga. 31304   Decatur, Ga. 31304

Questions 19-26.

DIRECTIONS: Each of Questions 19 through 26 has two lists of numbers. Each list contains three sets of numbers. Check each of the three sets in the list on the right to see if they are the same as the corresponding set in the list on the left. Mark your answers:
- A. if none of the sets in the right list are the same as those in the left list
- B. if only one of the sets in the right list is the same as those in the left list
- C. if only two of the sets in the right list are the same as those in the left list
- D. if all three sets in the right list are the same as those in the left lists

19. 7354183476   7354983476   19._____
    4474747744   4474747774
    5791430231   57914302311

20. 7143592185   7143892185   20._____
    8344517699   8344518699
    9178531263   9178531263

21. 2572114731   257214731   21._____
    8806835476   8806835476
    8255831246   8255831246

22. 331476853821   331476858621   22._____
    6976658532996   6976655832996
    3766042113715   3766042113745

23. 8806663315   88066633115   23._____
    74477138449   74477138449
    211756663666   211756663666

24. 990006966996   99000696996   24._____
    53022219743   53022219843
    4171171117717   4171171177717

25. 24400222433004   24400222433004   25._____
    5300030055000355   5300030055500355
    20000075532002022   20000075532002022

26. 61116664066001116   61116664066001116   26._____
    71113001170011007 33   71113001170011007 33
    26666446664476518   26666446664476518

26. 61116664066000 1116   61116664066001116   26._____

Questions 27-30.

DIRECTIONS: Questions 27 through 30 are to be answered by picking the answer which is in the correct numerical order, from the lowest number to the highest number, in each question.

27. A. 44533, 44518, 44516, 44547   27._____
    B. 44516, 44518, 44533, 44547
    C. 44547, 44533, 44518, 44516
    D. 44518, 44516, 44547, 44533

28. A. 95587, 95593, 95601, 95620   28._____
    B. 95601, 95620, 95587, 95593
    C. 95593, 95587, 95601. 95620
    D. 95620, 95601, 95593, 95587

29. A. 232212, 232208, 232232, 232223   29._____
    B. 232208, 232223, 232212, 232232
    C. 232208, 232212, 232223, 232232
    D. 232223, 232232, 232208, 232208

30. A. 113419, 113521, 113462, 113462   30._____
    B. 113588, 113462, 113521, 113419
    C. 113521, 113588, 113419, 113462
    D. 113419, 113462, 113521, 113588

KEY (CORRECT ANSWERS)

1.	C	11.	A	21.	C
2.	B	12.	C	22.	A
3.	D	13.	A	23.	D
4.	A	14.	A	24.	A
5.	C	15.	C	25.	C
6.	B	16.	B	26.	C
7.	D	17.	B	27.	B
8.	A	18.	B	28.	A
9.	D	19.	B	29.	C
10.	C	20.	B	30.	D

CODING

EXAMINATION SECTION

TEST 1

COMMENTARY

An ingenious question-type called coding, involving elements of alphabetizing, filing, name and number comparison, and evaluative judgment and application, has currently won wide acceptance in testing circles for measuring clerical aptitude and general ability, particularly on the senior (middle) grades (levels).

While the directions for this question-type usually vary in detail, the candidate is generally asked to consider groups of names, codes, and numbers, and, then, according to a given plan, to arrange codes in alphabetic order; to arrange these in numerical sequence; to rearrange columns of names and numbers in correct order; to espy errors in coding; to choose the correct coding arrangement in consonance with the given directions and examples, etc.

This question-type appears to have few parameters in respect to form, substance, or degree of difficulty.

Accordingly, acquaintance with, and practice in the coding question is recommended for the serious candidate.

DIRECTIONS: Column I consists of serial numbers of dollar bills. Column II shows different ways of arranging the corresponding serial numbers.
The serial numbers of dollar bills in Column I begin and end with a capital letter and have an eight-digit number in between. The serial numbers in Column I are to be arranged according to the following rules:
First: In alphabetical order according to the first letter.
Second: When two or more serial numbers have the same first letter, in alphabetical order according to the last letter.
Third: When two or more serial numbers have the same first and last letters, in numerical order, beginning with the lowest number.

The serial numbers in Column I are numbered (1) through (5) in the order in which they are listed. In Column II, the numbers (1) through (5) are arranged in four different ways to show different arrangements of the corresponding serial numbers. Choose the answer in Column II in which the serial numbers are arranged according to the above rules.

	Column I		Column II
1.	E75044127B	A.	4, 1, 3, 2, 5
2.	B96399104A	B.	4, 1, 2, 3, 5
3.	B93939086A	C.	4, 3, 2, 5, 1
4.	B47064465H	D.	3, 2, 5, 4, 1

In the simple question, the four serial numbers starting with B should be put before the serial number starting with E. The serial numbers starting with B and ending with A should be put before the serial number starting with B and ending with H. The three serial numbers starting with B and ending with A should be listed in numerical order, beginning with the lowest

2 (#1)

number. The correct way to arrange the serial numbers, therefore, is:
    3.   B93939086A
    2.   B96399104A
    5.   B99040922A
    4.   B47064465H
    1.   E75044127B

Since the order of arrangement is 3, 2, 5, 4, 1, the answer to the sample question is D.

	Column I	Column II	
1.	1. D89143888P 2. D98143838B 3. D89113883B 4. D89148338P 5. D89148388B	A. 3, 5, 2, 1, 4 B. 3, 1, 4, 5, 2 C. 4, 2, 3, 1, 5 D. 4, 1, 3, 5, 2	1.____
2.	1. W62455590E 2. W62455090F 3. W62405099E 4. V62455097F 5. V62405979E	A. 2, 4, 3, 1, 5 B. 3, 1, 5, 2, 4 C. 5, 3, 1, 4, 2 D. 5, 4, 3, 1, 2	2.____
3.	1. N74663826M 2. M74633286M 3. N76633228N 4. M76483686N 5. M74636688M	A. 2, 4, 5, 3, 1 B. 2, 5, 4, 1, 3 C. 1, 2, 5, 3, 4 D. 2, 5, 1, 4, 3	3.____
4.	1. P97560324B 2. R97663024B 3. P97503024E 4. R97563240E 5. P97652304B	A. 1, 5, 2, 3, 4 B. 3, 1, 4, 5, 2 C. 1, 5, 3, 2, 4 D. 1, 5, 2, 3, 4	4.____
5.	1. H92411165G 2. A92141465G 3. H92141165C 4. H92444165C 5. A92411465G	A. 2, 5, 3, 4, 1 B. 3, 4, 2, 5, 1 C. 3, 2, 1, 5, 4 D. 3, 1, 2, 5, 4	5.____
6.	1. X90637799S 2. N90037696S 3. Y90677369B 4. X09677693B 5. M09673699S	A. 4, 3, 5, 2, 1 B. 5, 4, 2, 1, 3 C. 5, 2, 4, 1, 3 D. 5, 2, 3, 4, 1	6.____

3 (#1)

	Column I	Column II	

7. 1. K78425174L
    2. K78452714C
    3. K78547214N
    4. K78442774C
    5. K78547724M

    A. 4, 2, 1, 3, 5
    B. 2, 3, 5, 4, 1
    C. 1, 4, 2, 3, 5
    D. 4, 2, 1, 5, 3

    7.____

8. 1. P18736652U
    2. P18766352V
    3. T17686532U
    4. T17865523U
    5. P18675332V

    A. 1, 3, 4, 5, 2
    B. 1, 5, 2, 3, 4
    C. 3, 4, 5, 1, 2
    D. 5, 2, 1, 3, 4

    8.____

9. 1. L51138101K
    2. S51138001R
    3. S51188222K
    4. S51183110R
    5. L51188100R

    A. 1, 5, 3, 2, 4
    B. 1, 3, 5, 2, 4
    C. 1, 5, 1, 4, 3
    D. 2, 5, 1, 4, 3

    9.____

10. 1. J28475336
    2. T28775363D
    3. J27843566P
    4. T27834563P
    5. J2843553D

    A. 5, 1, 2, 3, 4
    B. 4, 3, 5, 1, 2
    C. 1, 5, 2, 4, 3
    D. 5, 1, 3, 2, 4

    10.____

11. 1. S55126179E
    2. R51336177Q
    3. P55126177R
    4. S55126178R
    5. R55126180P

    A. 1, 5, 2, 3, 4
    B. 3, 4, 1, 5, 2
    C. 3, 5, 2, 1, 4
    D. 4, 3, 1, 5, 2

    11.____

12. 1. T64217813Q
    2. I64217817O
    3. T64217818O
    4. I64217811Q
    5. T64217816Q

    A. 4, 1, 3, 2, 4
    B. 2, 4, 3, 1, 5
    C. 4, 1, 5, 2, 3
    D. 2, 3, 4, 1, 5

    12.____

13. 1. B33886897B
    2. B38386882B
    3. D33389862B
    4. D33336887D
    5. B38888697D

    A. 5, 1, 3, 4, 2
    B. 1, 2, 5, 3, 4
    C. 1, 2, 5, 4, 3
    D. 2, 1, 4, 5, 3

    13.____

14. 1. E11664554M
    2. F11164544M
    3. F11614455N
    4. E11665454M
    5. F16161545N

    A. 4, 1, 2, 5, 3
    B. 2, 4, 1, 5, 3
    C. 4, 2, 1, 3, 5
    D. 1, 4, 2, 3, 5

    14.____

4 (#1)

    Column I   Column II

15.
   1. C86611355W
   2. C68631533V
   3. G88631533V
   4. C68833515V
   5. G68833511W

   A. 2, 4, 1, 5, 3
   B. 1, 2, 4, 3, 5
   C. 1, 2, 5, 4, 3
   D. 1, 2, 4, 3, 5

   15.____

16.
   1. R73665312J
   2. P73685512J
   3. P73968511J
   4. R73665321K
   5. R63985211K

   A. 3, 2, 1, 4, 5
   B. 2, 3, 5, 1, 4
   C. 2, 3, 1, 5, 4
   D. 3, 1, 5, 2, 4

   16.____

17.
   1. X33661222U
   2. Y83961323V
   3. Y88991123V
   4. X33691233U
   5. X38691333U

   A. 1, 4, 5, 2, 3
   B. 4, 5, 1, 3, 2
   C. 4, 5, 1, 2, 3
   D. 4, 1, 5, 2, 3

   17..____

18.
   1. B22838847W
   2. B28833874V
   3. B22288344X
   4. B28238374V
   5. B28883347V

   A. 4, 5, 2, 3, 1
   B. 4, 2, 5, 1, 3
   C. 4, 5, 2, 1, 3
   D. 4, 1, 5, 2, 3

   18.____

19.
   1. H44477447G
   2. H47444777G
   3. H74777477C
   4. H44747447G
   5. H77747447C

   A. 1, 3, 5, 4, 2
   B. 3, 1, 5, 2, 4
   C. 1, 4, 2, 3, 5
   D. 3, 5, 1, 4, 2

   19.____

20.
   1. G11143447G
   2. G15133388C
   3. C15134378G
   4. G11534477C
   5. C15533337C

   A. 3, 5, 1, 4, 2
   B. 1, 4, 3, 2, 5
   C. 5, 3, 4, 2, 1
   D. 4, 3, 1, 2, 5

   20.____

21.
   1. J96693369F
   2. J66939339F
   3. J96693693E
   4. J966T3933E
   5. J69639363F

   A. 4, 3, 2, 5, 1
   B. 2, 5, 4, 1, 3
   C. 2, 5, 4, 3, 1
   D. 3, 4, 5, 2, 1

   21.____

22.
   1. L15567834Z
   2. P11587638Z
   3. M51567688Z
   4. O55578784Z
   5. N53588783Z

   A. 3, 1, 5, 2, 4
   B. 1, 3, 5, 4, 2
   C. 1, 3, 5, 2, 4
   D. 3, 1, 4, 4, 2

   22.____

5 (#1)

	Column I		Column II	

   Column I   Column II

23. 1. C83261824G   A. 2, 4, 1, 5, 3   23.____
     2. C78361822C   B. 4, 2, 1, 3, 5
     3. G83261732G   C. 3, 1, 5, 2, 4
     4. C88261823C   D. , 3, 5, 1, 4
     5. G83261743C

24. 1. A11710107H   A. 2, 1, 4, 3, 5   24.____
     2. H17110017A   B. 3, 1, 5, 2, 4
     3. A11170707A   C. 3, 4, 1, 5, 2
     4. H17170171H   D. 3, 5, 1, 2, 4
     5. A11710177A

25. 1. R26794821S   A. 3, 2, 4, 1, 5   25.____
     2. O26794821T   B. 3, 4, 2, 1, 5
     3. M26794821Z   C. 4, 2, 1, 3, 5
     4. Q26794821R   D. 5, 4, 1, 2, 3
     5. S26794821P

KEY (CORRECT ANSWERS)

1. A   11. C
2. D   12. B
3. B   13. B
4. C   14. D
5. A   15. A

6. C   16. C
7. D   17. A
8. B   18. B
9. A   19. D
10. D   20. C

21. A
22. B
23. A
24. D
25. A

TEST 2

Questions 1-5.

DIRECTIONS: Questions 1 through 5 consist of a set of letters and numbers located under Column I. For each question, pick the answer (A, B, C, or D) located under Column II which contains ONLY letters and numbers that appear in the question in Column II. *PRINT THE LETTER OF THE CORRECT ANSWER IN THE SPACE AT THE RIGHT.*

SAMPLE QUESTION

Column I

B-9-P-H-2-Z-N-8-4-M

Column II

A. B-4-C-3-R-9
B. 4-H-P-8-6-N
C. P-2-Z-8-M-9
D. 4-B-N-5-E-Z

Choice C is the correct answer because P,2,Z,8,M and 9 all appear in the sample question. All the other choices have at least one letter or number that is not in the question.

Column I

1. 1-7-6-J-L-T-3-S-A-2

2. C-0-Q-5-3-9-H-L-2-7

3. P-3-B-C-5-6-0-E-1-T

4. U-T-Z-2-4-S-8-6-B-3

5. 4-D-F-G-C-6-8-3-J-L

Column II

1.
A. J-3-S-A-7-L
B. T-S-A-2-6-5
C. 3-7-J-L-S-Z
D. A-7-4-J-L-1

2.
A. F-9-T-2-7-Q
B. 3-0-6-9-L-C
C. 9-L-7-Q-C-3
D. H-Q-4-5-9-7

3.
A. B-4-6-1-3-T
B. T-B-P-3-E-0
C. 5-3-0-E-B-G
D. 0-6-P-T-9-B

4.
A. 2-4-S-V-Z-3
B. B-Z-S-8-3-6
C. 4-T-U-8-L-B
D. 9-3-T-Z-1-2

5.
A. T-D-6-8-4-J
B. C-4-3-2-J-F
C. 8-3-C-5-G-6
D. C-8-6-J-G-L

1.____

2.____

3.____

4.____

5.____

Questions 6-12.

DIRECTIONS: Each of the questions numbered 6 through 12 consist of a long series of letters and numbers under Column I and four short series of letters and numbers under Column II. For each question, choose the short series of letters and numbers which is entirely and exactly the same as some part of the long series.

	Column I		Column II	
6.	IE227FE383L4700	A. B. C. D.	E27FE3 EF838L EL4700 83LE70	6.____
7.	77J646G54NPB318	A. B. C. D.	NPB318 J646J5 4G54NP C54NPB	7.____
8.	85887T358W24A93	A. B. C. D.	858887 W24A93 858W24 87T353	8.____
9.	E104RY796B33H14	A. B. C. D.	04RY79 E14RYR 96B3H1 RY7996	9.____
10.	W58NP12141DE07M	A. B. C. D.	8MP121 W58NP1 14DEO7 12141D	10.____
11.	P473R365M442V5W	A. B. C. D.	P47365 73P365 365M44 5X42V5	11.____
12.	865CG441V21SS59	A. B. C. D.	1V12SS V21SS5 5GC441 894CG4	12.____

KEY (CORRECT ANSWERS)

1. A
2. C
3. B
4. B
5. D
6. D
7. A
8. B
9. A
10. D
11. C
12. B

TEST 3

DIRECTIONS: Each question from 1 through 8 consists of a set of letters and numbers. For each question, pick as your answer from the column to the right the choice has ONLY numbers and letters that are in the question you are answering.

To help you understand what to do, the following sample question is given:

SAMPLE: B-9-P-H-2-Z-N-8-4-M

A. B-4-C-3-E-9
B. 4-H-P-8-6-N
C. P-2-Z-8-M-9
D. 4-B-N-R-E-A

Choice C is the correct answer because P, 2, Z, 8, M-9 are in the sample question. All the other choices have at least one letter or number that is not in the question.

Questions 1 through 4 are based on Column I.

<u>Column I</u>

1. X-8-3-I-H-9-4-G-P-U   A. I-G-W-8-2-1   1._____

2. 4-1-2-X-U-B-9-H-7-3   B. U-3-G-9-P-8   2._____

3. U-I-G-2-5-4-W-P-3-B   C. 3-G-I-4-S-U   3._____

4. 3-H-7-G-4-5-1-U-B   D. 9-X-4-7-2-H   4._____

Questions 5 through 8 are based on Column II.

<u>Column II</u>

5. L-2-9-Z-R-8-Q-Y-5-7   A. 8-R-N-3-T-Z   5._____

6. J-L-9-N-Y-8-5-Q-Z-2   B. 2-L-R-5-7-Q   6._____

7. T-Y-3-3-J-Q-2-N-R-Z   C. J-2-8-Z-T-5   7._____

8. 8-Z-7-T-N-L-1-E-R-3   D. Z-8-9-3-L-5   8._____

KEY (CORRECT ANSWERS)

1. B   5. B
2. D   6. C
3. C   7. A
4. C   8. A

TEST 4

DIRECTIONS: Questions 1 through 5 have lines of letters and numbers. Each letter should be matched with its number in accordance with the following table.

Letter:	F	R	C	A	W	L	E	N	B	T
Matching Number:	0	1	2	3	4	5	6	7	8	9

From the table you can determine that the letter F has the matching number 0 below it, the letter R has the matching number 1 below it, etc.

For each question, compare each line of letters and numbers carefully to see if each letter has its correct matching number. If all the letters and numbers are matched correctly in none of the line of the question, mark your answer A; only one of the lines in the question, mark your answer B; only two of the lines of the question, mark your answer C; all three lines of the question, mark your answer D.

```
WBCR    4826
TLBF    9580
ATNE    3986
```

There is a mistake in the first line because the letter R should have its matching number 1 instead of the number 6. The second line is correct because each letter shown has the correct matching number.
There is a mistake in the third line because the letter N should have the matching number 7 instead of the number 8. Since all the letters and numbers are matched correctly in only one of the lines in the sample, the correct answer is B.

1. EBCT   6829
    ATWR   3962
    NLBW   7584

2. RNCT   1729
    LNCR   5728
    WAEB   5368

3. STWB   7948
    RABL   1385
    TAEF   9360

4. LWRB   5417
    RLWN   1647
    CBWA   2843

5. ABTC   3792
    WCER   5261
    AWCN   3417

1.____

2.____

3.____

4.____

5.____

KEY (CORRECT ANSWERS)

1. C
2. B
3. D
4. B
5. A

TEST 5

DIRECTIONS: Assume that each of the capital letters in the table below represents the name of an employee enrolled in the city employees' retirement system. The number directly beneath the letter represents the agency for which the employee works, and the small letter directly beneath represents the code for the employee's account.

Name of Employee:	L	O	T	Q	A	M	R	N	C
Agency:	3	4	5	9	8	7	52	1	6
Account Code:	r	f	b	i	d	t	g	e	n

In each of the following Questions 1 through 10, the agency code numbers and the account code letters in Columns 2 and 3 should correspond to the capital letters in Column 1 and should be in the same consecutive order. For each question, look at each column carefully and mark your answer as follows:

if there are one or more errors in Column 2 only, mark your answer A;
if there are one or more errors in Column 3 only, mark your answer B;
if there are one or more error in Column 2 and one or more errors in Column 3, mark your answer C;
if there are NO errors in either column, mark your answer D.

The following sample question is given to help you understand the procedure.

Column 1	Column 2	Column 3
TQLMOC	583746	birtfn

In Column 2, the second agency code number (corresponding to letter Q) should be "9," not "8." Column 3 is coded correctly to Column 1. Since there is an error only in Column 2, the correct answer is A.

	Column 1	Column 2	Column 3	
1.	QLNRCA	931268	ifegnd	1.____
2.	NRMOTC	127546	egftbn	2.____
3.	RCTALM	265837	gndbrt	3.____
4.	TAMLON	578341	bdtrfe	4.____
5.	ANTROM	815427	debigt	5.____
6.	MRALON	728341	tgdrfe	6.____
7.	CTNQRO	657924	ndeigf	7.____
8.	QMROTA	972458	itgfbd	8.____

2 (#5)

	Column 1	Column 2	Column 3	
9.	RQMCOL	297463	gitnfr	9._____
10.	NOMRTQ	147259	eftgbi	10._____

KEY (CORRECT ANSWERS)

1. D   6. D
2. C   7. C
3. B   8. D
4. A   9. A
5. B   10. D

TEST 6

DIRECTIONS: Each of Questions 1 through 6 consist of three lines of code letters and numbers. The numbers on each line should correspond to the code letter on the same line in accordance with the table below.

Code Letter:	D	Y	K	L	P	U	S	R	A	E
Corresponding Number:	0	1	2	3	4	5	6	7	8	9

On some of the lines an error exists in the coding. Prepare the letters and numbers in each question carefully. If you find an error or errors on
    only one of the lines in the question, mark your answer A;
    any two lines in the question, mark your answer B;
    all three lines in the question, mark your answer C;
    none of the lines in the question, mark your answer D.

SAMPLE QUESTION
    KSRYELD   2671930
    SAPUEKL   6845913
    RYKADLP   5128034

In the above sample, the first line is correct since each code letter listed has the correct corresponding number. On the second line, an error exists because code letter R should have the number 2 instead of number 1. On the third line, an error exists because the code letter R should have the number 7 instead of the number 5. Since there are errors on two of the three lines, the correct answer is B.

Now answer the following questions using the same procedure.

1.   YPUSRLD   1456730   1._____
     UPSAEDY   5648901
     PREYDKS   4791026

2.   AERLPUS   8973456   2._____
     DKLYDPA   0231048
     UKLDREP   5230794

3.   DAPUSLA   0845683   3._____
     YKLDLPS   1230356
     PUSKYDE   4562101

4.   LRPUPDL   3745403   4._____
     SUPLEDR   6543907
     PKEYDLU   4291025

5.   KEYDESR   2910967   5._____
     PRSALEY   4678391
     LRAYSK   3687162

6. YESREYL   1967913
   PLPRAKY   4346821
   YLPSRDU   1346705

6._____

KEY (CORRECT ANSWERS)

1. A   4. A
2. D   5. B
3. C   6. A

NAME AND NUMBER CHECKING
EXAMINATION SECTION
TEST 1

DIRECTIONS: Each question or incomplete statement is followed by several suggested answers or completions. Select the one that BEST answers the question or completes the statement. *PRINT THE LETTER OF THE CORRECT ANSWER IN THE SPACE AT THE RIGHT.*

Questions 1-10.

DIRECTIONS: Questions 1 through 10 below present the identification numbers, initials, and last names of employees enrolled in a city retirement system. You are to choose the option (A, B, C, or D) that has the identical identification number, initials, and last name as those given in each question.

<u>SAMPLE QUESTION</u>

B145695 JL Jones
   A. B146798 JL Jones   B. B145698 JL Jonas
   C. P145698 JL Jones   C. B145698 JL Jones

The correct answer is D. Only option D shows the identification number, initials, and last name exactly as they are in the sample question. Options A, B, and C have errors in the identification number or last name.

1. J297483 PL Robinson
 A. J294783 PL Robinson B. J297483 PL Robinson
 C. K297483 PL Robinson D. J297843 PL Robinson

 1.____

2. S497662 JG Schwartz
 A. S497662 JG Schwarz B. S497762 JG Schwartz
 C. S497662 JG Schwartz D. S497663 JG Schwartz

 2.____

3. G696436 LN Alberton
 A. G696436 LM Alberton B. G696436 LN Albertson
 C. G696346 LN Albertson D. G696436 LN Alberton

 3.____

4. R774923 AD Aldrich
 A. R774923 AD Aldrich B. R744923 AD Aldrich
 C. R774932 AP Aldrich D. R774932 AD Allrich

 4.____

5. N239638 RP Hrynyk
 A. N236938 PR Hrynyk B. N236938 RP Hrynyk
 C. N239638 PR Hrynyk D. N239638 RP Hrynyk

 5.____

6. R156949 LT Carlson
   A. R156949 LT Carlton
   B. R156494 LT Carlson
   C. R159649 LT Carlton
   D. R156949 LT Carlson

7. T524697 MN Orenstein
   A. T524697 MN Orenstein
   B. T524967 MN Orinstein
   C. T524697 NM Ornstein
   D. T524967 NM Orenstein

8. L346239 JD Remsen
   A. L346239 JD Remson
   B. L364239 JD Remsen
   C. L346438 JD Remsen
   D. L346239 JD Remsen

9. P966438 SB Rieperson
   A. P966438 SB Reiperson
   B. P966438 SB Rieperson
   C. R996438 SB Rieperson
   D. P966438 SB Rieperson

10. D749382 CD Thompson
    A. P749382 CD Thompson
    B. D749832 CD Thomsonn
    C. D749382 CD Thompson
    D. D749823 CD Thomspon

Questions 11-20.

DIRECTIONS: Each of Questions 11 through 20 gives the identification number and name of a person who has received treatment at a certain hospital. You are to choose the option (A, B, C, or D) which has EXACTLY the same identification number and name as those given in the question.

SAMPLE QUESTION

123765 Frank Y. Jones
A. 123675 Frank Y. Jones
B. 123765 Frank T. Jones
C. 123765 Frank Y. Johns
D. 123765 Frank Y. Jones

The correct answer is D. Only option D shows the identification number and name exactly as they are in the sample question. Option A has a mistake in the identification number. Option B has a mistake in the middle initial of the name. Option C has a mistake in the last name.

Now answer Questions 11 through 20 in the same manner.

11. 754898 Diane Malloy
    A. 745898 Diane Malloy
    B. 754898 Dion Malloy
    C. 754898 Diane Malloy
    D. 754898 Diane Maloy

12. 661818 Ferdinand Figueroa
    A. 661818 Ferdinand Figeuroa
    B. 661618 Ferdinand Figueroa
    C. 661818 Ferdnand Figueroa
    D. 661818 Ferdinand Figueroa

13. 100101 Norman D. Braustein
    A. 100101 Norman D. Braustein   B. 101001 Norman D. Braustein
    C. 100101 Norman P. Braustien   D. 100101 Norman D. Bruastein

    13.____

14. 838696 Robert Kittredge
    A. 838969 Robert Kittredge   B. 838696 Robert Kittredge
    C. 388696 Robert Kittredge   D. 838696 Robert Kittridge

    14.____

15. 243716 Abraham Soletsky
    A. 243716 Abrahm Soletsky   B. 243716 Abraham Solestky
    C. 243176 Abraham Soletsky   D. 243716 Abraham Soletsky

    15.____

16. 981121 Phillip M. Maas
    A. 981121 Phillip M. Mass   B. 981211 Phillip M. Maas
    C. 981121 Phillip M. Maas   D. 981121 Phillip N. Maas

    16.____

17. 786556 George Macalusso
    A. 785656 George Macalusso   B. 786556 George Macalusso
    C. 786556 George Maculasso   D. 786556 George Macluasso

    17.____

18. 639472 Eugene Weber
    A. 639472 Eugene Weber   B. 639472 Eugene Webre
    C. 693472 Eugene Weber   D. 639742 Eugene Weber

    18.____

19. 724936 John J. Lomonaco
    A. 724936 John J. Lomanoco   B. 724396 John J. Lomonaco
    C. 724936 John J. Lomonaco   D. 724936 John J. Lamonaco

    19.____

20. 899868 Michael Schnitzer
    A. 899868 Micheal Schnitzer   B. 898968 Michael Schnizter
    C. 899688 Michael Schnitzer   D. 899868 Michael Schnitzer

    20.____

Questions 21-28.

DIRECTIONS: Questions 21 through 28 consist of lines of names, dates, and numbers which represent the names, membership dates, social security numbers, and members of the retirement system. For each question you are to choose the option (A, B, C, or D) which exactly matches the information in the question.

SAMPLE QUESTION

Crossen 12/23/56 173568929 25349
  A. Crossen 2/23/56 173568929 253492
  B. Crossen 12/23/56 173568719 253492
  C. Crossen 12/23/56 173568929 253492
  D. Crossan 12/23/56 173568929 258492

4 (#1)

The correct answer is C. Only option C shows the name, date, and numbers exactly as they are in Column I. Option A has a mistake in the date. Option B has a mistake in the social security number. Option D has a mistake in the name and in the membership number.

21. Figueroa 1/15/64 119295386   21._____
    A. Figueroa 1/5/64 119295386 147563
    B. Figueroa 1/15/64 119295386 147563
    C. Figueroa 1/15/64 119295836 147563
    D. Figueroa 1/15/64 119295886 147563

22. Goodridge 6/19/59 106237869 128352   22._____
    A. Goodridge 6/19/59 106287869 128332
    B. Goodrigde 6/19/59 106237869 128352
    C. Goodridge 6/9/59 106237869 128352
    D. Goodridge 6/19/59 106237869 128352

23. Balsam 9/13/57 109652382 116938   23._____
    A. Balsan 9/13/57 109652382 116938
    B. Balsam 9/13/57 109652382 116938
    C. Balsom 9/13/57 109652382 116938
    D. Balsalm 9/13/57 109652382 116938

24. Mackenzie 2/16/49 127362513 101917   24._____
    A. Makenzie 2/16/49 127362513 101917
    B. Mackenzie 2/16/49 127362513 101917
    C. Mackenzie 2/16/49 127362513 101977
    D. Mackenzie 2/16/49 127862513 101917

25. Halpern 12/2/73 115205359 286070   25._____
    A. Halpern 12/2/73 115206359 286070
    B. Halpern 12/2/73 113206359 286070
    C. Halpern 12/2/73 115206359 206870
    D. Halpern 12/2/73 115206359 286870

26. Phillips 4/8/66 137125516 192612   26._____
    A. Phillips 4/8/66 137125516 196212
    B. Philipps 4/8/66 137125516 192612
    C. Phillips 4/8/66 137125516 192612
    D. Phillips 4/8/66 137122516 192612

27. Francisce 11/9/63 123926037 152210   27._____
    A. Francisce 11/9/63 123826837 152210
    B. Francisce 11/9/63 123926037 152210
    C. Francisce 11/9/63 123936037 152210
    D. Franscice 11/9/63 123926037 152210

28. Silbert 7/28/54 118421999 178514
    A. Silbert 7/28/54 118421999 178544
    B. Silbert 7/28/54 184421999 178514
    C. Silbert 7/28/54 118421999 178514
    D. Siblert 7/28/54 118421999 178514

28.____

KEY (CORRECT ANSWERS)

1.	B	11.	C	21.	B
2.	C	12.	D	22.	D
3.	D	13.	A	23.	B
4.	A	14.	B	24.	B
5.	D	15.	D	25.	A
6.	D	16.	C	26.	C
7.	A	17.	B	27.	B
8.	D	18.	A	28.	C
9.	D	19.	C		
10.	C	20.	D		

TEST 2

DIRECTIONS: Each question or incomplete statement is followed by several suggested answers or completions. Select the one that BEST answers the question or completes the statement. *PRINT THE LETTER OF THE CORRECT ANSWER IN THE SPACE AT THE RIGHT.*

Questions 1-3.

DIRECTIONS: Items 1 through 3 are a test of your proofreading ability. Each item consists of Copy I and Copy II. You are to assume that Copy I in each item is correct. Copy II, which is meant to be a duplicate of Copy I, may contain some typographical errors. In each item, compare Copy II with Copy I and determine the number of errors in Copy II. If there are:
no errors, mark your answer A;
1 or 2 errors, mark your answer B;
3 or 4 errors, mark your answer C;
5 or 6 errors, mark your answer D;
7 errors or more, mark your answer E.

1.   1.____

COPY I
The Commissioner, before issuing any such license, shall cause an investigation to be made of the premises named and described in such application, to determine whether all the provisions of the sanitary code, building code, state industrial code, state minimum wage law, local laws, regulations of municipal agencies, and other requirements of this article are fully observed. (Section B32-169.0 of Article 23.)

COPY II
The Commissioner, before issuing any such license shall cause an investigation to be made of the premises named and described in such application, to determine whether all the provisions of the sanitary code, bilding code, state industrial code, state minimum wage laws, local laws, regulations of municipal agencies, and other requirements of this article are fully observed. (Section E32-169.0 of Article 23.)

2.   2.____

COPY I
Among the persons who have been appointed to various agencies are John Queen, 9 West 55th Street, Brooklyn; Joseph Blount, 2497 Durward Road, Bronx; Lawrence K. Eberhardt, 3194 Bedford Street, Manhattan; Reginald L. Darcy, 1476 Allerton Drive, Bronx; and Benjamin Ledwith, 177 Greene Street, Manhattan.

2 (#2)

COPY II
Among the persons who have been appointed to various agencies are John Queen, 9 West 56th Street, Brooklyn, Joseph Blount, 2497 Dureward Road, Bronx: Lawrence K. Eberhart, 3194 Belford Street, Manhattan; Reginald L. Barcey, 1476 Allerton drive, Bronx; and Benjamin Ledwith, 177 Green Street, Manhattan.

3.   3.____

COPY I
Except as hereinafter provided, it shall be unlawful to use, store or have on hand any inflammable motion picture film in quantities greater than one standard or two sub-standard reels, or aggregating more than two thousand feet in length, or more than ten pounds in weight without the permit required by this section.

COPY II
Except as herinafter provided, it shall be unlawful to use, store or have on hand any inflamable motion picture film, in quantities greater than one standard or two substandard reels or aggregating more than two thousand feet in length, or more than ten pounds in weight without the permit required by this section.

Questions 4-6.

DIRECTIONS: Items 4 through 6 are a test of your proofreading ability. Each question consists of Copy I and Copy II. You are to assume that Copy I in each question is correct. Copy II, which is meant to be a duplicate of Copy I, may contain some typographical errors. In each question, compare Copy II with Copy I and determine the number of errors in Copy II. If there are:
no errors, mark your answer A;
1 or 2 errors, mark your answer B;
3 or 4 errors, mark your answer C;
5 or 6 errors or more, mark your answer D;

4.   4.____

COPY I
It shall be unlawful to install wires or appliances for electric light, heat or power, operating at a potential in excess of seven hundred fifty volts, in or on any part of a building, with the exception of a central station, sub-station, transformer, or switching vault, or motor room; provided, however, that the Commissioner may authorize the use of radio transmitting apparatus under special conditions.

COPY II
It shall be unlawful to install wires or appliances for electric light, heat or power, operating at a potential in excess of seven hundred fifty volts, in or on any part of a building, with the exception of a central station, sub-station, transformer, or switching vault, or motor room, provided, however, that the Commissioner may authorize the use of radio transmitting apperatus under special conditions.

3 (#2)

5.

COPY I
The grand total debt service for the fiscal year 2006-27 amounts to $350,563,718.63, as compared with $309,561,347.27 for the current fiscal year, or an increase of $41,002,371.36. The amount payable from other sources in 2006-07 shows an increase of $13,264,165.47, resulting in an increase of $27,733,205.89 payable from tax levy funds.

COPY II
The grand total debt service for the fiscal year 2006-07 amounts to $350,568,718.63, as compared with $309,561,347.27 for the current fiscel year, or an increase of $41,002,371.36. The amount payable from other sources in 2006-07 show an increase of $13,264,165.47 resulting in an increase of $27,733,295.89 payable from tax levy funds.

5._____

6.

COPY I
The following site proposed for the new building is approximately rectangular in shape and comprises an entire block, having frontages of about 721 feet on 16th Road, 200 feet on 157th feet, 721 on 17th Avenue and 200 feet on 154th Street, with a gross area of about 144,350 square feet. The 2006-07 assessed valuation is $28,700,000 of which $6,000,000 is for improvements.

COPY II
The following site proposed for the new building is approximately rectangular in shape and comprises an entire block, having frontage of about 721 feet on 16th Road, 200 feet on 157th Street on 17th Avenue, and 200 feet on 134th Street, with a gross area of about 114,350 square feet. The 2006-07 assessed valuation is $28,700,000 of which $6,000,000 is for improvements.

6._____

KEY (CORRECT ANSWERS)

1.	D	4.	B
2.	E	5.	D
3.	E	6.	C

TEST 3

DIRECTIONS: Each question or incomplete statement is followed by several suggested answers or completions. Select the one that BEST answers the question or completes the statement. *PRINT THE LETTER OF THE CORRECT ANSWER IN THE SPACE AT THE RIGHT.*

Questions 1-8.

DIRECTIONS: Each of the questions numbered 1 through 8 consists of three sets of names and name codes. In each question, the two names and name codes on the same line are supposed to be exactly the same.
Look carefully at each set of names and cods and mark your answer
A. if there are mistakes in all three sets
B. if there are mistakes in two of the sets
C. if there is a mistake in only one set
D. if there are no mistakes in any of the sets

SAMPLE QUESTION

The following sample question is given to help you understand the procedure.

Macabe, John N. – V53162	Macade, John N. – V53162
Howard, Joan S. – J24791	Howard, Joan S. – J24791
Ware, Susan B. – A45068	Ware, Susan B. – A45968

In the above sample question, the names and name codes of the first set are not exactly the same because of the spelling of the last name (Macabe – Macade). The names and name codes of the second set are exactly the same. The names and name codes of the third set are not exactly the same because the two name codes are different (A45068 – A45968). Since there are mistakes in only 2 of the sets, the answer to the sample question is B.

1. Powell, Michael C. – 78537F   Powell, Michael C. – 78537F   1.____
   Martinez, Pablo J. – 24435P   Martinez, Pablo J. – 24435P
   MacBane, Eliot M. – 98674E   MacBane, Eliot M. – 98674E

2. Fitz-Kramer Machines, Inc. – 259090   Fitz-Kramer Machines, Inc. – 259090   2.____
   Marvel Cleaning Service – 482657   Marvel Cleaning Service – 482657
   Donato, Carl G. – 637418   Danato, Carl G. - 687418

3. Martin Davison Trading Corp –   Martin Davidson Trading Corp. –   3.____
      43108T   43108T
   Cotwald Lighting Fixtures -76065L   Cotwald Lighting Fixtures – 70056L
   R. Crawford Plumbers – 23157C   R. Crawford Plumbers – 23157G

4. Fraiman Engineering Corp. – M4773   Friaman Engineering Corp. – M4773   4.____
   Neuman, Walter B. – N7745   Neumen, Walter B. – N7745
   Pierce, Eric M. – W6304   Pierce, Eric M. – W6304

5. Constable, Eugene – B64837   Comstable, Eugene – B6437   5.____
   Derrick, Paul – H27119   Derrik, Paul – H27119
   Heller, Karen – S4966   Heller, Karen – S46906

6. Hernando Delivery Service Co. -   Hernando Delivery Service Co. –   6.____
   D7456   D7456
   Barettz Electrical Supplies -   Barettz Electrical Supplies –
   N5392   N5392
   Tanner, Abraham – M4798   Tanner, Abraham – M4798

7. Kalin Associates – R38641   Kaline Associates – R38641   7.____
   Sealey, Robert E. – P63533   Sealey, Robert E. – P63553
   Seals! Office Furniture – R36742   Seals! Office Furniture – R36742

8. Janowsky, Philip M. – 742213   Janowsky, Philip M. – 742213   8.____
   Hansen, Thomas H. – 934816   Hanson, Thomas H. – 934816
   L. Lester and Son Inc. – 294568   L. Lester and Son Inc. - 294568

Questions 9-13.

DIRECTIONS: Each of the questions numbered 9 through 13 consists of three sets of names and building codes. In each question, the two names and building codes on the same line are supposed to be exactly the same.
If you find an error or errors on only one of the sets in the question, mark your answer A; any two of the sets in the question, mark your answer B; all three of the sets in the question, mark your answer C; none of the sets, mark your answer D.

SAMPLE QUESTION

Column I
Duvivier, Anne P. – X52714
Dyrborg, Alfred – B4217
Dymnick, JoAnne – P482596

Column II
Duviver, Anne P. – X52714
Dyrborg, Alfred – B4267
Dymnick, JoAnne – P482596

In the above sample question, the first set of names and building codes is not exactly the same because the last names are spelled differently (Duvivier – Duviver). The second set of names and building codes is not exactly the same because the building codes are different (B4217 – B4267). The third set of names and building codes is exactly the same. Since there are mistakes in two of the sets of names and building codes, the answer to the sample question is B.

Now answer the questions using the same procedure.

Column I
9. Lautmann, Gerald G. – C2483   Lautmann, Gerald C. – C2483   9.____
   Lawlor, Michael – W44639   Lawler, Michael – W44639
   Lawrence, John J. – H1358   Lawrence, John J. – H1358

Column II

3 (#3)

Column I	Column II	
10. Mittmann, Howard – J4113 Mitchell, William T. – M75271 Milan, T. Thomas – Q67553	Mittmann, Howard – J4113 Mitchell, William T. – M75721 Milan, T. Thomas – Q67553	10.____
11. Quarles, Vincent – J34760 Quinn, Alan N. – S38813 Quinones, Peter W. – B87467	Quarles, Vincent – J34760 Quinn, Alan N. – S38813 Quinones, Peter W. – B87467	11.____
12. Daniels, Harold H. – A26554 Dantzler, Richard – C35780 Davidson, Martina – E62901	Daniels, Harold H – A26544 Dantzler, Richard – 035780 Davidson, Martin – E62901	12.____
13. Graham, Cecil J. – I20244 Granger, Deborah – T86211 Grant, Charles L. – G5788	Graham, Cecil J. – I20244 Granger, Deborah – T86211 Grant, Charles L. – G5788	13.____

KEY (CORRECT ANSWERS)

1.	D	6.	D	11.	D
2.	C	7.	B	12.	C
3.	A	8.	C	13.	D
4.	B	9.	B		
5.	A	10.	A		

TEST 4

DIRECTIONS: In Questions 1 through 10 there are five pairs of numbers or letters and numbers. Compare each pair and decide how many pairs are exactly alike. *PRINT THE LETTER OF THE CORRECT ANSWER IN THE SPACE AT THE RIGHT.*
  A. if only one pair is exactly alike
  B. if only two pairs are exactly alike
  C. if only three pairs are exactly alike
  D. if only four pairs are exactly alike
  E. if all five pairs are exactly alike.

1. 73-F.....F-73   FF-73.....FF-73   1.____
   F-7373.....F-7373   373-FF.....337-FF
   F-733.....337-F

2. 0-17158.....0-17158 0-71518.....0-71518   2.____
   0-11758.....0-11758 0-15817.....0-15817

3. 1A-7908.....1A-7908 7A-8901.....7A-8091   3.____
   71-891.....7A-891   1A-9078.....1A-9708
   9A-7018.....9A-7081

4. 2V-6426.....2V-6246 2N-6246.....2N-6246   4.____
   2V-6426.....2N-6426 2N-6624.....2N-6624
   2V-6462.....2V-6562

5. 3NY-56.....3NY-65   5NY-356.....3NY-356   5.____
   6NY-3566.....3NY-3566 5NY-6536.....5NY-6536
   3NY-5663.....5NY-3663

6. COB-065.....COB-065 BCL-506.....BCL-506   6.____
   LBC-650.....LBC-650 DLB-560.....DLB-560
   CDB-056.....COB-065

7. 4KQ-9130.....4KQ-9130 4KQ-9310.....4KQ-9130 7.____
   4KQ-9031.....4KQ-9301 4KQ-9301.....4KQ-9301
   4KQ-9013.....4KQ-9013

8. MK-89.....MK-98   98-MK.....89-MK   8.____
   MSK-998.....MSK-998 MOSK.....MOKS
   SMK-899.....SMK-899

9. 8MD-2104.....SMD-2014 2MD-8140.....2MD-8140 9.____
   814-MD.....814-MD   4MD-8201.....4MD-8201
   MD-281.....MD-481

10. 161-035.....161-035 150-316.....150-316   10.____
    315-160.....315-160 131-650.....131-650
    165-301.....165-301

180

KEY (CORRECT ANSWERS)

1.	B	6.	D
2.	E	7.	D
3.	B	8.	B
4.	C	9.	C
5.	A	10.	E

TEST 5

DIRECTIONS: Each question or incomplete statement is followed by several suggested answers or completions. Select the one that BEST answers the question or completes the statement. *PRINT THE LETTER OF THE CORRECT ANSWER IN THE SPACE AT THE RIGHT.*

Questions -5.

DIRECTIONS: Questions 1 through 5, inclusive, consist of groups of four displays representing license identification plates. Examine each group of plates and determine the number of plates in each group which are identical. Mark your answer sheets as follows:
    If only two plates are identical, mark answer A.
    If only three plates are identical, mark answer B.
    If all four plates are identical, mark answer C.
    If the plates are all different, mark answer D.

EXAMPLE
ABC123   BCD123   ABC123   BCD235

Since only two plates are identical, the first and third, the correct answer is A.

#					
1.	PBV839	PVB839	PVB839	PVB839	1.____
2.	WTX083	WTX083	WTX083	WTX083	2.____
3.	B73609	D73906	BD7396	BD7906	3.____
4.	AK7423	AK7423	AK1423	A81324	4.____
5.	583Y10	683Y10	583701	583710	5.____

Questions 6-10.

DIRECTIONS: Questions 6 through 10 consist of groups of numbers and letters similar to those which might appear on license plates. Each group of numbers and letters will be called a license identification. Choose the license identification lettered A, B, C, or D that EXACTLY matches the license identification shown next to the question number.

SAMPLE
NY 1977
ABC-123

A. NY 1976   B. NY 1977   C. NY 1977   D. NY 1977
   ABC-123   ABC-132   CBA-123   ABC-123

2 (#5)

The license identification given is NY 1977.
ABC-123
The only choice that exactly matches it is the license identification next to the letter D. The correct answer is therefore D.

6. NY 1976
QLT-781

   A. NJ 1976 QLT-781   B. NY 1975 QLT-781   C. NY 1976 QLT-781   D. NY 1977 QLT-781

7. FLA 1977
2-7LT58J

   A. FLA 1977 2-7TL58J   B. FLA 1977 2-7LTJ58   C. FLA 1977 2-7LT58J   D. LA 1977 2-7LT58J

8. NY 1975
OQC383

   A. NY 1975 OQC383   B. NY 1975 OQC833   C. NY 1975 QCQ383   D. NY 1977 OCQ383

9. MASS 1977
B-8DK02

   A. MISS 1977 B-8DK02   B. MASS 1977 B-8DK02   C. MASS 1976 B-8DK02   D. MASS 1977 B-80KD2

10. NY 1976
ZV0586

   A. NY 1976 2V-0586   B. NY 1977 ZV0586   C. NY 1975 ZV0586   D. NY 1976 ZU0586

KEY (CORRECT ANSWERS)

1. B   6. C
2. C   7. C
3. D   8. A
4. A   9. B
5. A   10. C

TEST 6

DIRECTIONS: Assume that each of the capital letters in the table below represent the name of an employee enrolled in the city employees' retirement system. The number directly beneath the letter represents the agency for which the employee works, and the small letter directly beneath represents the code for the employee's account.

Name of Employee	L	O	T	Q	A	M	R	N	C
Agency	3	4	5	9	8	7	2	1	6
Account Code	r	f	b	i	d	t	g	e	n

In each of the following questions 1 through 3, the agency code numbers and the account code letters in Columns 2 and 3 should correspond to the capital letters in Column 1 and should be in the same consecutive order. For each question, look at each column carefully and mark your answer as follows:
If there are one or more errors in Column 2 only, mark your answer A.
If there are one or more errors in Column 3 only, mark your answer B.
If there are one or more errors in Column 2 and one or more errors in Column 3, mark your answer C.
If there are NO errors in either column, mark your answer D.
The following sample question is given to help you understand the procedure.

Column 1   Column 2   Column 3
TQLMOC   583746   birtfn

In Column 2, the second agency code number (corresponding to letter Q) should be "9", not "8". Column 3 is coded correctly to Column 1. Since there is an error only in Column 2, the correct answer is A.

	Column 1	Column 2	Column 3	
1.	Q L N R C A	9 3 1 2 6 8	i r e g n d	1.____
2.	N R M O T C	1 2 7 5 4 6	e g f t b n	2.____
3.	R C T A L M	2 6 5 8 3 7	g n d b r t	3.____

KEY (CORRECT ANSWERS)

1. D
2. C
3. B

POLICE SCIENCE NOTES

POLICE RECORDS

TABLE OF CONTENTS

	Page
COMMENTARY	1
FILING	1
FILING BY CLASSIFICATION AND CASE	2
STATISTICS	3
MOTOR VEHICLE ACCIDENTS	4
UNIFORM TRAFFIC TICKETS	4
JUVENILE AND YOUTH POLICE RECORDS	4

POLICE SCIENCE NOTES

POLICE RECORDS

Records are of vital importance to a law enforcement agency, whether large or small. A records system should be centralized for a law enforcement agency as a whole. Separate sets of independent records in various sections or divisions of an agency or department are less useful and less desirable than centralized records. For example, a uniformed patrolman's initial report on a store burglary and a later investigative report on the same burglary prepared by the detective assigned to a case should be filed together, rather than in separate files, in the Uniform Division and the Detective Division.

FILING

All reports, memoranda, letters, etc., should be filed with other documents relating to the same case or matter, in chronological order. By this means, the entire experience of the department in connection with any particular case or classification of cases or matters can be readily located for review and analysis, as desired. In addition, it simplifies locating reports when the names or subjects involved are unknown or have been forgotten.

In order to permit filing of reports, letters, memoranda, and other documents in a logical, usable way (i.e., burglary cases in the burglary classification files, assaults in the assault classification files, correspondence on police uniforms with similar correspondence, in the "uniforms" classification file, etc.), it is necessary to assign classifications to reports and other documents to be filed. In order to do so, a list of "file classifications" and "file classification numbers" must be prepared and used. The classification list of each department will depend on size, specific needs, and on the variety of classifications assigned to administrative things (all police departments should have approximately the same classifications for crimes, since all are governed by the same law).

A usable classification system, for example, could begin with classifications such as: 1 - Applicant, 2 – Alcoholic Beverage Control Law, 3 – Abandonment, 4 – Accidents, etc. The system should segregate crimes into classifications by kind of crime.

Each report, memorandum, letter or document to be filed should be assigned an unvarying classification number (e.g., anything to do with an abortion case would be marked "3"), followed by the number assigned the particular case or matter, and, if desired, a serial number.

Thus, a uniformed officer's report from an informant concerning child abandonment by a Mr. X, which would begin a new case, would be marked (on the first page only, usually at lower right) with "3" for the classification abandonment followed by a dash and a number following the number of the last case in file (e.g., "3-42").

If serial numbering is desired, the report would be marked "3-42-1". The next document filed would be "3-42-2," etc. The "1" shows the report is the first document put in file 3-42.

Files, of course, may be kept loose in individually numbered folders, or as documents permanently put together with patent fasteners of various kinds, or in files with covers, without covers, etc. A secure method should be adopted and used uniformly.

Where a classification system is used, it permits clerical filing "by the numbers" with accuracy, insuring that (for example) all abandonment cases and correspondence or other material relating to them not only go in the same place in files, but that pieces of a particular case are filed in proper order with the case and not someplace else where they have to be hunted and may be lost. Procedure should be the same for any classification, whether it is "ABC Law," "Supply of Uniforms," "Vehicle Maintenance," or anything else.

FILING BY CLASSIFICATION AND CASE

Reports, letters, memoranda, and other documents should be identified, for filing and finding, by classification, file and serial number, in that order (e.g., 3-42-1).

1. Classification Number: The first digit or digits of a complete "file number." It identifies the classification. In the example given, the classification number "3" indicates the case reported relates to abandonment.

2. Case Number: The second digit or digits of the file number. It identifies the particular case concerned. Case numbers should be assigned consecutively (to initial reports or documents of cases in the same classification as they are received). Once a case has been assigned a case number, all reports in that case should carry the same number. In the example given, the number 42 indicates that the case is the 42nd case report in this particular classification.

   Each classification should also have a zero (0) case file and a double zero (00) case file.

   a. Zero (0) Case File: The zero case file should contain material of a non-specific nature which relates to a particular classification but does not relate to any particular case in the classification. This will be material on which no cases need be opened.

   b. Double Zero (00) File: A double zero file should be used solely for rules and instructions relating to the particular classification (not pertaining to any specific case but to the classification generally).

3. Serial Number: A serial number indicates the order in which the report or other document was received in relation to other reports or documents in the same case file. Serial numbers should be assigned consecutively, as the material is received for filing. They permit permanent accounting for all items in file.

Reports should be classified and assigned their classification and case numbers as they are received. Reports should, of course, be reviewed by supervisory personnel for content, errors, etc. When corrections are required, they should be brought to the attention of the responsible officer for appropriate action. If a report is satisfactory, it may then be indexed, given a serial number, and filed.

Files in each classification should be kept in numerical order, behind a divider which identifies the classification.

In the file room, names of the title or heading of the first report or document filed should be indexed. Thereafter, only changes or additions need be indexed. Any other names which appear in an investigation or document which are desirable to index, should be underlined by the officer or reviewing supervisor (on file copy) in red ink or pencil, with a red check mark on the first page of the report as a flag to file room personnel that there is indexing required. Supervisors should be alert to ensure that all necessary indexing is marked on file copies before they are sent to the file room. The index cards in all instances must show the name of the person or item, and the file number (classification and case numbers). Brief identifying data may also be entered (e.g., "fem, born 8/12/61").

In cases where there are any exhibits or evidence in file which are not to be retained as a permanent part of the case, a report should be placed in file showing the final disposition of them. Supervisors should ensure that evidence and exhibits are promptly disposed of when they have served their purpose. Appropriate receipts should be obtained when property is disposed of by means other than by destruction.

STATISTICS

All police agencies maintain certain crime and arrest statistics covering their jurisdiction. They must submit these statistics to the Department every calendar month on forms supplied by the Department. No police agency is exempted by reason of its size or lack of personnel.

Statistics are required concerning felonies, misdemeanors, and other offenses and on all persons arrested for such crimes and offenses, as specified by the Department in its statistical forms.

The statistics must show the number of offenses known to the police, how many were determined to be unfounded, and how many were "cleared by arrest." The data on arrested persons must include the county of arrest, the specific crime or offense charged, their sex, and their age. Forms and instructions may be secured directly from the Department of Corrections.

The Federal Bureau of Investigation, U.S. Department of Justice, Washington, D.C., also collects crime statistics on a monthly basis, for the national Uniform Crime Reports. Police agencies not contributing should consider doing so. Necessary details, instructions, and forms may be secured by writing to the Director, Federal Bureau of Investigation, U.S. Department of Justice, Washington, D.C., or by contacting the nearest F.B.I. office.

In order to comply with state law and to provide the basic minimum records necessary, even the smallest department must maintain a record of complaints received and a notation of action taken thereon. It must also maintain a record of persons arrested.

Such records may be maintained in their simplest form in a "blotter" or other bound volume. They are better and more useful on a separate form for each complaint and for each arrest. Separate forms may be filed in separate files by case and by classification, for various administrative uses and analyses. Such an arrangement is a bare minimum. Departments desiring to establish new and better record systems or to alter and improve old ones may obtain a "Manual of Police Records" from the Director, Federal Bureau of Investigation, U.S. Department of Justice, Washington, D.C., free of charge.

Data entered on complaint forms should always include notation as to the action taken, by whom taken, and the final disposition of the matter.

MOTOR VEHICLE ACCIDENTS

The Vehicle and Traffic Law requires all officers to investigate every motor vehicle involving a personal injury which is reported to them within five days after the accident. They must make a report of their investigation to the Commissioner of Motor Vehicles on forms furnished by the Department of Motor Vehicles.

All reports and records of any accident (not alone motor vehicle) which are kept by the State Police or by the police force of any county, city, town, or village or other district of the State, shall be open to the inspection of any person having an interest therein or his attorney or agent, except that any report or reports may be withheld from inspection if their disclosure would interfere with the investigation or prosecution of a crime involved in or connected with the accident. All departments, therefore, must keep their accident files in proper order, so that the reports may be readily located when required. This may be done by numbering and indexing or by filing by place and date of accident.

UNIFORM TRAFFIC TICKETS

Under the Vehicle and Traffic Law and the Regulations of the Commissioner of Motor Vehicles, all police must use the prescribed Uniform Traffic Ticket. In addition, they are required to maintain a file of Part IV of the uniform ticket. This is one of the copies delivered to the court by the issuing officer; on it the court notes the disposition and forwards it to the department of the issuing officer.

JUVENILE AND YOUTH POLICE RECORDS

All records of police relating to juvenile delinquents, persons in need of supervision or youthful offenders must be kept confidential. They may, however, be inspected upon order from the court wherein the subject was adjudged, or, without a court order, by the institution to which a youth has been committed.

Juvenile Delinquency and Persons in Need of Supervision police records must be kept by police in files separate and apart from similar files on adults. Youthful Offender files need not be separately maintained by police.

www.ingramcontent.com/pod-product-compliance
Lightning Source LLC
Chambersburg PA
CBHW082039300426
44117CB00015B/2538